CROWN INSIDERS' GUIDE™ TO BRITAIN

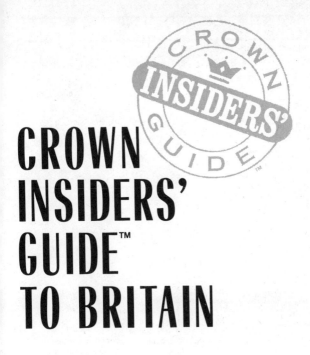

CROWN INSIDERS' GUIDE™ TO BRITAIN

Patricia and Lester Brooks

Robert C. Fisher
General Editor

Crown Publishers, Inc.
New York

The authors wish to extend thanks to the following friends and associates for their invaluable help, counsel, and encouragement:

Peter ffrench-Hodges of the British Tourist Authority, London; Bedford Pace of the British Tourist Authority, New York; John Lampl of British Airways; Elaine Heller; and Peter Senn.

At this writing the exchange rate of dollars for pounds is $1.50/£1, but the rate has gyrated from $1.20 to $1.60 during the past year alone. Rates change daily, and you will find them posted in bank and exchange dealers' windows. Remember that the lowest posted rate is not necessarily the best deal.

Published by Crown Publishers, Inc., 225 Park Avenue South, New York, New York 10003 and represented in Canada by the Canadian MANDA Group.

CROWN and CROWN INSIDERS' GUIDE are trademarks of Crown Publishers, Inc.

Manufactured in the United States of America

Library of Congress Cataloging-in-Publication Data

Brooks, Patricia
  Crown insiders' guide to Britain.

  Includes index.
  1. Great Britain—Description and travel—1971–
Guide-books.   I. Brooks, Lester.   II. Fisher, Robert C.,
1930–   .   III. Title.
DA650.B898   1987   914.1'04858   86-24378
ISBN 0-517-56571-4

10 9 8 7 6 5 4 3 2 1

First Edition

CONTENTS

BRITAIN INSIDE OUT

THE REGIONS OF ENGLAND

List of Maps

EDITOR'S NOTE

Americans can't seem to get enough of Britain, especially England. They flock to these sceptered isles in greater numbers than to any other overseas destination (some 6 million yearly, by last count), and more than half are repeat travelers, says the British Tourist Authority. It certainly isn't just the so-called ethnic traveler, either, even though Americans of British ancestry still are the largest group constituting the population of the United States. Plenty of visitors dig around a little for their roots, but most can't be bothered. Certainly, Americans of non-British background, who still get goosebumps at royal weddings or would kill for an invitation to the Queen's garden party, care little for lineage or heraldry.

What unites nearly all Americans is the desire to study our cultural roots, whether they be linguistic, legal, or literary. The glory and the maddening complexity of the English language intrigues us, and we want to examine the original on the site. The sheer horror of our juridical system, once awesome rather than awful, makes us want to sit in on a session at Old Bailey. Finally, the dazzling insight of authors such as Shakespeare, the Brontës, or Milton almost compels us to see English theater or visit the settings of the classics on their home ground.

A trip abroad helps make an education whole, or more so than not. And a perfect place for any first overseas visit is Britain, more specifically England, where we need not worry about the language, the drinking water, or embarrassingly exotic customs. (We might get run over by left-handed traffic because we forget first to look right instead of left, but that's a relatively rare event.)

I lived in the British capital for 8 happy years during the Carnaby Street period, when the Beatles were at their zenith, and *Time* magazine coined the phrase "swinging London." I went to England a skeptic; I had been sent to do a job there, and I grumbled because my first choice for a European assignment had been Paris. Though my father was of British stock, I had no interest in looking up long-withered, possibly decayed, or even deliberately hidden roots, despite the entreaties of some family members to investigate a mysterious gap in the genealogy. I arrived in London expecting to be bored to death, and quickly.

How wrong I was! And how much fun it was to be proved in error! London then, as today, was the most tolerant capital on earth. Already a doddering 35-year-old, I was accepted by young and old, aristocrat and cockney, and practically nobody asked me what I did for a living. Now, as then, if you are interested in theater, music, army bands, hard rock, gardening, primal screaming, batik dyeing, Romanesque churches, motorbikes, mud wrestling, Zen, or kick-boxing, the British will welcome you, your opinion, and even your accent. Contrary to what you may have heard about the English, they are not interested in categorizing you, but just in you, for yourself. So I advise you to go into a pub, order something to drink (even if it's wine or mineral water), and chat up someone of the opposite—or the same—sex. The regulars have all their lives to wait for someone else to initiate the conversation, but you don't. As soon as you open your mouth, the chances are nine out of ten that you'll have a sympathetic audience. If you talk for over three minutes and start a polite argument, you'll know you're in danger of making a friend for life. For underneath that so-called phlegmatic exterior, most English men and women are dying to talk to someone.

I left London a convert to the British Way of Life. Certainly not to the British economic system, to monarchy, or to the class structure. But I think the inhabitants of those isles off the European continent know a lot about how to live, how to tolerate differences of opinion, and how to be civil to each other under stress. They're also pretty good at having fun, as you'll see at their Christmas pantomines or Albert Hall sing-alongs. I can't think of any better place to go if you're going abroad.

The Crown Insiders' Guide™ Series

Knowing Britain inside out isn't enough, by itself, to make a good travel guide. A good writer has to get inside his subject, yet keep the perspective right. The best authors learn to think like the people they portray. At the same time, they can't be chameleons, all things to all readers. In this series the authors try to show the reader what each country looks like from the viewpoint of a trained observer, someone who knows the ground thoroughly but isn't blinded by tradition, connections, or misplaced loyalties. Our Insiders, in short, have to be Outsiders for the very reason that natives of the country have too many obligations, too much cultural baggage of their own, too little knowledge of what American readers want.

You'll learn from a Crown Insiders' guide the perils and pitfalls of travel, items that most travel books ignore. We'll make it a point to highlight the good things too, calling attention to special finds, such as a tourist superstore in London where you can get free information, make reservations, buy guidebooks, or place phone calls.

The Authors

The Crown Insiders' Guide authors have all lived in the countries they write about. The coauthors of this book on Britain, Patricia and Lester Brooks, are veteran travel writers who live in Connecticut, but spend more than one-third of each year traveling and reporting on various destinations for *Bon Appétit, Family Circle, Harper's Bazaar, House Beautiful, McCall's, Modern Bride,* the *New York Times, Travel & Leisure, Travel-Holiday, Vogue,* and many other publications. Between them, they are the authors of 20 books, including 7 on travel. In their travels, they combine their interests in food and wine, Pat as restaurant and food critic for the Connecticut section of the *New York Times,* Les as a beverage writer and member of the Sommelier Society of America.

The Brookses first met as students at the University of London. ("It was over a jugged hare," Les recalls.) Since then, as dedicated Anglophiles, they have lived and traveled extensively throughout Britain. Sometimes their travels have taken them in search of ancestral roots (Les to Ashby-de-la-Zouch in the Midlands, from which his great-grandparents emigrated in the mid-19th century, Pat to County Cork, Ireland, which her Grandfather Harrington left in the early 1900s). Once their pursuit of a story led them to don overalls to work in a London archaeological dig. ("We'll plumb any depths for a good story," says Pat.) Another time they rented a house in a Somerset village, Wedmore, in pursuit of ghosts. Their love affair with Britain is unending.

Other contributors to this book include Christopher Brooks (beer and ale) and Jim Brooks (Scotland and Wales).

THE INSIDERS' RATING SYSTEM

The authors and the editor jointly award 1, 2, 3, 4, or 5 crowns to hotels, restaurants, and such places as museums, monuments, churches, palaces, and other sights or sites that seem important to them. Here is our interpretation of the awards:

Hotels and Restaurants

♛ ♛ ♛ ♛ ♛	Best in the country
♛ ♛ ♛ ♛	Outstanding
♛ ♛ ♛	Excellent
♛ ♛	Very Good
♛	Recommended

Sights and Sites

♛ ♛ ♛ ♛ ♛	Once-in-a-lifetime
♛ ♛ ♛ ♛	A "must see"
♛ ♛ ♛	Worth a considerable detour
♛ ♛	Important
♛	Interesting

Become an Insider

Nobody's perfect, and though our Insiders have tried to include everything worthwhile, omit the tourist traps, and maintain up-to-date prices and other information, the ever-changing aspects of travel ensure that something in this book will change between the time we wrote about it and the time you read or visit. Let us know, by writing to the authors and/or the editor at Crown Insiders' Guides, Crown Publishers, Inc., 225 Park Avenue South, New York, New York 10003. We'll be grateful for corrections, suggestions for new listings, or any comments you care to make.

GREAT BRITAIN

ATLANTIC OCEAN

Shetland Islands

Lerwick

N

Orkney Islands

Kirkwall

John O'Groats

Wick

Outer Hebrides

Stornoway

Ullapool

Uig

Isle of Skye

Kyle of Lochalsh

Inverness

Banff

Barra

Aviemore

Ballater

Aberdeen

NORTH SEA

Mallaig

Fort Williams

SCOTLAND

Oban

Perth

Dundee

St. Andrews

Stirling

Rothesay

Glasgow

Edinburgh

Isle of Arran

Prestwick

Berwick-upon-Tweed

Dumfries

Gretna

Carlisle

Newcastle-upon-Tyne

Durham

Isle of Man

Kendal

Scarborough

Douglas

ENGLAND

IRISH SEA

Blackpool

NORTHERN IRELAND

Leeds

Liverpool

Manchester

Isle of Anglesey

Llandudno

Sheffield

Lincoln

Sherwood Forest

Stoke-on-Trent

Derby

Nottingham

Boston

WALES

Stafford

Leicester

Norwich

Aberystwyth

Birmingham

Coventry

Cardigan

Rugby

Northampton

Aldeburgh

Fishguard

Llandrindod Wells

Stratford-upon-Avon

Cambridge

St. David's

Hereford

Colchester

Ipswich

Milford Raven

Gloucester

Oxford

St. Albans

Southend-on-Sea

Swansea

Newport

Cirencester

Margate

Cardiff

Bristol

Bath

LONDON

Ramsgate

Glastonbury

Wells

London Heathrow

Canterbury

Dover

Tunbridge Wells

Rye

Folkestone

Southampton

Brighton

Hastings

Bournemouth

Isle of Wight

Newquay

Torquay

St. Ives

Penzance

Falmouth

Isles of Scilly

ENGLISH CHANNEL

ST. GEORGE'S CHANNEL

Channel Islands

FRANCE

SCALE OF MILES

0   50   100

BEFORE YOU GO

WHY YOU SHOULD VISIT BRITAIN NOW

The good news is that Britain is *in*.

That's really non-news, because it always has been in (with some transitory exceptions, circa 1776–1816).

Events such as royal weddings are recent reminders of the innumerable elements that make Britain so appealing to so many, over such a wide spectrum of interests. Royal lives and letters, even the occasional funeral or distant scandal, are, in effect, mere samples.

The Queen's Guards, the Beefeaters, the Horse Guards, banner-hung halls, medieval castles, heraldry, wigged judges, pealing bells, and robed Parliamentarians are part of daily life. The art and furniture in the "Treasure Houses" exhibit, which entranced Washington, D.C. in 1985, were items from a mere handful of the hundreds of "stately homes" you are invited to visit—after you've gorged yourself on the incomparable museum collections and exhibitions in royal palaces.

To visit handsome and historic country palaces such as Chatsworth, Knole, Leeds, and Longleat has long been a summer pastime with Britons themselves. Now it is a new and satisfying goal of Britain's visitors, who are surprised to find how accessible these provincial stately homes are.

When it comes to shopping, *in*, as always, is Harvey Nichols, the Knightsbridge department store that is considered Britain's most stylish. Of course, you can't go wrong at the Scotch House, almost across the street, for woolens, or at fabulous Harrods—for anything and everything.

In the knife-and-fork department, Hilaire's Restaurant's *nouvelle cuisine* is rated *numero uno* at the moment by London cognoscenti.

As top-drawer as ever are the Connaught, Claridge's, the Berkeley, the Dorchester, the Inn on the Park, and the Ritz. Some, however, consider it more chic to book into the hotel Lillie Langtry once owned (and where Oscar Wilde used to stay), the Cadogan Thistle on Sloane Street.

One of the diversions attracting posh customers is a polo party in which you travel in a chauffeur-driven Jaguar or Daimler to a Guards Polo Club match in Windsor. The one-day outing includes a champagne lunch while polo-watching and an optional look-in at Windsor Castle or a stately home.

And then there's the theater—one of the glories of the English-speaking world and an outstanding feature of British life. Extravagantly staged musicals pack them in at West End theaters, before moving on to New York. Meanwhile, at the British Museum, one of the recent big attractions is ancient—a 2,000-year-old man whose remains were found only in 1984, and exhibited just now.

Not to be overlooked is the sheer excitement of seeing people and places you've read about and recognize from photos, films, and books—the actual (nonmediated), living, breathing experience of it all. Rain or shine, day or night, there's nothing to compare with the best of Britain—and that's what we've tried to capture and convey in the pages that follow.

HISTORY IN A HURRY
Dynasties of England and Britain

827–A.D. 1066	Anglo-Saxons and Danes
1066–1154	Normans
1154–1399	House of Plantagenet
1399–1461	House of Lancaster (Red Rose)
1461–1485	House of York (White Rose)
1485–1603	House of Tudor
1603–1714	House of Stuart
1714–1901	House of Hanover
1901–1910	House of Saxe-Coburg
1910–	House of Windsor

Key Events in Britain's Past

300,000–8000 B.C.	The Paleolithic (Old Stone Age) era. Hunters and gatherers in small bands.
8000–3000 B.C.	Mesolithic (Middle Stone Age) era. Melting

	ice cap separates Britain from the European landmass; increase in population, forests, game.
3000–1800 B.C.	Neolithic (New Stone Age) era. Farmer immigrants arrive from northern and western Europe.
1800–550 B.C.	Bronze Age. New immigrants arrive from the Low Countries; wheat and barley cultivation; Wessex trade in gold and tin; Celts arrive from northern France.
550 B.C.–A.D. 43	Iron Age. Immigrants, including Brythons (Britons) arrive, and population increases; fortified villages appear.
55 B.C.–A.D. 412	Roman Britain. Caesar invades in 55–54 B.C. for reconnaissance. The A.D. 43 Roman conquest installs garrisons, Hadrian's Wall, the Antonine Wall, Coloniae (settlements of retired troops at modern-day Lincoln, York, Colchester, and Gloucester), Roman law, roads, agriculture, and trade. In 412, the last Roman legions leave.
440–A.D. 1066	Anglo-Saxon era: Angles, Saxons, and Jutes drive the Celts to the coasts of Wales, Cornwall, and Brittany. British knight Arthur defeats invaders, giving rise to the legend of King Arthur.
597	St. Augustine lands at Thanet, Kent, to convert the English, who worship Odin and Thor. Irish-Scottish Christianity, independent of Rome, spreads in northern Britain.
796	King Offa of Mercia completes Offa's Dyke, a Welsh/English frontier earthwork.
865	The Danish army lands, by 870 captures all of East Anglia, much of Northumberland and York.
878	Alfred the Great defeats the Danes, and a treaty gives the Danes control northeast of the Chester-London line. He codifies laws, forms a navy, establishes schools and fortified towns, starts the Anglo-Saxon Chronicle.
981	The Danes defeat the forces of Ethelred the Unready, annex England. King Canute (Cnut) the Great marries Ethelred's widow, and is accepted as the English king.
1042	Canute's stepson Edward the Confessor becomes king (1042–1066).
1066	Edward dies and his first cousin once-removed, William, Duke of Normandy, defeats the Anglo-Saxons at the Battle of Hastings. William ruthlessly consolidates control, introduces Norman feudalism, installs Norman landholders and churchmen.

1071–1138	Norman kings: William II, called Rufus (1087–1100), Henry I (1100–1135), Stephen (1135–1154).
1154	Henry Plantagenet (1154–1159) invades England and is crowned Henry II.
1170	Thomas à Becket, Archbishop of Canterbury, is murdered in Canterbury Cathedral by four of Henry II's knights.
1189	Henry II is defeated at Chinon, France, by his heir, Richard, crowned Richard I (the Lion-Hearted, 1189–1199).
1199	King John (1199–1216), youngest son of Henry II, is crowned. He loses Normandy, wins the sobriquet "Lackland."
1215	King John is forced by his barons to sign the Magna Carta at Runnymede.
1216	Henry III (1216–1272) ascends the throne, battles rebellious barons.
1265	The first Parliament assembles.
1272	Edward I (1272–1307) conquers Wales, backs John de Baliol in a battle with Robert the Bruce for the Scottish throne. Bruce is defeated.
1295	Parliament is established.
1301	At Caernarvon, Edward I presents his son as the first Prince of Wales and heir to the throne.
1307	Edward II (1307–1327) succeeds to the throne at his father's death, but, defeated by Robert the Bruce at Bannockburn, is deposed and murdered.
1327	Edward III (1327–1377) becomes king at age 14. Scotland is recognized as a separate kingdom in 1328.
1337	Edward claims the French throne; the Hundred Years War with France begins.
1348	The Black Death sweeps Europe.
1356	The French king is taken prisoner at Poitiers by Edward the Black Prince, the son of Edward III. English possessions in France are lost after the Black Prince dies.
1377	Edward II is succeeded by his 14-year-old grandson, Richard II (1377–1399), who subdues the Peasant Rebellion of 1381.
1399–1413	Bolingbroke usurps power as Henry IV (1399–1413), first of the Lancaster kings.
1413	Henry V (1413–1422), Henry IV's son, renews the claim to the French throne. He dies during the siege of Meaux.
1422	The infant Henry VI (1422–1461) succeeds his father, Henry V. Joan of Arc inspires French resistance.

1431	Joan of Arc is burned at the stake.
1453	The Hundred Years War ends, with France lost to the English.
1455	The Wars of the Roses begin between the houses of York and Lancaster battling for the throne. Competing warlords create near-anarchy.
1461	Edward of York defeats Henry VI, is enthroned as Edward IV (1461–1483). His son succeeds him as Edward V (1483), but is murdered with his younger brother in the Tower of London.
1483	The throne is seized by the Duke of Gloucester, who becomes Richard III (1483–1485).
1485	Henry Tudor defeats Richard III at the Battle of Bosworth, becomes Henry VII (1485–1509), joining Wales to England. He marries the daughter of (Yorkist) Edward IV, ends the Wars of the Roses.
1509	Henry VIII (1509–1547) succeeds his father, breaks away from Roman Catholicism, establishes the Church of England, confiscates monasteries.
1534	Henry VIII divorces Catherine of Aragon (mother of Mary I).
1536	Henry's second wife, Anne Boleyn (mother of Elizabeth I), is executed.
1537	Henry's third wife, Jane Seymour, dies as the future Edward VI is born.
1540	Henry marries Anne of Cleves; the marriage is annulled and he marries Catherine Howard.
1542	Catherine Howard is executed.
1543	Henry marries Katherine Parr, his sixth and last wife.
1547	Edward VI (1547–1553) succeeds Henry VIII, supports the Church of England.
1553	Mary I, "Bloody Mary" (1553–1558), restores Catholicism and persecutes Protestants.
1554	Mary marries Philip II of Spain.
1558	At Mary's death, Elizabeth I (1558–1603) becomes Queen, reestablishes Church of England, supports exploration, the arts, and the sciences.
1561	Mary Stuart, Queen of Scots, returns to Scotland from France.
1565	Mary marries Lord Darnley.
1566	Darnley murders Rizzio, Mary's secretary.
1567	The Earl of Bothwell murders Darnley, Mary marries Bothwell, the Scots revolt against Mary.
1568	Mary's troops are defeated, and she flees to England.

1577	Sir Francis Drake sails around the world.
1587	Mary Queen of Scots is executed.
1588	The Spanish Armada is defeated.
1603	James I (1603–1625), son of Mary Queen of Scots, a descendant of Henry VII, is also James VI of Scotland, uniting England and Scotland.
1605	Guy Fawkes's plot to blow up Parliament is thwarted (the discovery is celebrated even today by children begging for money on Guy Fawkes Day, Nov. 4).
1620	The *Mayflower* sails for America.
1625	Charles I (1625–1649) ascends the throne, tries to govern without Parliament (1629–1640).
1642–1649	Civil war in which Parliamentarians, called "Roundheads," are victorious. Charles I is executed.
1649–1660	Puritan Commonwealth, headed by Oliver Cromwell (1653–1658) and Richard Cromwell (1658–1659).
1660	The monarchy is restored, Charles II (1660–1685) returns to England and the throne.
1665	Bubonic plague strikes England again.
1666	The Great Fire of London burns 13,000 houses in five days.
1685	Accession of James II (1685–1688), whose daughter Mary married William of Orange. William invades England. James flees to France.
1688	William III and Mary II rule (1688–1702).
1689	Bill of Rights establishes Parliament's supremacy.
1702	Anne, Mary's sister, James II's daughter, becomes queen (1702–1714), the last of the Stuarts.
1702	The War of Spanish Succession begins, involving England against France.
1706–1709	The Duke of Marlborough is victorious over the French.
1707	The Treaty of Union between England and Scotland unites their parliaments.
1714	George I (1714–1727), a German descendant of James I, becomes King by Parliamentary decree.
1727	George II (1727–1760) becomes king.
1745	Charles Edward Stuart, "Bonnie Prince Charlie" (b. 1720, d. 1788), the "Young Pretender" in Scotland, attempts to regain the throne for the Stuarts.
1746	The Battle of Culloden crushes the Scots uprising. Charles Stuart flees to France.
1756–1763	Britain defeats the French in Canada.

1760	George III (1760–1820) succeeds to the throne.
1776–1783	The American War of Independence.
1789	The French Revolution begins.
1805	Nelson defeats a Franco-Spanish fleet at Trafalgar.
1807	England abolishes the slave trade.
1811–1820	The Regency Period begins while George III is still king; his son becomes regent and succeeds as George IV (1820–1830), followed by William IV (1830–1837).
1815	Wellington defeats Napoleon at Waterloo.
1825	The first railway opens in England.
1832	Voting rights are extended to the middle class by the Reform Bill.
1837	Victoria (1837–1901) ascends the throne.
1851	The Great Exhibition, in London, shows wonders of the Industrial Revolution.
1854–1856	The Crimean War.
1861	Prince Albert dies.
1887	Victoria is named Empress of India.
1899–1902	The Boer War is fought in South Africa.
1901	Edward VII (1901–1910) succeeds Victoria.
1910	George V (1910–1936) ascends the throne.
1914–1918	World War I.
1918	An act of Parliament gives women the right to vote.
1922	The Irish Free State is established; Ulster (Northern Ireland) remains part of the United Kingdom.
1926	A General Strike of workers cripples the nation.
1936	Edward VIII abdicates and is succeeded by his brother, George VI (1936–1952).
1939–1945	World War II. Winston Churchill is Prime Minister.
1945	A Labour government is elected.
1947	India is granted independence; the British Empire is dismantled.
1949	Britain joins the North Atlantic Treaty Organization (NATO).
1952	Elizabeth II (1952–) becomes queen.
1973	Britain joins the European Economic Community.
1979	Margaret Thatcher becomes the first woman Prime Minister.
1981	Royal Wedding of Prince Charles and Lady Diana Spencer.
1982	Britain retakes the Falkland Islands from Argentina.
1986	Royal wedding of Prince Andrew and Sarah Ferguson.

BRITISH CULTURE IN A CAPSULE
Architecture

ARCHITECTURAL PERIODS IN BRITAIN

3000–43 B.C.	Prehistoric
43 B.C.–412 A.D.	Roman
412–1066	Anglo-Saxon Romanesque
1066–1190	Norman Romanesque
1190–1300	Gothic (Early English)
1300–1340	Gothic (Decorated)
1340–1500	Gothic (Perpendicular)
1485–1603	Tudor
1558–1603	Elizabethan
1603–1625	Jacobean
1625–1688	Stuart (Palladian, neoclassical)
1688–1714	Queen Anne
1714–1830	Georgian
1810–1820	Regency
1837–1901	Victorian
1901–1914	Edwardian
1915–present	Contemporary

The British have been great builders, as the surviving
fortresses, churches, castles, manors, and royal or government buildings show. The following are examples of the
periods listed above:

Prehistoric. Impressive and mysterious circles of
dressed stones at sites such as Stonehenge and Silbury.

Roman. Hadrian's Wall, amphitheaters at Chester and
Caerleon, spa complex at Bath, villas at Chedworth,
Bignor.

Saxon. Few, such as the church at Bradford-on-Avon, or a
tower, crypt, or chapel incorporated in another structure.

Norman. Fortresses, castles, and churches, such as the
inner Tower of London; St. Bartholomew the Great in
London; Winchester Cathedral; and especially Durham
Cathedral; Edward I's castles in Wales.

Monastic orders brought Gothic architecture to Britain.
It is seen in the Early English, Decorated, and Perpendicular styles that evolved from the 1170s through the
1540s.

Gothic (Early English). Salisbury Cathedral.

Gothic (Decorated). Exeter Cathedral.

Gothic (Perpendicular). King's College Chapel at
Cambridge.

Tudor and Elizabethan. "Stately homes" era—buildings for nobles, wealthy merchants, using brick, timber, many chimneys, leaded windows—as at Knole, Burghley House, Hatfield House; palaces such as Hampton Court.

Jacobean and Stuart. Neoclassicism introduced in Palladian designs by Inigo Jones and Christopher Wren, as in London's Banqueting Hall, St. Paul's Cathedral, and the Royal Naval College at Greenwich.

Georgian. (including Queen Anne and Regency) Many styles, from severe and plain to baroque, using materials ranging from brick to dressed stone and grand urban designs, as at Bath. Palatial "stately homes" proliferated. Leading architects: John Vanbrugh, Nicholas Hawksmoor, James Gibbs, Robert and James Adam, John Wood, Sr. and Jr., Lord Burlington, James Wyatt, Henry Holland, John Nash. Examples: Castle Howard, Yorkshire; Blenheim, Oxfordshire; Royal Crescent, Bath; St. Martin-in-the-Fields; Osterley Park House; Regent Street, London; Royal Pavilion, Brighton.

Victorian and Edwardian. Wide-ranging styles, from monumental neoclassical to decorated neo-Gothic, often using new materials such as steel and ceramics, by architects such as Robert Smirke, John Soane, and Charles Barry. Structures include Parliament, the British Museum, Kensington museums, the Albert Bridge, major railway terminals.

Contemporary. Generally solid and cautious, with perhaps fewer pleasures for the eye (London's South Bank complex) than motes (Barbican Arts Centre; Shell Building) and a limited number of experimental successes (Sainsbury Centre, Norwich; Burrell Collection, Glasgow).

Sculpture and Painting

When sculpture and painting began in Britain, no one knows. Surviving early examples are primarily stone sculpture in Roman motifs and Celtic crosses.

Church and monastic buildings, which required figures of deities and saints for altars, roodscreens, doorways, and façades, as well as effigies for tombs, gave tremendous impetus to figurative sculpture in Britain. The sculptors of Nottingham, who specialized in alabaster, were so skilled that their works were prized on the Continent.

Meanwhile, church walls were painted with murals, and monks were at work illuminating manuscripts (such as the 12th-century Winchester Bible and the 14th-century Luttrell Psalter).

The Reformation and Henry VIII's break with Rome released art in Britain from the grip of religious themes. Suddenly, in Tudor times, portraits of living persons proliferated. Most famous artists of this period are imported portraitists such as Hans Holbein and, in the Stuart era, Anthony Van Dyck, Godfrey Kneller, and Peter Lely.

Patrons—royal and otherwise—of the arts continued to import painters and purchase works abroad until the 18th century, largely because home-grown talent had not achieved equal capability. But in the 18th century, James Thornhill won the commission to do the dome of St. Paul's Cathedral, and the social satirist William Hogarth and the visionary William Blake emerged.

The portraitists Joshua Reynolds, Thomas Gainsborough, and George Romney scored great successes with royal and noble patrons, and established the Royal Academy of Arts in 1768. Landscapes flowed from the brushes of Richard Wilson and Thomas Jones and (in the 19th century), John Constable, J. M. W. Turner, Francis Danby, Samuel Palmer, John Martin, and Edwin Landseer. The anatomist George Stubbs painted animals, especially horses, as none had before him. Thomas Lawrence was the preeminent portraitist in the first third of the 19th century, but his heroic style gave way to the Pre-Raphaelites, Dante Gabriel Rossetti, J. E. Millais, Sir Edward Burne-Jones, and W. H. Hunt, who brought medieval legend and fantasy into their works.

In the 1880s, British artists with continental training reacted against the Royal Academy and formed the New English Art Club, which used current French techniques and promoted regional themes and pride. The Scots George Henry, John Lavery, and James Guthrie won fame at this time.

At the turn of the century, Walter Sickert and the American James McNeill Whistler were among the leading exponents of British Impressionism.

By 1911, British Post-Impressionists Roger Fry, Harold Gilman, Spencer Gore, and Robert Bevan exhibited as the Camden Town Group.

In this century, leading British painters have included Augustus John, Ben Nicholson, Francis Bacon, J. D. Innes, and David Hockney. Some major sculptors have been Jacob Epstein, Barbara Hepworth, John Davies, and Henry Moore.

Dance and Music

Britain is an incredibly rich, nearly nonstop fountain of music. Whether it's the latest in electronic-augmented rock or the most ancient of monastic chants, the newest West End musical or medieval minstrelsy, you're likely to find it in performance. And during spring and summer, music festivals blossom throughout the land. For our listing of the major ones, see below.

Dance. British dancing is interesting in its folk variations, competent in its contemporary West End musical form, and remarkable, often inspired, in its ballets.

To put it another way, if you look for Scottish sword dances and Irish jigs, Morris and country dances, you will probably find them. You are certain to see dance sequences well done in current West End productions—but they are as likely to be the products of American choreography as British. It is nearly certain that somewhere in Britain you will find excellent ballet troupes in action.

Since the Ballets Russe captivated London in 1911, the development of British ballet—at first as the Royal Ballet Company—has surprised and delighted millions in and out of Britain.

From the days when it provided the dance sequences for Sadler's Wells operas, the Royal Ballet has come far. Today it is internationally famous and has a permanent home base in Covent Garden, which it shares with the Royal Opera Company.

But it is not alone. Perhaps even better known abroad is its offshoot, the Sadler's Wells Ballet, which is often on international tour. In fact, the world learned about British ballet largely through the tours of the Sadler's Wells Ballet and the immensely popular film *The Red Shoes.* And there were stars such as ballerinas Moira Shearer and

Margot Fonteyn and choreographer Frederick Ashton. The company is usually found in London in May and again in September and October at the Sadler's Wells Theatre.

Like all dynamic performing arts, dance in Britain is constantly changing, and dance aficionados will need to follow closely reports of new dance companies and their presentations to keep up with evolving work in this field. During the summer in London, outdoor dance performances are frequent at stages such as the Serpentine in Hyde Park and the Holland Park open-air theater.

For current dance information, see the publications suggested under "Information Sources" on page 15.

Music. The musical creativity of British composers such as Benjamin Britten, Frederick Delius, Ralph Vaughan Williams, and Sir Edward Elgar has won appreciative audiences. But in the past century it is in more popular genres that British music has scored its greatest successes and won its most enthusiastic followings.

Building on the robust British music-hall tradition, Sir William Gilbert and Sir Arthur Sullivan collaborated on a series of wildly successful comic operas from 1875 on. Produced at the Savoy Theatre with enormous success by Richard D'Oyly Carte and his successors for nearly three generations, the Gilbert and Sullivan operettas (*The Pirates of Penzance, Patience, Iolanthe,* and *The Mikado* among them), with their witty satire and tuneful melodies, captivated a world audience.

In the first half of the 20th century Noël Coward was a leading crafter of British popular music. But it was the Liverpudlian Beatles who revolutionized the world's popular music in the sixties. And British innovation continues with such pop groups as the Rolling Stones in one genre and Andrew Lloyd Webber and his associates (*Evita, Cats, Jesus Christ Superstar, Starlight Express*) in another.

The music-performing Britons are remarkable in quantity as well as quality. There are so many of them and they sing and/or play so well that you can't miss or overlook music in Britain.

Whether it's amateur or professional, jazz or classical, recitals or oratorios, performed by church choirs or buskers, you'll find musicians concertizing from lunchtime on, almost every day of every week somewhere within earshot.

And that is true not only of London, but of many towns and cities across the land.

In summer, the British Isles seem to be swept with live music performances, not only in the conventional sites, but in the perennial enthusiasms known as festivals that erupt everywhere. The major ones you will have heard of—Edinburgh, Glyndebourne, Malvern, Bath—but the countryside is alive with festivals from May through September. In a surprising number of instances, what seem to be remote places manage to feature nationally-known musicians or groups. And even when the performers are local only, the level of musicianship is usually high.

One of the delights of a British visit for music lovers is the opportunity to indulge their interests many times over. And when the festival is in a lovely setting—Harrogate or Chester or Greenwich, for instance—the pleasure of the music is multiplied.

There is no central clearinghouse for all the concerts taking place around Britain—there are too many, and most are local. In your travels you must be alert to posters stuck in shop and restaurant windows, pinned to church and school bulletin boards, pasted on fences. These will be notices about candlelight concerts in castles, recitals in stately homes, jazz in chapels, chamber works in churches and libraries. All of these are in addition to the well-advertised festivals and concert-hall appearances.

Some of the regular venues are as follows (see London theater listings for addresses and telephone numbers):

Opera at Royal Opera House, Covent Garden, by the Royal Opera Company and at the London Coliseum by the English National Opera Company.

Chamber music and recitals at Wigmore Hall and chapels and churches.

Symphonic and classical music at Royal Albert Hall, Royal Festival Hall, Barbican Hall, large churches and cathedrals.

"Early" music is sung and played in smaller halls and churches. Check sources below for listings.

Outdoor concerts in summer. In London, try St. James's, Regent's, Hyde, and Kensington parks (especially on Sundays), and Greenwich Park, Lincoln's Inn Fields, and the steps of St. Paul's on Thursdays at noon.

Jazz is as improvisational in scheduling as in performance, with concerts around Britain at various halls and times. One sure venue is Ronnie Scott's in London. Check "Information Sources" suggested below.

The Proms, or Promenade Concerts, July through September every year. Top-notch performers, lowest possible prices; friendly queue begins about 6 P.M. at Royal Albert Hall.

Easter and Christmas music. Each church in the land seems to field the finest presentation of seasonal music that it can afford. Consequently, the entire country is a musical feast at these times. See local newspapers for listings.

Festivals and Special Concerts (Our suggestions, from the scores offered):

- English Bach Festival: London in early May; Oxford in late May.
- Malvern Festival, Malvern, Worcestershire: Shaw's plays, Elgar's music; May–June.
- Bath Festival, Bath, Avon: orchestral, choral music; May–June.
- Glyndebourne Festival Season, Glyndebourne, Sussex: Mozart and other operas; black ties and picnic suppers; May–August.
- Aldeburgh Festival, Aldeburgh, Suffolk: Britten operas, classical music, films; June.
- International Music Eisteddfod, Llangollen, Wales: choirs, folk dancing, and song competition; July.
- Edinburgh International Festival, Edinburgh, Scotland: the oldest and biggest, with opera, orchestral and chamber music, dance, mime, theater; August–September.
- Brighton Festival, Brighton, East Sussex: opera, classical, rock, pop, jazz, dance, films; May.
- Greenwich Festival, Greenwich, Greater London: classical, jazz, and folk music; June.
- Chichester Festival, Chichester, West Sussex: classical and jazz music, films; July.
- Chester Festival, Chester, Cheshire: classical and jazz music; July.
- Harrogate Festival, Harrogate, North Yorkshire: classical music, dance, theater; August.
- Belfast Festival, Belfast, Northern Ireland: opera, classical, jazz, dance, and theater in Ireland's biggest arts festival; November.

INFORMATION SOURCES

Check *What's On and Where to Go in London*, *Time Out*, and listings in the *Daily Telegraph*, the *Times*, the *Guardian*, and tourist information offices. For festivals, contact: Coordinator, BAFA, 23 Orchard Road, London N6 5TR.

Literature

For English speakers, a visit to Britain is like coming home. We share the same literature, theater history, and literary figures and heroes. The byways of Britain are peopled with names and references that evoke pleasurable associations. For many of us, some of the greatest touring pleasures come from visits to the homes, haunts, or habitats of Keats, Byron, Kipling, Dickens, and other literary giants, and from watching Royal Shakespeare Company actors bringing *Twelfth Night* to life, or a National Theatre production of a seldom-seen Restoration comedy by Etherege.

English literature is a richly veined and mined mother lode going back to *Beowulf*. Much later, Alfred the Great ordered the Anglo-Saxon Chronicles, which were compiled in the 9th century by monks working in Canterbury, Winchester, Peterborough, and other centers.

The medieval period of language, poetry, and the theater of Mystery and Miracle plays (in which Gospel events were retold and dramatized) is revived today in festivals such as the York Mystery Cycle. Memories of Chaucer's *Canterbury Tales* are evoked with each visit to Canterbury. In the 14th century, along with Chaucer, came William Langland with *Piers Plowman*.

Thomas Malory's *Morte d'Arthur*, written in the 15th century, told the legends of King Arthur's era, which a visit to Glastonbury brings to mind.

When the Tudor monarchs consolidated their power, a golden age of literature flowered. Its luminaries were Edmund Spenser, with his poetic *Faerie Queene*, the dramatists William Shakespeare, Christopher Marlowe, Ben Jonson, Thomas Middleton, John Webster, and the team of Francis Beaumont and John Fletcher. You may think of Fletcher while having tea in his house in Rye. The Marlowe Theatre in Canterbury is a reminder of that town's native son. And visiting tranquil Penshurst Place in Kent, where Sir Philip Sidney was born, one can understand the inspiration for his sonnets.

The Reformation and Cromwellian times introduced a more serious note in literature, with works like John Milton's *Paradise Lost*, as well as the poetry of Robert Herrick and John Donne.

Wit and satire took center stage in the late 17th century with the Restoration, and the vanities and vices of the nobility were wittily portrayed on stage in comedies like William Congreve's *The Way of the World*, William Wycherley's *The Country Wife*, and George Etherege's *The Man of Mode*, as well as others by poet laureate John Dryden and architect-playwright John Vanbrugh. Their works are revived regularly on the current British stage, bringing that licentious era vibrantly to life. Even if you miss seeing Vanbrugh's *The Provok'd Wife* performed, his architectural work is clearly visible at Blenheim, Castle Howard, and the Haymarket Theatre in London. Samuel Pepys is better known for his famous diary than for his work as an Admiralty official.

The 18th century introduced another great era of literature in England, with the irreverence of Alexander Pope's *Dunciad*, Jonathan Swift's satirical *Gulliver's Travels*, and John Gay's *Beggar's Opera* (which we see more often in Brecht's version, *The Threepenny Opera*).

The English novel as we know it had 18th-century antecedents in Daniel Defoe's *Robinson Crusoe* and *Moll Flanders*, followed by such riches as Henry Fielding's *Tom Jones*, Laurence Sterne's *Tristram Shandy*, Samuel Richardson's *Pamela*, and the novels of Jane Austen. The Bath of Austen's day has changed a little, but you can still follow her footsteps through the city she knew so well.

Other 18th-century milestones were playwright Oliver Goldsmith's *She Stoops to Conquer* and the poems of Thomas Gray, William Cowper, and Robert Burns. While Samuel Johnson compiled his famous dictionary and *Lives of the Poets*, his friend and biographer, James Boswell, followed him around London, taking notes for his *Life of Samuel Johnson*. Traces of their London are still visible in Holborn and the City.

The 19th century was another age of literary abundance, with the romantic poetry of John Keats, Percy Shelley, Lord Byron, William Wordsworth, Samuel Taylor Coleridge, and Thomas de Quincey, and novels by Thomas Hardy, William Thackeray, George Eliot, Charles Dickens, the Brontë sisters, Sir Walter Scott, and Robert Louis Stevenson.

Dickens left a trail the visitor can follow even today, both in London and throughout Mr. Pickwick's Kent. Oscar Wilde's London was a more fashionable one, but it lives, too, in Victorian salons. Echoes of Rudyard Kipling's India reverberate at Bateman's, his home in Kent.

Admirers of Thomas Hardy are impressed by their first views of Dorset and how vividly the novelist recreated its landscape in *Tess of the D'Urbervilles, The Return of the Native, Jude the Obscure,* and his other novels.

English authors have always been able to evoke a special "sense of place" that is so tangible we recognize it even *before* we visit it for the first time—like the moors of Emily and Charlotte Brontë, the lakes of Wordsworth's Lake District, Coleridge's Devon, D. H. Lawrence's Nottinghamshire, Robert Burns's Scotland, and the Wales of Dylan Thomas.

Visits to Oxford and Cambridge remind us of the early-20th-century writings of Aldous Huxley and Evelyn Waugh and the more recent times and novels of C. P. Snow. Walking in London's Mayfair, we see people right out of Nancy Mitford's pages, and in Bloomsbury we are reminded of the world of Virginia Woolf, Vita Sackville-West, and Lytton Strachey.

Contemporary English literature continues to thrive, with current plays by Tom Stoppard, Harold Pinter, Michael Frayn, and Peter Shaffer, and novels by Lawrence Durrell, Kingsley Amis, Graham Greene, John Le Carré, John Fowles, and Anthony Burgess. It is more than likely that, in time, other tourists will be following *their* trails through the English countryside.

Folk Art and Handicrafts

The craft tradition is alive in Britain. In many towns and villages you will find exhibitions by local craftsmen, as well as many shops featuring well-designed, original contemporary handicrafts. Ceramics in England and weaving in Scotland and Wales are particularly strong, drawing on long traditions.

Much of the craft revival stems from the 19th-century Arts and Crafts movement spearheaded by William Morris and his associates as a reaction against the Industrial Revolution and its emphasis on machine-made goods rather than handwork. Morris, Sir Edward Burne-Jones, and others enjoyed considerable vogue, and their achievements are admired today. Craft aficionados will want to make a pilgrimage to the William Morris Gallery. (See the section on "Excursions from London.")

The current English revival of pottery stems largely from the influence of the late Bernard Leach, an internationally known potter. Leach's grandson John carries on the family tradition with a pottery and shop in the tiny Somerset town of Muchelney.

Pottery and handweaving are by no means the only handicrafts you will see in Britain. Woodwork, silver, jewelry, glass—virtually every craft viable in the United States, Canada, or Australia has its exponents in Britain as well.

For an introduction to the contemporary craft scene, drop by the Crafts Council, 12 Waterloo Place, London SW1; tel. 930-4811. Just two minutes from Piccadilly Circus, the council's information center has changing exhibitions as well as books and other publications containing extensive data about contemporary crafts and craftsmen in England and Wales. It also distributes an invaluable "Crafts Map" that identifies and locates dozens of workshops, stores, and galleries that specialize in high-quality contemporary crafts on exhibit and sale. The council has checked each of them for quality and high standards. Thus, as you travel through the countryside, you can plan your craft stops accordingly.

"Folk art," in the sense of indigenous or people's art, has pretty much died out in Britain, though in village fairs you may see corn-husk "dollies," and rustic carvings made by local hobbyists.

A remarkable example of indigenous folk art is that of the "pearlies," those cockney Londoners who adorn themselves with pearl buttons sewn on every inch of their clothing so they almost literally shine. You may still encounter the Pearly King or Pearly Queen, but the tradition is fading.

A DAY IN THE LIFE . . .

Come along and spend a day with an average middle-class British family. Though three-quarters of Britain is agricultural, only 3 percent of its citizens live on farms. The overwhelming majority live in cities and towns and work in manufacturing, mining, or service jobs.

John and Alice Wensley, both 43 years old, are "modern" Britons. They met at college in the Midlands, where he earned his accounting degree and she studied English literature. Married 17 years, they live with their children Eleanor, 16, and Arthur, 14, and a Scottie dog and a tabby cat, in a semidetached tract house in Ealing, west of London.

The Wensleys own their home, like most Britons (only one in five lives in an apartment). The house was built after World War II, as were 40 percent of all British houses, and has a tiny, well-kept garden on the street next to the driveway. Inside, on the ground floor you will find a living room, kitchen, and dining room, and upstairs are three bedrooms. There is a small patio and yard in the rear of the house, for Alice's vegetable and flower gardens.

A typical day starts off with family breakfast, a serial event. John wolfs down toast, a boiled egg, and tea at 7:30, then walks the six blocks to the Underground station where he buys the *Daily Telegraph* before boarding the train to Whitehall and his work as a government clerk. There are 667,000 like him with government jobs; in all, there are 4½ million people who work in London.

Alice sips tea while preparing porridge for the children, who eat quickly before catching the bus to the comprehensive (middle-track public) school, where classes begin at 9 A.M. and end at 4 P.M. The Wensleys have a full-scale English breakfast only on weekends and holidays when there is ample time for grapefruit, cereal, eggs, and bacon or kippers, toast, marmalade, and tea.

Alice works three mornings a week as a typist at a local real-estate office, but today she has arranged to meet an old schoolmate for lunch at a trendy new restaurant near

Harrods and shop in the city for new slipcovers for her living room sofa. Normally she would do all her grocery shopping at the supermarket and greengrocer's near home, but having made the trip to South Kensington via Underground, she buys the family some treats—blue Cheshire cheese and a hazelnut torte—at Harrods' famous Food Halls. Lunch—prawn salad, tea, and a pastry—is not cheap and the two ladies walk to the V&A (Victoria and Albert Museum) for a quick look at the latest show—handwoven rugs from Uzbekistan—and old favorite exhibits in the permanent collection.

At about 4:30 P.M., the children return (unless there is a club meeting or intramural ball game). Eleanor and her girlfriend grab biscuits and sodas to fortify themselves for homework. Arthur and his chum explore a new computer program in the electronics corner of his bedroom.

By the time John Wensley arrives home about 6:15, Alice has ready an uncomplicated meal of linguini with homemade meat sauce, garden string beans and carrots, and the Harrods pastry. At dinner, the only time in the weekday the family spends together, conversation shifts from politics (Eleanor likes to take a Liberal line to provoke her Conservative Party parents) to plans for a Saturday drive in the family Ford to Brighton, and perhaps a swim, if the weather is warm enough. They also talk about a vacation to Spain's Costa del Sol for a week in midwinter. John and Alice want to escape Britain's rainy and chilling weather during the midterm break, and have saved for this for a year. Choosing among several inexpensive package tours to Benidorm prompts some lively discussion.

After dinner there is a brief debate about which of the four channels on TV the family will watch. The unanimous choice would be either a cricket or football (soccer) game, but none is scheduled. The decision (the children's votes are not as weighty as their parents'), therefore, is a symposium on the future of Britain in the European Economic Community. Arthur and Eleanor flee to their rooms (she is studying for exams that will determine whether she qualifies for university, where she wants to study Greek classics) until the American gangster movie scheduled at 9 P.M. comes on.

John and Alice have had their quota of movie mayhem,

and instead of watching the nine o'clock movie, they walk three blocks to their "local," the Green Man pub. There they meet neighbors and friends and chat over a pint or two of bitter until the 10:30 P.M. closing time. Then it's home again to walk the dog and remind the children it is bedtime and close up the house before turning in for the night.

THE MOOD OF THE PEOPLE

Friendly. In a word, that's the mood of Brits toward you who are about to visit. In fact, not to put too fine a point on it, they love Americans and most other English-speaking people almost as much as their "cuppa" and daily pint.

Cynics would have you believe that it's their folding green that endears tourists to Britons. Like many half-truths, that's far from the whole story.

Those who were in Britain during the Great Dearth (1986, when fear of terrorism kept Americans away in droves) can testify that the yearning to have more Yanks peering through their windows, poking about their gardens, and parading around their museums and palaces was all but palpable. And it was far from commercial. The attitude was (and is) like that reserved for the prodigal son that the family considers a bit daft but dear and enjoys having about, regardless of his foibles.

Britain has its share of triumphs (royal weddings, theater, art exhibits, opera, ballet, music) and vicissitudes (oil slump, high unemployment, limping economy). But it is complex enough, driven by enough countervailing cross-currents, and resilient enough to have a citizenry that copes with life as it is—and prevails, with good spirit. You'll see.

HOW MUCH WILL IT COST?

The quick and accurate answer is "It's impossible to tell." That's because only you know what you are willing to spend (what your marginal cost point is on transportation, accommodations, eating, etc.), what season you will be there, how much British prices may have risen (what their inflation rate is), and what the exchange rate of the dollar will be when you make your trip.

However, we can lay out some of the possibilities and you can make some reasonable estimates as to where your needs and wants follow or diverge from these.

Airfare ranges from the ultimate luxury of a Concorde flight to the bare-bones round trip via a discounter, with extra charges for each bag, and for a box lunch or refreshments. As you know, prices vary according to season (low, shoulder, and peak). In addition, some airlines offer stand-by fares, available on the day of departure.

Via ship, your options are limited primarily to the *Queen Elizabeth 2*'s regularly scheduled transatlantic crossings. It has two fare structures, for first and transatlantic classes and youth fares for travelers under 26 years of age.

Here are some figures from which you can estimate your potential costs per person per day:

	Deluxe	Moderate	Inexpensive
Hotel (w/continental breakfast, double rm.)			
London	$150–250	$90–150	$60–80
Provinces	90–120	60–80	40–50
Restaurant (lunch and dinner w/o drinks)			
London	45–70	20–40	10–15
Provinces	25–40	15–20	6–10
DAILY TOTALS:			
London	$195–320	$110–190	$70–95
Provinces	115–160	75–100	46–60

Hotels are plentiful (except during peak season, when some international convention is in the place you've chosen) and range across a wide price spectrum. In general, hotels of comparable quality are more expensive in London and tourist magnet areas than in smaller towns and villages.

Restaurants range from posh to nosh. You can find the finest cuisine with prices to match, or subsist on finger food and tea—or pitch your dining decisions anywhere in between.

Transportation is not cheap in Britain. Reasonable and

cheaper than major U.S. cities, yes. But you will want to watch your transportation outlays carefully.

Balance all that against the many delights that are free—many museums, most churches, all government buildings, schools, libraries, and parks, lunchtime and foyer concerts, walks and hikes, as well as those serendipitous pleasures you happen upon without plan—and your sightseeing in Britain can be a bargain.

Many British hotels, especially the hotel chains, offer attractive package deals at bargain prices. This is true even of some of the most prestigious hotels (though seldom the small deluxe-class country hotels). Most hotels offer discounts for children and many hotels offer discounts for senior citizens (the British call them "pensioners"). It pays to ask.

There are special deals ("breaks," the British call them) on rail and bus transportation. See the sections on "Getting to Britain (By Train)" and "How to Get Around."

THE BEST TIME TO GO

Oh, to be in England
Now that April's there.

Easy for Robert Browning to write, and in sunny Italy. He remembered the bursts of color from blossoming crocuses, daffodils, and orchards chroming the English countryside from doorstep gardens to lambent valleys. He took poetic license with the rain.

T. S. Eliot may have been nearer the mark when he wrote, "April is the cruellest month." Though he was not referring to the weather specifically, the statement is apt. Chaucer focused on its central feature in saying "Aprille with his shoures sote / The droghte of Marche hath percéd to the rote."

The fact is, an English spring can wrap you in rain, sleet, hail, snow, or fog (or any combination of them), all within minutes. Then, as you are about to resign yourself to such punishment, rotten weather may whimsically sweep away and you may be bathed in glorious sunshine.

British spring weather is changeable. It can be blustery and chilly with a surprising variety of precipitation.

Summers in the south (including London) can be hot and sticky, but are usually temperate, with sun and light rain alternating. It's still light at 10 P.M. in June and July, and from June through August London's daytime temperatures range from 63 to 77 degrees, on average. Wear cottons and lightweight clothing, but don't forget your raincoat and a jacket or sweater for cooler evenings.

Fall weather is cooler and generally wetter. Winter's warm days are usually cloudy with rain; colder days may bring sleet. Highest humidity (averaging 85–86 percent) is from October through January. Roses blooming in December in London are no rarity. July's average temperatures are the highest (63 degrees) and January's the lowest (39 degrees).

PERILS & PITFALLS

All in all, 'tis a brave or foolhardy traveler who visits Britain without either rain gear or umbrella. May, June, and September have the fewest days with rain (averaging 12 per month) and October, November, and December the most (averaging 16).

When are you likely to find this small island country least crowded? Not in August or at Easter and Bank Holidays (which are the first and last Mondays in May and the last Monday in August). These are the great British migration times, when the natives take to roads, rails, and runways in huge numbers. The competition for hotel, restaurant, and theater bookings is intense at these times. A careful visitor notes this and plans ahead.

Christmas, in contrast, is a quiet family time in Britain. This means that theaters, restaurants, and businesses close up tight December 24–27. Even transportation—buses, Underground, and trains especially—are on limited schedules.

Yet Christmas is usually an interesting time to visit. You will enjoy it if you plan to spend Christmas itself quietly out of town. Country hotels and inns offer special Christmas holiday packages that feature traditional yule logs, caroling, coach or sleigh rides, fox hunts, feasting, and the peculiar British "pantomimes."

Public holidays include January 1, Good Friday, Easter Monday, May Day, Spring Bank Holiday (in May), Summer Bank Holiday (in August), Christmas Day (December 25), and Boxing Day (December 26).

HOW TO GO

For English-speaking people, Britain is unquestionably one of the easiest and pleasantest countries in which to travel.

After all, we can read the street signs, maps, guide books, tickets, and directions—and when all else fails, we can ask, can't we? As for personal safety, the hazards to life and limb are demonstrably fewer than in the major cities of the United States. In Britain a woman can travel alone with complete confidence, unlike some other areas of the world, where she would be harassed.

The facility and safety of Britain differentiate it from other destinations. When you visit a country whose language and customs are alien, it's often advisable or even necessary to go as part of a group, letting someone else take care of the essentials, providing explanations and translations.

Why would anyone need a package tour to Britain? The advantages of tours are cost, convenience, and companionship. A package tour often costs less than individual arrangements and usually takes care of booking hotels, meals, seats, and details such as baggage transfers. The question is whether the tour's format is a straitjacket or includes features that appeal to you—a question that requires you to review specifically what's included in the tour and to analyze what you want most. If you are a single traveler, the built-in companionship of a tour might be comforting.

Our belief is that for the person with an inquiring mind who finds it exhilarating to be on his or her own in a foreign land, a self-designed trip can be much more rewarding. By studying this book, by securing current travel data from the British Tourist Authority's offices, and by working with a travel agent, you can custom-tailor a satisfying trip to your own interests and specifications at reasonable cost. Furthermore, you will move at your pace, not in lockstep with others.

Between the covers of this book you will find much of

what you need to know about the mechanics of going to Britain and getting around while there. We have included information about specific restaurants and accommodations to help you make judicious choices. And you will find brief descriptions of places and pleasures with our evaluations of them to guide you in selecting things to do and see.

If you augment this with data from BTA and your local library, you can outline an itinerary that a knowledgeable travel agent can then implement. Furthermore, if you are a truly independent person, you will find in this book addresses and telephone numbers that can aid you in making your own arrangements.

DOCUMENTATION

A valid passport is required to visit Britain if you are from a Commonwealth country, the United States, or a non–European Economic Community nation. No International Health Certificate is necessary.

If you are bringing in a pet, you'll need to get a license for the animal before you arrive in Britain. It can be secured by mail from HM Customs and Excise, Kent House, Upper Ground, London SE1 9PS.

A valid U.K. firearms certificate is necessary if you are taking in firearms for sporting purposes. Details of the procedure are available from HM Customs and Excise, Kent House, Upper Ground, London SE1 9PS.

There are no restrictions on the amount of currency, bank notes, or travelers checks you may bring in or take out of Britain.

WHAT TO PACK

Essentials: At least one dress-up outfit—tie and jacket for men—for those dinners at special 4- or 5-star restaurants. Casual clothes for sightseeing should be neat, not beach casual. Include comfortable walking shoes and rain gear for those inevitable soggy days. Women should include a kerchief or hat for sea or mountain areas.

Drip-dry shirts, blouses, stockings, and underwear will save cleaning money, time, and inconvenience. Many luxury hotels and country houses equip each suite with an electrical device that presses pants and skirts.

A travel iron (or any electrical device) can be a source of frustration unless it is (a) able to function on 220-volt AC current; and (b) equipped with a British two- or three-pronged plug.

Most 4- and 5-star hotels have 110-volt AC outlets for electric razors; they also furnish hair dryers and have heated towel racks for drying clothes. Their amenities usually include a terrycloth robe (not to be taken), shampoo, bubble bath, comb, tissues, and a sewing kit. Many hotels, such as Trusthouse Forte, equip each room with a "teamaker," an electric kettle plus teabags and instant coffee packets.

You'll find all the familiar brands of cosmetics, drugs, vitamins, soaps, and personal-hygiene items in British shops, plus famous English and Continental brands.

Cigarettes, cigars, and tobacco are available, but at higher prices than in America. The same is true of bourbon and other American liquors. The bargains are in Scotch and Irish whiskey, British gin, sherry, port, and the superlative ales.

HINTS ON YOUR HEALTH

If you become ill or injured, there is a 24-hour-a-day emergency facility at London University College Hospital, Gower Street W1, tel. 837-9300. Away from London, call the police to locate the nearest emergency medical care.

Britain's National Health Service may cover certain emergency medical or dental treatment without charge. Nonemergency treatment is not covered. Check with the hospital, clinic, or doctor before any services are rendered to verify in what mode they will be done—whether for a fee or covered by NHS.

When you need a doctor, you will find a list of them at the nearest post office. Be sure to phone for an appointment, and expect to pay for services or prescriptions rendered.

For emergency dental work, there are three clinics open 24 hours a day in London. For the nearest one, phone 584-1008.

Pharmacies—chemist shops—are open during normal shopping hours. However, in every district or town, at least one "dispensing chemist" stays open late and for one hour on Sundays and public holidays.

TRAVEL FOR THE HANDICAPPED

Most British hotels and restaurants are equipped to make handicapped guests welcome and comfortable. Your travel agent can determine which places accommodate handicapped travelers, and to what extent (some may not be able to accept wheelchairs, for instance). It's advisable to give as much advance notice as possible to the hotel or restaurant about the nature of the handicap and services required.

The Holiday Care Service is designed to help persons who are elderly or disabled. This nonprofit, free service will advise on appropriate accommodations, as well as travel and other facilities. It will not book or make reservations. You can reach the Holiday Care Service at 2 Old Bank Chambers, Station Road, Horley, Surrey RH6 9HW; tel. 0293-774-535.

The British Tourist Authority issues a booklet concerning travel in Britain by disabled people.

GETTING TO BRITAIN

IF YOU'RE TAKING A PACKAGE TOUR

There's probably no other country in the world with Britain's wealth of tour offerings. Package tours run the gamut from general, once-over-lightly, first-time tours to special-interest ones focused on food, theater, art, antiques, and walking tours, conducted by experts. Which tour you choose depends on your interests.

As a rule of thumb, general tours are less expensive than more specialized ones, which often involve special arrangements and expert guides. Tours that stay at the most deluxe hotels and include most meals and many extras cost more than tours using adequate hotels with minimal frills.

A number of tour operators offer custom packages to Britain. These are not group tours, but independent packages in which you travel pretty much at your own speed, doing what you like, but your package price includes airfare, hotel, usually a half-day sightseeing tour, and perhaps a meal or two. British Airways, TWA, and British Caledonian Airways offer such packages, as does American Express. The package price is usually lower than the cost of making your own arrangements.

For inexpensive group tours that highlight major sights, Cosmos Tours is bargain-priced. Globus-Gateway and American Express offer good value and paint London's attractions with a broad brush.

Among the luxury tours, those offered by Abercrombie & Kent, such as a 16-day "Collectors and Collections" car (rather than coach) tour to some of England's great houses and art collections, and Maupintour, in its 16-day "Homes and Gardens of Britain," receive high marks for quality.

Cruising is an unusual way to see Britain, but Royal Viking Lines' "British Isles Cruises" makes it a pampered, luxurious experience, calling at Southampton, Loch Ness, Edinburgh, and the Isle of Man, with land trips as well. On a smaller scale, Esplanade Travel offers "Cruising Through Rural England" via its canals on a nine-person hotel-boat.

All of the above can be booked through your travel agent.

An example of special-interest tour diversity is "Cotswolds Way," one of 20 different walks offered by The Wayfarers, in which the pace is leisurely and you needn't be an expert hiker. Contact The Wayfarers, c/o Moira Lubbock, 535 W. 110 St., New York, NY 10025; tel. 212-678-0024. And for erudite, academic-led literary tours, those arranged through Plantagenet Tours are highly regarded and typical of the genre. Contact Plantagenet Tours, c/o Peter Gravgaard, 85 The Grove, Moordown, Bournemouth, Dorset BH9 2TY, England; tel. 0202-521-895.

The following is a list of addresses of major tour operators who specialize in and/or offer British itineraries:

- Abercrombie & Kent Travel International, 1420 Kensington Road, Suite 111, Oak Brook, IL 60521; tel. 800-323-7308.
- American Express Co., P.O. Box 5014, Atlanta, GA 30302; tel. 800-241-1700.
- Esplanade Tours, 38 Newbury Street, Boston, MA 02116; tel. 800-343-7184.
- Globus-Gateway/Cosmos, 95-25 Queens Boulevard, Rego Park, NY 11374; tel. 800-221-0090.
- Maupintour, P.O. Box 807, Lawrence, KS 66044; tel. 800-255-4266.
- Thomas Cook Travel, USA, 380 Madison Avenue, New York, NY 10017; tel. 212-916-0471. In Canada: Thomas Cook Travel (Canada, Ltd.), 14 Queen Street East, Toronto, Ont. M5C 2R8; tel. 416-863-6841/6.

AIRLINES

The good news for travelers is that fares on the North Atlantic routes have been driven down by intense competition, helped by lower energy costs. At this time, the lowest-priced flights are promotional one-way, scheduled, no-frills flights from Newark, N.J., to London's Gatwick airport for $199. You have to reserve these at least 21 days ahead. The regular economy fare at press time is $388 to $494 one way, and economy-class APEX fares from New York to London are $468 to $738 round trip.

The premium-priced trip is on British Airways' Concorde, whose round-trip New York–London fare is $5,490. (It also flies from both Miami Airport and Washington's Dulles Airport to London three times a week for $5,170 and $5,196 respectively.)

Regular first-class fares between New York and London are $2,087 one way.

"Business" class fares for the New York–London run are about $1,063 one way.

Some charter trips offer remarkable bargains. Typically, they fly into smaller, less convenient cities and include meals and drinks aloft, plus baggage transfers on the ground. Checking with your travel agent, scanning the travel pages of your local newspaper and travel magazines, or calling your college alumni association will almost always turn up attractively priced charter trips or group tours to England.

At this time, the following airlines serve Britain from the United States:

British Airways, British Caledonian Airways, Delta Airlines, World Airways, Northwest Orient Airlines, TWA, Pan Am, American Airlines, Air New Zealand (from Honolulu), Continental Airlines, Virgin Atlantic Airways, People Express Airlines, Air India, El Al, and Kuwait Airways.

From Canada: Air Canada, British Airways, Wardair.

SHIPS AND CRUISES

Cunard's *Queen Elizabeth 2* is the only regularly scheduled passenger liner sailing from Britain (Southampton) to New York and return. Cruise lines such as Royal Viking devise itineraries that include British ports of call.

To reach Britain from the Continent, you have a wide selection of ports and surface craft. Among the car ferries, hovercraft, jetfoils, and steamers, the major ones use the ports of Plymouth, Dover, Southampton, Folkestone, Harwich, Holyhead, Stanraer, Felixstowe, and Fishguard from Scandinavia, West Germany, France, Belgium, Holland, and Ireland.

AIR OR FLY/SAIL FARES

	High	Moderate	Low
Air fare, New York to London (round trip, low season)	$5,490*	$2,126†	$398‡
Ship passage (New York to London by ship, return by air)	7,195	3,610	1,350

*Concorde (First Class: $4,174)
†Business Class
‡No-frills

BY TRAIN

Yes, you can reach Britain by train—*boat* train—from the Continent and Ireland. British Rail offers rail/hovercraft and rail/ship service from Brussels, the Netherlands, and Channel ports, with multiple departures daily. BritRail offices have all the necessary information.

BY CAR

You can take your car to Britain via the car ferry services from the Continent (see the section on "Ships and Cruises").

To use your own car in Britain, you'll need the auto's registration papers, an insurance policy or green card, a current driver's license, and a sticker or plaque showing nationality (get these from your nearest American Automobile Association office).

ARRIVING IN BRITAIN

A LITTLE GEOGRAPHY

That the United Kingdom is divided into three countries (England, Scotland, and Wales) is a point nobody overlooks. What many Americans don't always note, however, is that the full title of the U.K. is the United Kingdom of Great Britain and Northern Ireland. Nobody publishes a guide book and calls it *The United Kingdom*, because it doesn't roll off the tongue as nicely as the older, more famous "Great Britain" or just plain "Britain."

The Insiders' guide is titled "Britain," but really touches also on Northern Ireland, if only briefly. Regardless of politics, the northern six counties of the island of Ireland are linked to Great Britain, quite apart from the independent Republic of Ireland to the south. Although tourism to Northern Ireland remains down since the troubles began in 1968, many Americans continue to visit, if only to dig for their roots. (A large number of Irish-Americans, including six presidents, come from that part of the world.)

We also include the Channel Islands, which lie off the coast of France, but which have belonged first to England, then to Great Britain for centuries. Connoisseurs of travel to Britain may want to visit Jersey, Guernsey, or even Sark.

IMMIGRATION AND CUSTOMS

You're welcome in Britain if you have a valid American or Commonwealth passport or EEC identity card.

For adult (over age 17) visitors from outside Europe who plan to stay less than six months, customs regulations allow you to bring in duty- and tax-free:

- 400 cigarettes, 200 cigarillos, 100 cigars, or 500 grams of tobacco

33

- 1 liter of spirits, and 2 liters of wine at 38.8 proof, or 2 liters of still table wine
- 50 grams of perfume
- ¼ liter of toilet water
- £28 worth of other goods

Don't try to bring in illicit drugs, firearms, fireworks, ammunition, explosives, weapons, or "obscene" publications.

PERILS & PITFALLS

It is illegal to bring drugs such as marijuana, hashish, cocaine, and heroin into Britain. If you are caught, you won't ride the "Midnight Express," but you could duplicate actor Stacy Keach's one-year enforced "vacation" behind bars.

Dogs, cats, and other mammals brought in must stay in quarantine for 6 months, to prevent the spread of rabies. Birds can wing it after only 35 days.

From a practical point of view, you will encounter British Customs at the air terminal or port of entry. At Heathrow, for example, after your passport is checked, you have a choice of two exits marked NOTHING TO DECLARE and GOODS TO DECLARE. If you choose the former, chances of your luggage being inspected are remote. Only spot checks are made of travelers passing through that exit.

Some countries have stringent controls on money. Britain doesn't. You may bring in or take out almost any amount of any currency, including British pounds.

MEASUREMENTS

WOMEN'S DRESSES AND SUITS

British	8	10	12	14	16	18
American	6	8	10	12	14	16
Continental	38	40	42	44	46	48

WOMEN'S SHOES

British	3	4	5	6	7	8
American	4½	5½	6½	7½	8½	9½
Continental	36	37	38	39	40	41

MEN'S SUITS AND COATS

British	36	38	40	42	44	46	48
American	36	38	40	42	44	46	48
Continental	46	48	50	52	54	56	58

MEN'S SHOES

British	7	8	9	10	11	12	13
American	7½	8½	9½	10½	11½	12½	13½
Continental	41	42	43	44	46	47	48

U.S., ENGLISH, AND METRIC

Linear Measure

1 mile (8 furlongs)=1.6093 kilometers
1 kilometer=.62137 mile
To convert kilometers to miles, multiply by ⁸⁄₅
To convert miles to kilometers, multiply by ⁵⁄₈

Weight

1 pound=453.59 grams=.454 kilograms
1 kilogram=2.679 pounds

LIQUID MEASURE

U.S.	*English*	*Metric*
1 pint (16 oz.)		.473 liter
1 quart (32 oz.)	.832 Brit. imperial quart	.946 liter
1 gallon (128 oz.)	.832 Brit. imperial gallon	3.785 liter
33.8 oz.		1 liter
1.2 gallons	1 Brit. imperial gallon	4.546 liter

Temperature

0° Celsius or centigrade = 32° Fahrenheit
–17.8° Celsius or centigrade = 0° Fahrenheit
100° Celsius or centigrade = 212° Fahrenheit
To convert Celsius to Fahrenheit, multiply by ⁹⁄₅ and add 32.
To convert Fahrenheit to Celsius, subtract 32 and multiply by ⁵⁄₉.

GETTING TO LONDON FROM THE AIRPORT

Your Heathrow-to-London options are as follows:

Taxi. Queue for them just outside the terminal. By law, you will have to pay only what the meter registers.

PERILS & PITFALLS

As you exit from Customs, touts ("hustlers" in American terms) will call to you, asking if you want a taxi. Avoid them. They are selling unregistered "gypsy cab" rides that are sure to be no bargains.

Ask at the terminal information counter if you have questions about where the taxis are. Taxi fare to London currently is between £10 and £20 ($15–$30).

Bus. "Flightline" express buses run to the Victoria Coach Station, for £2.75 ($4.13) and "Airbus," for £3 ($4.50). Airbuses pick up passengers just outside Terminals 1, 2, 3, and 4, and depart as often as every 10 minutes, depending on time of day.

The Airbuses run from 6:35 A.M. to 9:55 P.M. daily to designated stops near major hotel locations in central London. The trip usually takes about 40 minutes and fares can be paid in U.S., Canadian, French, or German currency on the bus.

INSIDERS' TIPS

For £3.50 ($5.25), you can buy a "One Day Rover" London Transport pass at the transportation counter in Heathrow. That entitles you to a ride via Airbus into the city, plus unlimited travel on London's buses and Underground trains for the balance of the day.

Underground or "Tube." There is a tube connection to all Heathrow terminals. It is on the Piccadilly line, which connects to other tube lines so you can reach all 268 stations of the London Underground system.

Tube trains run from 5:07 A.M. to 11:50 P.M. weekdays and Saturdays, and from 6:48 A.M. to 10:57 P.M. on Sundays, at the rate of at least 8 trains per hour. The trip to central London takes about 45 minutes.

The tube is fine if you have your own luggage cart or are carrying only hand luggage or a single bag. To reach the trains from the terminals you have to roll or lug your bags a long distance and carry them up many stairs at your transfer or destination station. The fare to central London stations, one way, is currently £1.50 ($2.25).

If you arrive at Gatwick, there is a BritRail "Gatwick Express" train every 15 minutes to Victoria Station from 6:30 A.M. to 10:30 P.M., then one per hour. The trip takes only 30 minutes. The current one way fare is about £5 ($7.50).

THE MONEY

The basic monetary unit is the pound sterling (£) which is made up of 100 pence (p). There are banknotes for £1, £5, £10, £20 and £50 (each one a different color) and there are coins for £1 (gold color), 50p, and 20p (both 7-sided), 10p, 5p (silver color), 2p, 1p and ½p (bronze).

If you should happen to receive an old 2-shilling piece, it is still good and has the value of the modern 10p coin. Likewise, the old 1-shilling piece is equal to the modern 5p coin and is still valid "coin of the realm."

PERILS & PITFALLS

Several British coins are nearly identical in size. Though the gold-colored £1 coin is twice as thick, it can be confused with the silver 5p, which has a milled edge. The 50p 7-sided coin can be mistaken for the round 10p, and so can the 7-sided 20p for a 1p coin. It pays to double-check them.

You may convert foreign currency into British money freely. (Exchange dealers and banks usually ask to see your passport and then record the transaction, however.)

In our experience, Lloyd's Bank generally has very favorable rates and low commission charges. Be wary of small, obscure banks and money changers; many of them make a flat charge plus a commission on each exchange. Keep in mind that you will receive a slightly better rate for traveler's checks than for dollar notes, and there is no charge if you exchange American Express traveler's checks at American Express offices.

TIPPING

For the porter at the airport terminal, figure 20p or 30p (30¢ or 45¢) per suitcase, or £1 ($1.50) for four or more.

No tips are expected on the bus to the city.

Taxi drivers may try for more on the airport trip (which may average £17 or $25.50), but a tip of £1.50 or £2 ($2.25 or $3) should be adequate. On most taxi rides, figure 15p (23¢) on fares under £1 ($1.50) and about 10 to 15 percent of fares above £1, or round the tip off to the next 10p (15¢).

PERILS & PITFALLS

At Heathrow Airport, Bureau de Change windows are operated around the clock (at this writing) by private companies, not banks. They charge a minimum of 1½ percent or £1.50 ($2.25) for each dollar transaction, or £2 ($3) for each traveler's check transaction, which makes small-denomination exchanges very expensive.

Many restaurants, inns, and hotels add a service charge of 10 to 15 percent to your bill. This is usually, but not always stated. (In case of doubt, ask.)

If the restaurant does not add a service charge, tip 12 to 15 percent of the check, as service warrants. If it's a minimum-service, quick-eats place, 20p (30¢) might be generous. If it's a "medieval banquet," do not tip; when the price says "all-inclusive," it should be. When the tab goes on your hotel bill, service is generally added by the management (if this is unclear, ask the waiter). If it is not included, 12 to 15 percent is appropriate at all cloth-napery, flower-decorated restaurants.

At the hotel, you may find it more comfortable to keep 50p (75¢) coins handy to tip the bellhop or porter who wrestles your luggage from front desk to your room. The room maid will appreciate a token 50p (75¢) per person per day, if you're so inclined. Doormen and cloakroom attendants should receive small change.

Hairdressers and barbers should receive 10 percent of their fee. Tips are not needed for ushers, elevator operators, bartenders, or guides. (At a pub, you may choose to leave the few pence change from your banknote, but it is not necessary.)

THE INSIDERS' BRITAIN

WHERE TO STAY

When it comes to types of accommodations, you name it, Britain's got it. The range is extraordinary, from hostels and inexpensive farm and guest-house B&Bs (bed-and-breakfasts) to modern high-rise hotels, condominiums, and apartments, from seaside cottages and old-fashioned Victorian resort hotels to quaint village inns, country-house hotels, and converted palaces and castles.

In the sky's-the-limit price category are the private stately homes, in which, for a celestial fee, Lord and Lady Noblesse Oblige will greet you at the door, offer a palatial room, and deign to have tea or possibly dinner with you on their very best china. Less rarefied arrangements are possible through a number of rental agencies. The British Tourist Authority has brochures of many such agencies, as well as farmhouse and B&B listings.

If you yearn to stay in a historic property—a castle, palace, gatehouse, or former church—it is a definite possibility in England. Landmark Trust has scores of such properties, which are generally rented by the week, with many booked months in advance. You do your own house-keeping and cooking, but the properties are completely furnished and usually sleep at least four, making them especially suitable for a large family or several couples traveling together. For information, write the Landmark Trust, Shottesbrooke, Maidenhead, Berkshire, England.

When it comes to the more traditional lodgings for travelers—hotels—there is enormous variety. London hotels are expensive. Though Britain does not have an official national system of classification of hotels (as does Spain, for instance), the Automobile Association rates hotels by categories, and their ratings are close to the mark of our own evaluations.

Our ratings and listings are not encyclopedic; we have cited those hotels and inns that we think offer special quality. Charm, furnishings, service, historic associations—any and all of these are part of the ambience. We consider them important, but no more so than cleanliness, housekeeping, good reading lights, firm mattresses, and plumbing that works without coaxing.

Some of the pleasantest places to stay, outside of London, are village inns, usually layered with history and atmosphere, and country-house hotels. The latter are often individually owned, by couples escaping the rat race of city life (much as refugees from New York open New England inns). The food is often excellent, and accommodations are gracious or even luxurious. You'll find a number of these hotels in Scotland, too.

Though the comforts of living like the gentry do not come cheap, we feel that a stay at a really lovely place in or near a historic town contributes to a travel experience and helps make it memorable.

If you crave more modest accommodations, we enthusiastically recommend the vast network of farmhouses and B&Bs throughout Britain. The prices are usually low and the welcomes warm. English, Welsh, and Scottish Tourist Offices are usually very helpful in finding accommodations for you on the spot.

WHERE TO EAT

Just as food-consciousness has risen in the U.S. and Canada, so it has also in Britain. This is evident, in part, in many fancy and expensive *haute cuisine* and *nouvelle cuisine* French restaurants in London and most major cities.

Paralleling this is a renewed interest in traditional foods. A "Taste of Britain" campaign, launched a few years ago, encouraged restaurants around the country to feature old-fashioned regional dishes. Thus, in Somerset, for example, you can sometimes find stargazer pie (see the

---

INSIDERS' TIPS

A Taste of England Restaurant Guide, listing participating restaurants and their specialties, is available for a few pence at BTA in New York or the English Tourist Board in London.

Glossary of British Food Terms) and dishes made with scrumpy, the local cider. The Scots and Welsh have their own national specialties, as you will note in these sections of the book.

In London you can find the cuisine of your choice in virtually any price range. At the top are deluxe establishments as elegant as any in the world, with decor and prices as rarefied as the food. Some of these are in London's poshest hotels, but many are small, stylish, chef-owned places. At the other end of the spectrum, if you yearn for a McSomething, you will find many American fast-food chains, as well as English versions offering burgers, pizzas, and fish 'n' chips.

In between are moderate-priced restaurants of all kinds, including those in department stores, museums, and stately homes. There are ethnic restaurants by the hundreds—Greek, Italian, Mexican, Chinese, Thai, Japanese, Russian, Scandinavian, and so many Indian and Pakistani restaurants that they often specialize in a particular culinary style.

PERILS & PITFALLS

The best British ethnic restaurants are authentic and excellent. However, Chinese restaurants are an exception. In our experience, their food rarely measures up to the finest Chinese cuisine one can find in New York, San Francisco, Los Angeles, Chicago, Vancouver, or Sydney.

One of the open secrets of dining in Britain is that Indian restaurants are usually excellent. The food is authentically spicy, and the prices are usually considerably lower than in other comparable eateries. If your taste buds can tolerate incendiary food, Indian is a real delight. For families traveling on a budget, Indian restaurants can be a real bonanza.

Britain's better restaurants are hospitable to women traveling alone. You aren't shunted to a back-of-the-restaurant "Siberia," and you'll find so many other singles you won't feel like an odd woman out.

Restaurant dress codes are much as at home. Deluxe establishments generally expect men to wear a jacket and tie at dinner, and sometimes at lunch. Informal places are as casual as similar places would be at home, though we can't think of any place that would welcome scruffy T-shirts and bare feet.

INSIDERS' TIPS

Better restaurants and country hotels serve after-dinner coffee with a tiny plate of petits fours. Often we skip a heavy dessert (to save calories) and opt for the tidbits of candied ginger, chocolate truffles, or cookies—just sweet enough to tame one's sweet tooth.

Two British institutions are a boon to travelers: the tea room and the pub.

English tea is a delightful tradition, recommended to every visitor. Between 3 and 5 P.M. is a nice time to pause in a busy day of sightseeing or shopping for a pick-me-up that will bridge the gap between a late English breakfast and dinnertime. In London, tea can be the hunger-stopper that keeps you going from late afternoon through an early theater performance to an after-theater supper.

Sometimes you don't want to spend too much time or money on a midday meal. Try a pub lunch. More and more pubs, even in the country, now offer hot dishes (sometimes local specialties) at lunchtime. These are usually displayed at a counter so you can examine before ordering. Usual choices might include shepherd's pie, quiche, a casserole, or game or pork pie. If in doubt, a quick and filling option is a "ploughman's lunch." This consists of a large slice of cheese, a small green salad, chutney, butter, and crusty bread. Nothing delicate about it, but the £1.50 ($2.25) price is modest.

Pubs are also the best places for sampling the *vin du pays*. The "wine of the country" comes not from the grape, but the hop. Beer, ale, stout, bitter—these are Britain's glory. If you are inclined to experiment, ask in each pub for the local brew.

In recent years there has been a resurgence of indigenous winemaking in Britain. In our view, it still has a way to go (see our comments later on). French and Italian wines are widely available, as well as Spanish sherries and Portuguese port and madeira. You'll find in better restaurants a fine range of Bordeaux (called claret here, when red) and Burgundies at prices comparable to U.S. prices.

PERILS & PITFALLS

If you persist in ordering bourbon or Canadian whiskey, you will pay dearly. Unless you are a hard core bourbonite, go with the flow of local beverages. The range is wide, the discoveries great.

FOOD AND DRINK

English food gets a bad rap, proving that you can't keep a cliché down. The canards survive long after they have even a whisper of truth left in them.

True, there was a time when English food may have deserved the labels that visitors tagged it with—atrocious, overcooked, and underseasoned. Even English writers joined the "bash English food" campaign. Somerset Maugham once said that the only way to survive in England was to have breakfast three times a day.

In the past 15 years, all that has changed, and anyone who derides English food hasn't been paying attention. What has happened is that a subtle infiltration of European chefs has taught a whole new generation of Englishmen how to cook. They in turn have fanned out and trained others, and good restaurants have spawned others, first in London and now all over England, Scotland, and, to a lesser extent, Wales.

The aristocracy once showed their indifference to food by letting others prepare it. They imported their own chefs from the Continent, or ate at their private clubs. The average middle-class English homemaker who once thought a culinary triumph was being able to bring shirred eggs and canned asparagus warm to the table now has learned the pleasures of wild mushrooms, sun-dried tomatoes, and chevre, and is busy exploring exotic gastronomic landscapes dotted with such dishes as sushi, spanakopita, and carpaccio.

Like their counterparts in North America, the English have joined the culinary revolution. This has produced a generation of middle-class English men and women who appreciate good food, and are eating out more. A more discerning clientele in the dining room produces higher standards in the kitchen.

Let's clear up a possible misunderstanding: good food in England is not confined to French restaurants. Along with the raised culinary consciousness has come a desire to preserve the best dishes from England's own past. A new British cooking style combines techniques of the French *nouvelle cuisine* (attractive presentation, smaller portions, fresh ingredients, and sometimes unusual combinations) with traditional English recipes and use of the best of home-grown products.

Small as England is, it still retains many local specialties. You will have trouble in Yorkshire in a public place finding a decent Yorkshire pudding, but look instead for "fat rascals" (currant scones, eaten with a slice of Wensleydale cheese), Brontë cake (a type of sweet fruitcake), and parkin (treacle-based cake).

In the Lake District, keep taste buds alert for "rum Nicky," a tart filled with dates and ginger and doused in rum. In Kent, land of apples and cherries, look for "lardy Johns" (currant dough squares), "twice laid" (mashed potatoes and fried codfish rolls), and, in Sussex, "Sussex plum heavies" (baked raisin cakes served hot, sprinkled with sugar).

In the northwest, you will find Shrewsbury simnel cakes (with meringue filling and marzipan icing), Warwick scones (served with local honey), and perhaps Coventry Godcakes (glazed puff-pastry triangles filled with almonds, raisins, mincemeat, chopped apples, and brandy).

In Cornwall, the Cornish pasties are sometimes called Tiddy Oggys. Bath has numerous specialties. You will find Bath Olivers (biscuits eaten with cheese), Bath buns (with sugar on top), Bath chaps (made from pig's cheeks), and Bath polonies (spicy pork sausage).

The old-time names of English dishes were often more imaginative than the dishes themselves. How could sausage in a puff pastry surpass its label as "toad-in-the-hole"? Would you ever guess that "yarb" is a leek-and-green-vegetable pudding?

Among England's national culinary specialties, cheeses are standouts. Justifiably famous among many hard, crumbly, often pungent varieties, are Cheddar, Stilton, Cheshire, Double Gloucester, and Leicester. Wales's most famous cheese is Caerphilly, and in Scotland you will find

Crowdie, similar to cottage cheese.

Many regions have their own special cheeses, often named after the county in which they were originally made, such as Blue Cheshire, Lancashire, and green-veined Sage Derby. As you travel through the countryside, look for the local specialties, such as Wensleydale and a new version called Blue Wensleydale in Yorkshire. The recent upsurge of interest in English cheeses has led to many new ones. There are varieties of goat and ewe cheeses and a delicious cheese called Lymeswold, modeled after soft, mold-ripened European cheeses like Brie and Camembert.

At many of Britain's better restaurants, a cheese course is served between entree and dessert. With the cheese you will be offered stalks of celery. The contrast of flavors and textures is surprisingly refreshing.

In Britain you will enjoy some of the best lamb in the world; all kinds of game, including hare, pheasant, venison, squab, duck, and goose; and free-range (farm-fresh) eggs that really have flavor. English bacon is cut thicker than the U.S. variety and more closely resembles what Americans call Canadian bacon. In Scotland, the salmon is world-renowned, as are minuscule plover eggs. Kippers, finnan haddie, and steak-and-kidney pie are all popular British dishes. A favorite pub lunch is a meat (pork) or game pie. (These vary from fresh, meaty, and delicious to stale and dreadful. Unfortunately, you can't always tell by looking.) The British also like curries, a taste that dates from the days of the Raj, along with chutney, kedgeree, and mulligatawny soup.

Then there is the British sweet tooth, which, judging by the numerous candy and sweet shops, needs constant appeasing. Regional sweets are legion, from Banbury cake (puff pastry filled with rum, currants, orange peel, and nutmeg) to "Richmond maids of honour" (little rich cheese-cakes named for Elizabeth I's greedy ladies-in-waiting).

A sweet tooth is best tamed at tea time. Of course there are teas and teas. You will see advertised at tea shops throughout the island "cream tea" or a "real Devonshire tea." These feature clotted cream (which sounds awful, but is rich and delicious), tea, scones, jam, butter, and/or assorted cakes and thinly sliced cucumber, ham, and cheese sandwiches.

After dinner, you will be asked if you would like a pudding or a "pud." Don't take this literally. The English refer to all desserts as puddings, though at least one real "pud" will be on the menu, along with cakes, tarts, and fruit salad (a mixture of fresh, diced fruit).

PERILS & PITFALLS

Sadly, brewed tea is becoming obsolete, except in better hotels and tea shops that make tea a specialty. Instead, you will be confronted with a modern convenience that would have been unthinkable in Britain 20 years ago: the ubiquitous tea bag. What price "progress"?

The English breakfast that Maugham referred to is still a mainstay of private and hotel life. At its best, a hearty English breakfast is still one of the world's pleasures, with a choice of eggs, sausage and/or bacon, broiled tomato or mushroom slices, possibly kippers, toast, and jam. It does help one through the morning.

At noontime, the English often pop into a pub for a quick lunch. Pubs are places to discover some traditional English fare—such dishes as shepherd's pie, Scotch egg, Lancashire hot pot, and bubble-and-squeak. At their best, these can be homey and tasty; alas, they aren't *always* at their best. Sometimes they are soggy, tired, or day-old.

One thing you can usually count on in a pub is a good choice of potables. Wine is often a companion to an English restaurant meal and the wine of choice is usually Bordeaux, commonly known as claret.

But a word about Britain's home-produced wines: In recent years, adventurous English vintners have built upon the technology and expertise of Continental winemakers, and several are now producing respectable, very drinkable wines. Most of these are white wines, mostly from grapes widely grown in Germany. At this point they are competing in quality and price with German *Qualitatswein*.

Some English wines we have found enjoyable are Lamberhurst Priory, Three Choirs, Magdalen, and Pilton Manor.

The drink of choice in some parts of Britain is cider (or *cyder*). In apple-raising areas such as the southern counties, it will be available on tap, from kegs. Elsewhere, it is usually in bottles. There are three basic types of this delicious drink: sweet, dryer, and astringent. The latter, known as "scrumpy," doesn't travel—it's usually found only near cider mills and is decidedly an acquired taste. All the ciders are alcoholic, about like mild beer.

The *real* "wine of the country" throughout Britain is its nut-brown ale, and we urge you to try many different ones, because their variety is large and quality is deliciously high.

Ale is a British drink with a long provenance. There is a reference in the 10th-century epic *Beowulf* to beer halls. Flemish immigrants introduced the hop to England around 1500, but the British were suspicious of the plant's influence and preferred their own unhopped product. One writer, Andrew Boorde, noted: "The drink doth make a man fat, and inflate the bely, as it doth appere by the Dutche men's faces and belyes."

Hopped or home-grown, unhopped beer—or ale, as it is called in Britain—was the drink of choice for Queen Elizabeth I and was in widespread use throughout the country in those days, even as it is today.

Now let's try to sort out some of the brews you will encounter during your pub-crawls in Britain.

Ale is the generic term used to describe all brews consumed in Britain except lager. Ales are made using a yeast that ferments on the top of the liquid, at a warmer temperature than lager beer. The following are all types of ale:

- Bitter is considered the national beer of England. Served on draft in every pub, it's a copper-colored ale, often heavily hopped, and usually possessing a bitter, dry, fruity, and rich palate.
- Pale ale is basically the bottled counterpart of bitter.
- Mild ale is lightly hopped, and not as strong as bitter. This draft ale is usually the least expensive offering at the pub, and is quite popular in northwest England and the Midlands.
- Brown ale is basically the bottled version of a dark mild ale.
- Porter is a dark ale, a robust progenitor of stout, and has almost completely given way to its descendant.

- Stout comes in many forms. The most popular and well known is bitter stout, as typified by Guinness. Other kinds include milk stout, a sweet-palated dark ale (English law now forbids the use of the word *milk* on beer labels, so look for a bucolic description or phrase); and Russian stout, which sports a roasted-malt palate, but otherwise isn't much like other stouts; its potency is so great that it could be ranked with barley wine.
- Barley wine is a strong ale that usually improves in the bottle for several years. Most often a dark brew, though occasionally light in color, barley wine falls into the "winter warmer" category.
- Scottish ale is similar to the English bitter, though usually slightly stronger and with a drier, fruitier palate.

Lager *beer*, which, as noted above, is not considered an ale, is light-colored and most similar to the beer Americans are used to drinking at home. Lager has made large strides in popularity in England in recent years, especially among younger drinkers. Its most notable characteristics are a light, dry palate, and thirst-quenching capabilities.

If you plan to drink draft beer in a pub, seek a "free house" that stocks a variety of brews, and avoid those ales that are pumped via gas out of a metal container. To sample the most representative pub ales, look for traditional, cask-fermented brews. When in doubt, ask the publican if he has "real ale."

The Campaign for Real Ale (CAMRA) began some years ago as a grassroots protest against the big breweries' keg beers, which lacked the flavor of the real thing. Keg beer is filtered and pasteurized, with additives that preserve it, making long storage possible. In the process, all traces of yeast are removed and secondary fermentation is halted. Real ales, on the other hand, have a cask-conditioning that allows the flavor to develop and mature as the ale sits in its cask in the pub cellar. CAMRA created a real "brewha-ha" in Britain, generating such support that now many pubs advertise that they sell real ale, as opposed to the keg beers of Watney and other members of the "Big Six" breweries (Bass, Courage, Allied Breweries, Whitbreads, and Scottish & Newcastle).

Herewith are a few special brews to ask for in various regions:

London and the South

- Brakspear's Bitter/Pale Ale—a very hoppy ale.
- Fuller's Extra Special Bitter (ESB)—one of England's strongest bitters.
- Gale's Prize Old Ale—a bottle-conditioned (live-yeast) ale that is aged for one year in wooden barrels.
- Shepherd Neame's Bitter and Best—both extremely hoppy, sharp, fruity, flavorful, and most astringent.

The North

- Boddingtons Bitter—a highly respected ale from Manchester.
- Hartley's XB—an intriguing bitter brewed in Ulverston.
- Taylor Brewery of Keighley—cask-conditioned, all-malt ales of superb quality, especially Landlord and Porter.
- Tetley's Bitter—brewed near York, not quite as assertive as many bitters, but nevertheless typical of a Yorkshire brew.
- Thwaites Real Best Mild—an outstanding mild ale from Blackburn.
- Vaux Double Maxim—a potent brown ale from Sunderland.

The Midlands

- Banks Mild—a well-regarded ale with a well-rounded palate.
- Marston's Pedigree, Merrie Monk, and Owd Roger—all outstanding, produced using the Burton Union system of fermentation (by which barrels are interconnected, allowing the yeast to travel from one barrel to the next).
- Worthington White Shield—a bottle-conditioned ale produced by Bass. Also worthy of note is Bass No. 1 Barley Wine.

The West

- Courage's Bulldog Pale Ale—a fruity, tart-palated brew.
- Pope's Thomas Hardy's Ale—Britain's strongest beer, a distinctive barley wine, issued in a limited quantity of numbered bottles, which can then be stored like wine for several years.

The East

- Adnam's Bitter—a well-poised ale, made in Southwold, with a slightly briny character. In winter, look for Tally Ho, a barley wine, on draft.

- Greene King Abbot—a malty ale with hoppy bite, produced in Bury and Biggleswade by the family of author Graham Greene.

Scotland

- Belhaven products—all are worth sampling.
- Lorimer (Edinburgh)—produces a tasty ale called Golden.
- Maclay (in the brewing town of Alloa)—produces several good ales.
- Tennent's Fowler's Wee Heavy (Edinburgh)—a very good example of a traditional Scottish ale.
- Traquair—which we have noted in the section on Scotland.

Wales

- Brain's S.A.—a palatable though potent bitter.
- Felinfoel's Double Dragon—a well-rounded bitter from Llanelli.

A few final words: In a pub the usual order is for a pint or half-pint, usually served in a glass mug with a handle or in a tall handleless glass. And *pint* means an imperial pint (20 ounces).

HOW TO GET AROUND

London

The Underground. The "tube," as natives refer to the Underground (the term *subway* is reserved for walkways under streets), is a network of ten lines with 268 stations, and is often the quickest way to go from point to point in the city. Mercifully graffiti-free, remarkably safe, and reasonably accessible, the stations are connected by well-lighted, relatively quiet trains that seldom lurch, stop short, or subject you to unpredictable behavior that may be hazardous to safety. Route maps and directions are models of clarity—they're prominently posted in stations and train cars and are easily read and understood.

Tube trains run from about 6 A.M. to midnight. Fares start at 50p or 75¢ (20p or 30¢ for riders under 16), and are charged by the number of zones crossed. You purchase your ticket at the vending machine or ticket window before entering, and turn it in to the collector when you reach your destination. Youngsters under 16 ride for half-fare, and those under 5 travel free.

If you're returning to the same station, you'll save by buying a round-trip ("return") ticket. There are other special money-saving tickets for frequent travel.

Red Double-Decker Buses. These seem to go everywhere in metropolitan London, from about 6 A.M. to midnight. They are the least expensive public transportation. Bus stops are well marked, and often have shelters where placards spell out the route of each bus that stops there.

Fares are scaled according to distance. Minimum is 50p or 75¢ (15p or 23¢, 20p or 30¢ for children until 10 P.M.). Keep your ticket until you leave the bus. Youngsters under 14 pay a flat rate until 10 P.M. Buses tend to be slow. At peak traffic times, their speed would allow a caterpillar to clear the way.

INSIDERS' TIPS

The L2 "Red Bus Rover" ticket allows unlimited London Transport bus travel during the ticket's one-day validity. Buy them at Underground stations or London Transport Travel Information centers at Piccadilly Circus, Victoria, Charing Cross, St. James's Park, Oxford Circus, or farther afield, King's Cross, Euston, and Heathrow.

There are many sightseeing buses in London, but one of the most convenient is the red Official London Sightseeing Bus, which runs from 9 A.M. to 5 P.M. every day but Christmas and makes a 1½-hour circuit for £4.25 or $6.38 (under 16, £2.50 or $3.75), or with a ticket to Madame Tussaud's included, £7.25 or $10.88 (under 16, £5.50 or $8.25).

London Explorer Pass. This is a ticket for unlimited travel on all buses (except tour buses) plus nearly all stops on the Underground trains. Even the Airbus and tube to Heathrow can be ridden using these 1-, 3-, 4-, or 7-day tickets.

With each London Explorer ticket you receive a free "Mini-Guide" to London that includes discount coupons on many attractions, including Madame Tussaud's, the London Zoo, and the London Dungeon. Leaflets describing these specials plus bus, Underground, and Central London street maps are free at Underground ticket offices and London Transport Information Centres.

Current prices for the London Explorer Pass are:

	Adult	Child (5–15)
1 day	£3.50 ($5.25)	£1.30 ($1.95)
3 days	£9.00 ($13.50)	£3.00 ($4.50)
4 days	£11.50 ($17.25)	£3.50 ($5.25)
7 days	£16.00 ($24)	£4.00 ($6)

INSIDERS' TIPS

A 1-day London Explorer Pass for £3.50 ($5.25) is a true travel bargain. The day you are to fly out of London you might want to buy one. You can use it for unlimited bus and tube transportation in the city and finally use it for your Airbus trip to Heathrow. If bought separately, the London-to-Heathrow Airbus ride alone costs £3 ($4.50).

London Taxis. These have a high reputation for service, efficiency, and comfort. There are taxi stands at airports, at rail stations, and near many large hotels. You can also hail a taxi in the street or telephone for one (see the Yellow Pages under "Taxis"). When a cab is available, its TAXI or FOR HIRE sign is lighted. All legitimate taxis are licensed by the police. Fares are displayed on electronic meters, and authorized supplemental charges register on the meter also.

Afoot. London is a special joy for walkers. The sense of discovery when you find yourself by chance at a historic site, the onetime home of your favorite author, the pub mentioned in a book or seen in a film, and the delight of shops and store windows, quaint anachronistic signs, and Dickensian business names—these are the visual canapés that bring pleasure to the observant pedestrian's London diet.

When Nature Calls. Public restrooms in Underground and rail stations, bus and airline terminals are generally safe. Better facilities are found in hotels, restaurants, department stores, galleries, museums, and pubs.

Outside London

AIR TRAVEL

These are the London phone numbers of domestic airlines:

Air UK, 249-7073

British Airways, 897-4000

British Midland Airways, Ltd., 581-0864

Dan Air, 680-1011, 930-2782

Redcoat Express, 935-4100

Shuttle flights serving such cities as Glasgow, Edinburgh, Manchester, and London are frequent and do not require reservations. You simply check in 10 minutes before flight time.

British Rail. For shorter hauls, second-class tickets are adequate. For longer runs you may prefer first-class coach or overnight sleeper accommodations.

First-class tickets cost about 50 percent more than second-class. Be sure to check whether a reservation is advisable in addition to the basic ticket (there's a separate charge and an additional voucher).

BritRail also offers a premium service using the Simplon-Orient Express cars on luxury day trips from London. In antique splendor you are served champagne brunches and meals with wine to and from such popular destinations as Bath, Bournemouth, Leeds Castle, and Hever Castle.

On 50 routes your car can accompany you. Some of these start at ferry ports and can take you from boat to destination. One "Motorail" ticket covers shipment of the car plus your fare in coach or sleeper. There is an array of package holidays that offer all-inclusive accommodations at hotels and resorts along with the Motorail transportation. Details are available from British Rail.

There are BritRail Passes (Eurail Passes are not good in Britain) good for 7, 14, or 21 days, or 1 month, beginning the day the first trip is made. These allow unlimited travel on any of the 14,000 trains per day to any destination(s) in Britain. They are good also on Sealink ships to the Isle of Wight and Lake Windermere steamers.

Other BritRail bargains are its Youth Pass (for ages 16–25) and Sea Pass (which includes travel between London and the Continent or Ireland). These must be bought abroad. For information, contact BritRail Travel International, 630 Third Avenue, New York, NY 10017; tel. 212-599-5400. In Canada: 94 Cumberland Street, Suite 601, Toronto, Ont. M5R 1A3; tel. 416-929-3333.

INSIDERS' TIPS

Among the many special British Rail deals is a 6-day package for only $50. It includes transportation between Heathrow or Gatwick and London, 3 days of unlimited travel in London (Explorer Pass), and round-trip rail tickets from London to Canterbury, Cambridge, and Brighton. (Information as above.)

BritRail also offers "Britainshrinkers"—one- to six-day package tours to prime attractions from Scotland and Wales to Stonehenge and Windsor. They combine train and luxury coach travel with trained guides, light pub lunches, and entrance fees and tax.

Coaches. London Transport is only one of the coach tour operators offering excellent access to places such as Stratford, Sussex, Winchester, Warwick, and more. National Express (Britain's largest coach operator), may be found at Victoria Coach Station, Buckingham Palace Road, London SW1; tel. 730-0202.

By Water. Colorful, live-aboard canal boats can be booked through travel agents and U.K. Waterway Holidays, Ltd., Penn Place, Rickmansworth, Hertfordshire WD3 1EU, England; tel. 0923-770-040. Special canal-boat package tours are available.

Afoot. You may follow the footsteps of Roman legions, Norman invaders, or Lake District poets—or just ramble through parks, Pennines, and pleasure trails. Serious walkers will secure a copy of the *Countryside Access Charter,* which tells where you can go in England and Wales. It's available free from Countryside Commission, Publications Despatch Department, 19/23 Albert Road, Manchester M19 2EQ. For Scotland, check the free catalog of the Countryside Commission for Scotland, Battleby, Redgorton, Perth PH1 3EW, Scotland. Other sources of information for walkers: Ramblers' Association, 105 Wandsworth Road, London SW8 2XX; tel. 01-582-6878; The Wayfarers', 22 Maltravers Street, Arundel, West Sussex BN18

9BU, tel. Arundel 882-925; and British Travel Authority for up-to-date information about walking circuits, maps, outings, and other details.

When Nature Calls. In smaller towns and villages, the local hotels or pubs are your best bets.

SHOPPING

Napoleon once called Britain "a nation of shopkeepers." Most Brits would say "Amen."

Shopping is a way of life in Britain, and especially in England. There are shops everywhere: individual shops, trendy boutiques, department stores, and, of late, big shopping complexes. Major American credit cards are widely accepted.

What's to buy? Some of the best values are in woolens, knits as well as woven goods—men's cashmere and tweed jackets and overcoats, men's and women's suits, woolen accessories. The closer to the source, the better the prices. Better in Yorkshire, Scotland, and Wales than in London. Shoes and stylish boots are also excellent buys, and the varieties boggle the mind. Sheepskin—rugs, jackets, slippers—is the specialty of the Lake District.

Custom-made clothes, especially men's suits and shirts, are a London specialty, but not for budget-stretchers. Rain gear (something the Brits know a lot about)—coats, hats, clever umbrellas—are popular purchases.

PERILS & PITFALLS

We may speak the same language, more or less, but we use different numbers in our clothing and shoe sizes. Check the section on "Measurements."

Antiques, whether snuff boxes and other small *objets*, or silver, porcelain, glass, and furniture, can be found everywhere in Britain, especially England. Bath, Brighton, and York have a plethora of antique shops, London has entire antique arcades and various auction houses, Cotswold villages such as Broadway and Chipping Campden are veritable antique heavens, but the relatively "undiscovered" hunting grounds for the least pricy goods are the towns and villages of East Anglia.

Art—modern and traditional paintings, contemporary and Old Master prints—is everywhere, but don't expect bargains. Brass rubbings from church tombs are popular items to buy ready-made, even framed, but many people rub their own for a small fee at various churches. There are brass rubbing centers in London, Bath, York, and many other cities and towns all over England.

Handicrafts are another British specialty. In Scotland, Wales, and Northern Ireland, look especially for knitted and hand-woven items—scarves, stoles, gloves, caps—at very good prices. In England, the craft of choice is often pottery. Good starting places to look for contemporary pottery and other crafts are the Craft Centres in England, Scotland, Wales. Porcelain is represented by such distinguished names as Royal Doulton, Royal Worcester, Minton, and Wedgwood. Much of it is produced in the industrial Midlands around Stoke-on-Trent, but can be bought in retail shops and some "seconds" (called "reject") shops all over the country.

Books are fun to shop for in Britain, though new books are not the bargain they were ten years ago. (What is?) Still, the variety is extraordinary; old, rare, and used books can be found in every town and village.

We like to take food items home, for friends who are surfeited with bibelots. Tea, candies, biscuits packaged in attractive tins, and English cheeses all are appreciated.

Bargaining, or negotiating the retail price, is not a British custom. Don't attempt it in major stores and shops, but you might try it at used-book stalls, open-air markets, and antiques shops and fairs.

INSIDERS' TIPS

The VAT (Value Added Tax) of 15 percent on almost everything sold retail in Britain can be refunded on items sold to foreigners and transported abroad. Not all stores allow VAT rebates; others limit refunds to purchases totaling more than £50 ($75) or so. To get the refund, you must ask for the VAT form when you make your purchase. Then, in leaving Britain, you have the filled-out form certified at Customs. The refund check is mailed to you at home. On expensive items, the refund can make a considerable difference.

NIGHTLIFE

The problem of what to do at night in London is only a problem of choice as to which offerings to select from the perennially prolific menus.

Whatever your taste in entertainment, London has it— from Berlioz to burlesque, discos to divas, *Swan Lake* to strippers, cello concertos to country-and-western, *Goldberg Variations* to Gilbert and Sullivan, Shakespeare and Shaw to *Starlight Express.*

Live professional theater is one of the glories of Britain. London's theaters are concentrated in the West End, an easily walkable area centered on Leicester Square. There are two other major centers for theatrical performances: the National Theatre, across Waterloo Bridge in the South Bank Centre; and the Barbican Arts Centre (home of the Royal Shakespeare Company), near the City. In addition to evening performances, there are matinees at various theaters on Wednesdays, Thursdays, and Saturdays.

INSIDERS' TIPS

Get to the theater early enough to order your intermission drinks in advance from the bartender, and pay for them. They'll be waiting for you at the interval (intermission), usually on a table, with your name on a slip of paper. Enjoy your drink while others crowd around the bar, hoping to catch the bartender's eye before the next act. This convenience is not available in all theaters, but in many.

For most theater offerings you can book seats by phone, using your credit card, and pick them up at the box office half an hour before curtain. If you buy through a ticket service, expect to pay a fee of up to 20 percent of the ticket price. A convenient 24-hour-a-day telephone booking service ("First Call," 240-7200) will book seats via credit card and mail your tickets for a fee of £1.25 ($1.88) each. You can book before you go to Britain, through Keith Prowse & Co., 234 West 44 Street, New York, NY 10036; tel. 212-398-1430 or 800-223-4446.

There is a thriving "Fringe Theater"—equivalent to New York's Off-Broadway—of revivals, avant-garde, and experimental presentations. Although the theaters are scattered, there is a central booking office: Fringe Box Office, Duke of York's Theatre, 379-6002.

INSIDERS' TIPS

Theatergoers flock to the Half Price Ticket Booth in Leicester Square on Monday through Saturday, open from noon on for matinee tickets and from 2:30 to 6:30 P.M. for evening performances. Only same-day tickets are sold, for half-price plus a nominal fee, *cash only,* no credit cards. The signboards tell which shows are available. There is no telephone.

In the city where Mozart composed his first symphony and such giants as Haydn, Handel, and Mendelssohn scored triumphs, the tradition of classical music continues. With five symphony orchestras and two major opera companies in the city, plus innumerable smaller orchestras, soloists, and chamber music groups, concerts are to be enjoyed not only evenings, but afternoons and Sundays. Major concerts are at the Royal Albert Hall (Promenade Concert series each summer) and the South Bank and Barbican centers.

INSIDERS' TIPS

Lunchtime concerts, many of them free, are heard almost every day of the week at churches such as St. Martins-in-the-Fields. Phone 606-3030 for information. Free pre-theater concerts are standard in the foyers of the Royal Festival Hall and Barbican Centre. Look for announcements and schedules in the *Times, Telegraph,* and *Evening Standard.*

Opera is presented at the Royal Opera House, Covent Garden, and the English National Opera at the London Coliseum. The famed Royal Ballet and Sadler's Wells Ballet play these same theaters.

Jazz in many forms is found almost every night of the year, and Ronnie Scott's is acknowledged as one of Europe's leading jazz sites.

Pop concerts by British and international groups are continual features.

Nightclubs, cabarets, and floor shows are often found in

major hotels. If there are two bands or internationally known entertainers, expect the experience to be costly (£50 or $75 per person and up). You may be just as happy in a modest place listening to a quartet for one-third the price. Many pizza parlors, for instance, offer live music— jazz or rock.

There are movie houses (cinemas) aplenty in London. The first-run houses advertise with billboards and ads in the newspapers. If you're interested in offbeat, historic, and foreign films, check the National Film Theatre at 928-3232. No reservations or advance booking, but the tickets are bargain-priced.

For that special evening out, the 28th-floor Roof Restaurant at the London Hilton, or tea or dinner dancing at the Ritz are glamorous. There are discos all over London—the Hippodrome bills itself as "the greatest," and the Park may be the loudest. You can enjoy ethnic fun at such places as the Greek Fantasia or the Italian Concordia Notte or Tiberio. There is Scottish entertainment at the Caledonian Suite; Victorian music and cabaret at the Boulogne; Gilbert and Sullivan at the Grims Dyke Hotel; and good fun at the Cockney Cabaret and Music Hall. The King's Head offers Fringe theater in a pub setting. (See London listings for details on these.)

INSIDERS' TIPS

For current information on theater, concerts, jazz, dance, and opera, check the British Tourist Authority's "London Planner" listing; the periodic *London Theatre Guide* from the Society of West End Theatre; *Barbican Centre Diary,* the National Theatre's monthly schedule; *Virgin Guide to Music, Opera and Dance* from Rhinegold Publishing; and *Where* magazine. All these are free and found in tourist information, railway, travel, and airline offices, and/or hotels. *What's On and Where to Go* and *Time Out* magazines can be bought at newsdealers, along with the *Guardian,* the *Times,* the *Telegraph,* and the *Evening Standard.*

Outside London

Yes, there is cultural life after London. It not only exists away from the capital, it thrives. Major cities and towns—

Bath, Bristol, York, Cambridge, and others—have their own professional theaters. In addition, there are internationally known festivals of music and the arts throughout the country. Among these are:

- Aldeburgh Festival (June)
- Bath Festival (May–June)
- Belfast Festival (November)
- Brighton Festival (May)
- Cambridge Festival (July–August)
- City of London Festival (July)
- Edinburgh International Festival (August–September)
- Glyndebourne Festival (May–August)
- Greenwich Festival (June)
- Llangollen International Musical Festival, or Eisteddfod, (July)
- Malvern Festival (May–June)

For information on these and other festivals in Britain, write: Coordinator, BAFA, 23 Orchard Road, London N6 5TR.

PAMPERING THE BODY BEAUTIFUL

Most of London's deluxe hotels have beauty salons. In addition, department stores such as Harrods and Selfridge's have fashionable, outstanding beauty salons. Look also for the current salons of such internationally known health-and-beauty authorities as Dickins & Jones, Harvey, Nichols, Helena Rubenstein, Revlon, Vidal Sassoon, and Yardley.

There are health centers with saunas, massage, electrolysis, and beauty treatments in such spa towns as Cheltenham, Droitwich, Harrogate, and Tunbridge Wells. A booklet, *Britain's Spa Heritage*, available at the English Tourist Board or the BTA, lists specific facilities and addresses.

YOU AND YOUR MACHINES

Britain's electric current is 50-cycle, 240-volt AC, so appliances built for American 60-cycle, 120-volt current cannot be used without a transformer. (Hotel housekeeping may have such equipment.) Furthermore, new electric outlets in British hotel rooms require plugs with three rectangular prongs. Older outlets take plugs with two round prongs. You will need an adapter for either one, and you'll find them at the hall porter's desk or at electrical shops.

Many modern hotel bathrooms are equipped with hair dryers, and all have special electric-shaver outlets that supply both 110-volt AC (the standard American current) and British 240-volt AC. They accommodate both American and British plugs. For irons and other electrical appliances, check with hotel housekeeping.

You will find few bargains in British electrical appliances, because they are built for 240-volt current. Battery-operated equipment has no such handicaps. There are discount shops that feature all kinds of electronic gear from microrecorders and personal stereos to microcomputers and electric shavers.

DOING BUSINESS IN BRITAIN

For business information, the leading daily newspapers are the *Financial Times*, *The Times*, the *Guardian*, and the *Daily Telegraph*. And, for business news weekly, the *Sunday Times*, the *Observer*, and the *Sunday Telegraph*.

The major weekly business and economic magazines are *The Economist*, *Trade & Industry Journal*, *Investor's Chronicle*, and *Stock Exchange Gazette*.

For office temporaries and secretaries, London's 5-star hotels are accustomed to arranging for these for visiting businessmen. You will find listings in the telephone book business directory pages under this heading and under "Word Processing Services."

The American Chamber of Commerce (United Kingdom), Inc., publishes an annual *Anglo-American Trade Directory* of 17,000 companies with U.K./U.S. business links. The ACC's address is 75 Brook Street, London W1Y 2EB; tel. 493-0381.

Other helpful addresses:

- Department of Trade, 1 Victoria Street, London SW1H OET. (There are regional DOT offices for Scotland, Wales, Northern Ireland, and other sections of England.)

- Association of British Chambers of Commerce, 6 Dean Farrar Street, London, SW1; tel. 222-0201.
- London Chamber of Commerce, 69 Cannon Street, London, EC4N 5AB; tel. 248-4444.

TELEPHONE, TELEGRAPH, AND MAIL
Mail

Buy stamps at the hotel porter's desk; at stores with POST OFFICE signs; at post office buildings, weekdays from 9 A.M. to 5:30 P.M. and Saturdays from 9 A.M. to 12:30 P.M. London's Trafalgar Square post office, WC2, is open from 8 A.M. to 8 P.M. daily.

Postage: Air mail to America, per 10-gram letter, is 34p (51¢); postcard, 26p (39¢). Air mail to the Continent, per 20-gram letter, is 22p (33¢). In Britain, letters and postcards under 60 grams cost 17p (26¢).

For parcels sent out of Britain, a customs declaration form is necessary.

Mail letters at the hotel desk, red post boxes, and post offices.

Receive letters at hotels, addressed to you and marked POSTE RESTANTE or HOLD FOR ARRIVAL; c/o American Express, 6 Haymarket, London SW1Y 4BS, marked HOLD FOR ARRIVAL.

Telegraph

Send telegrams by telephone at any time. From your hotel, the amount will be added to your bill. From a pay phone, you will need the full amount in coins (the operator will estimate the price for you). And from major post offices you can send telegrams 24 hours a day, over the counter.

To send a telegram within Britain, dial 190; to send abroad, dial 193.

Telephone

You will need 10p coins to operate them. Dial your number first, and when you hear a series of high-pitched, rapid beeps, push a 10p piece in the slot. When you hear more rapid beeps, push in another coin to continue.

There are also pay telephones (at airports and central London) in which you put a 50p coin *before* dialing. The machine computes your charges and, after your call, returns the change due.

Still a third type of pay telephone is operated by a plastic "Phonecard" that you purchase in advance at post offices. You place the card in a special slot, make your call, and the charges are debited from the card electronically. They are available for £2.80, £7, or £14 ($4.20, $10.50, or $21).

You can dial directly from nearly all telephones in Britain. For local calls, no area code is needed. For other counties and for international calls you must dial the area code. The international operator number is 100.

PERILS & PITFALLS

Before you make any long-distance phone calls from your hotel room, check the tariff. Some hotels list rates for telephone calls in their "hotel services" card, but many do not. Certain hotels routinely savage guests by slapping whopping surcharges on long-distance calls.

The hotel switchboard will place long-distance and overseas calls for you if you request them, but to avoid heavy hotel surcharges, dial direct. Even better, arrange for your party to call you. Another alternative: the local post office building generally has a telephone section from which you can place calls at minimum expense.

The London information number ("directory enquiries" is 142; general information, 191; information ("directory enquiries") for other parts of Britain, 192. For calls outside London, 100; overseas calls, 107 or 108; Continental calls, 104 or 105. The emergency number (for police, fire, or medical help) is 999 all over Britain.

BUSINESS HOURS

Shopping, government, and business hours are 9 A.M. to 5 or 5:30 P.M., Monday through Saturday. In country towns, shops may open earlier and stay open later—and close a half or full day in midweek (often Wednesday or Thursday).

Banking hours are 9:30 A.M. to 3:30 P.M., Monday through Friday. Some banks are open Saturday mornings.

Many West End London shops remain open one evening a week, usually Thursday. Knightsbridge shops stay open Wednesday evenings. Harrods is open daily from 9 A.M. to 5 P.M., Wednesdays from 9:30 A.M. to 7 P.M., Saturdays from 9 A.M. to 6 P.M..

Pubs are open from 11 A.M. to 3 P.M. and from 5:30 P.M. to 11 P.M. daily; on Sundays from noon to 2 P.M. and from 7 to 10:30 P.M. Restaurant hours are similar.

West End theaters: No uniformity—check matinee days and curtain times. 7:30 P.M. is more or less standard.

Museums, stately homes, gardens, and art galleries in London are usually open from 10 A.M. to 5 or 6 P.M. weekdays, and from 2 to 6 P.M. Sundays and holidays. Outside of London, any time goes.

Because hours and days of opening change frequently, it is always best to inquire beforehand from your hotel concierge or local listings.

PERILS & PITFALLS

Nothing is more unpredictable than "open to view" days and hours at stately homes and gardens. Unless you phone and verify, you will often travel 30 miles to see a famous 18th-century estate and discover at the closed gate that it is open only from 2 to 3 P.M. the third Monday of months that begin with the letter *J*. Or half an hour on St. Swithin's day. Or any Wednesday *but* odd-numbered ones. Check carefully the listings in the current annual issue of *Historic Houses Castles & Gardens,* East Grinstead House, East Grinstead, West Sussex RH19 1XA; tel. 0342-26972. Or phone ahead.

MAKING FRIENDS WITH THE BRITISH

Forget those agonizing movie scenes of English railway compartments with half a dozen strangers intent on ignoring one another.

You usually won't experience anything like that with the Brits if you simply open a conversation with a conventional salutation and a simple question. The weather is always fair game, but ask about things that interest you:

how to reach your destination, what is the time of the cathedral concert or evensong, where to find a good restaurant, spot of tea, or pub lunch. Of course, if you get a really taciturn type, don't keep trying. Just back off and try with someone else.

The Briton's pub (his "local") is made for conversation. One sure-fire conversational gambit is to ask the advice of the publican (bartender) on the available brews. Another dialogue-starter: In any pub that appears to be more than 50 years old, ask, "Who is the resident ghost?" You're likely to find others chipping in and telling you about ghosts they've seen or heard about. (Buy the publican a drink if you do have a lengthy dialogue with him. The same applies to anyone who buys you one. It is bad form not to reciprocate.)

A comfortable and welcoming central meeting place is the English-Speaking Union, 37 Charles Street, London W1; tel. 668-9300. It has events and activities for members, who (in addition to Brits, of course) are generally from Commonwealth countries and the U.S. E-SU has scores of active branches in the U.S., and its American headquarters are at the English-Speaking Union of the United States, 16 East 69th Street, New York, NY 10021; tel. 212-879-6800.

Some of London's venerable, exclusive men's clubs open their doors on a reciprocal basis to members of the following American clubs: New York's Players, Coffee House, Knickerbocker, Century, and Lotos; Washington's Cosmos, Metropolitan, and Georgetown; Philadelphia's Union League and Rittenhouse; San Francisco's Press Club; Boston's Tavern, Harvard, St. Botolph's, and Somerset. A letter of introduction from the home club may allow use of the London counterpart's facilities.

Businessmen will home in on the American Chamber of Commerce in London, 75 Brook Street, W1; tel. 493-0381.

One sure-fire way to meet Britons who have similar interests is to contact by phone, letter, or personal call the organization in Britain that caters to your hobby or avocation. You'll find associations and societies for every imaginable interest, and some you can't imagine.

Start with the London phone book business directory pages for "Clubs & Associations." It lists organizations from A&A Social Club and the American Club to the Zinc Development Association, and includes the British Ornithologists Union, Burlesque Club, Contemporary Art Society, Dickens Fellowship, Royal Philatelic Society, Society for Psychical Research—and scores more.

STUDYING IN BRITAIN

Opportunities for brief studies in Britain seem unlimited.

Summer courses at Cambridge and Oxford universities on historical and literary subjects, with coach excursions and walking tours, are offered by University Vacations, 9602 NW 13 Street, Miami, FL 33172; tel. 800-792-0100. Registrants live and dine at university colleges.

See also the National Institute of Adult Continuing Education's calendar of short residential courses taught at various towns around Britain. Write NIACE at 19B De Montfort Street, Leicester LE1 7GE, enclose £1 ($1.50) plus postage.

For short courses available in the London area: City & Guilds of London Leisure Courses, 76 Portland Place, London W1N 4AA; tel. 580-3050.

The Victoria and Albert Museum offers various short courses. Catalog from the V&A, Cromwell Road, South Kensington, London SW7 2RL.

Christie's, the international auction firm, has evening courses taught by specialists, ranging from one to ten weeks in length. The £130 ($195) fee (plus 15 percent VAT) includes tuition, buffet supper, and wine after each of the ten sessions. (Christie's Fine Art Courses, 63 Old Brompton Road, London SW7 3JS; tel. 581-3933.)

Christie's Wine Courses, taught by experts such as Michael Broadbent, are open at fees averaging £100 ($150). (Christie's Wine Courses, 8 King Street, St. James's, London SW1Y 6QT.)

Cordon Bleu Cookery School (London), Ltd., offers courses one to four weeks in length. (Write to 114 Marylebone Lane, London W1; tel. 935-3503.)

For Oriental cooking, try the Chinese Cookery School, 3b Hyde Park Mansions, Transept Street, London NW1; tel. 258-0355.

Clothing design is taught at the London Academy of Dressmaking and Designing, 27 Westbourne Grove W2; tel. 727-2850.

Craftsmen will want to investigate the offerings of the Camberwell School of Arts and Crafts, Peckham Road, London SE5; tel. 703-0987; and the instruction available through the Association of British Craftsmen, 57 Coombe Bridge Avenue, Stoke Bishop, Bristol, Avon BS9; tel. 0272-686-417.

The Field Studies Council, Montford Bridge, Shrewsbury SY4 1HW, has information on short courses about birds, flowers, history, and myriad other subjects. You learn on campus at one of nine centers for a fee of £125 ($188) up.

SPORTS IN BRITAIN

To Americans who visit Britain, the native pastimes may seem peculiar if not downright indecipherable. Their "sports" are cricket, football (which we call soccer), rugby, and polo.

There are sports that surmount language barriers. These include tennis, badminton, squash, golf, rowing, riding, swimming, skating, cycling, basketball, boxing, and racing—motor, horse, greyhound, and human.

Spectator Sports

For tickets to the spectator sports listed below, book through your hotel hall porter. Alternatively, call or write the organizations listed, or try the Keith Prowse Ticket Agency, Banda House, Cambridge Grove, Hammersmith London W6 OLE; tel. 741-8989, and its U.S. office at 234 West 44 Street, New York 10036; tel. 212-398-1430 or 800-223-4446.

- Football (soccer): August through May; Wembley Stadium box office, tel. 902-1234.
- Cricket: Call National Cricket Association, tel. 289-1611; Lord's Cricket Ground (the most famous cricket ground of them all, at St. John's Wood Road, London

NW8), tel.289-1615; or Surrey CCC Oval Cricket Ground, tel. 582-6660.

- Rugby's home is Twickenham. Tel. 892-8161.
- Polo: Hurlingham Polo Association; tel. Lodsworth, (079-85) 277.
- Badminton: Call National Badminton Centre, Milton Keynes, tel. 0908-568-822.
- Basketball: English Basketball Association, Calomax House, Lupton Av., Leeds; tel. 0532-496-044.
- Boxing: Championship bouts in May; call British Boxing Board, tel. 828-2133.
- Bicycling: British Cycling Federation, 16 Upper Woburn Pl., London WC1; tel. 387-9320. If you want to train on the indoor track, call Eastway Cycle Circuit; tel. 534-6085.
- Racing:

  Horses (Ascot, Epsom, Derby): call Jockey Club at 486-4921.

  Motorcycles: Call Rugby, 0788-703-32.

  Greyhounds at Hackney Stadium, tel. 986-3511; Wembley Stadium, tel. 946-5361.

  Autos: RAC Motor Sports Association, Ltd., tel. 235-8601.

  Stock cars: Call 946-5361 or Aldershot 0252-201-82.

- Rowing: *The* event is the Oxford vs. Cambridge race in March or April. Check *British Rowing Almanack.*
- Tennis: Wimbledon fortnight in June. Tickets: All England Lawn Tennis & Croquet Club, Church Rd., London SW19; tel. 946-2244.

Participant Sports

For general information, call the Sports Council's Information Centre, 16 Upper Woburn Place, London WC1; tel. 388-1277. Some possibilities:

- Golf: British Tourist Authority publishes a booklet listing golfing holiday tours and hotels that provide golf (see "Useful Addresses and Telephone Numbers" section for BTA address).
- Gymnasiums: Fitness Centre, 11 Floral Street, London WC2; tel. 379-6613; and Westside Health Club, 201 Kensington High St., London W8; tel. 937-5386.

- Riding: Bathurst Riding Stables, 63 Bathurst Mews, London W2; tel. 723-2813; Roehampton Gate Stables, Richmond Park, tel. 876-7089; British Horse Society, Stoneleigh, Kenilworth, Warwickshire CV8 2LR.
- Skating: National Skating Association of Great Britain, 15 Gee St., London EC1; tel. 253-3824.
- Squash: Squash Rackets Association, Francis House, Francis St., London SW1; tel. 828-3064.
- Swimming: Several new hotels have pools for guests. Otherwise, it's the so-called Public Baths at Chelsea Manor, tel. 352-6985; Ironmonger Row, tel. 253-4011; Kensington New Pools, tel. 727-9923; Porchester Baths, tel. 229-3226 and Seymour Place, tel. 723-8018; and outdoor pools from May to September.
- Tennis: Public courts in the parks, or call the Lawn Tennis Association for the closest member club, tel. 385-2366.

A note to football fanatics: If you're in Britain during the American football season, you'll be able to see an NFL game each week on Channel 4. There's a growing audience for football in Britain, and there are now two amateur leagues with more than 100 teams (in case you want to see how the Brits play this American sport). You can keep up in the magazines *Gridiron U.K.* and *Touchdown*.

TRAVELING WITH CHILDREN

Britain is one of the best foreign countries in the world for children to visit, even young ones.

Language and food are familiar (mostly), the natives are friendly, and many activities are geared to young interests.

Travel for children under 5 is free, and those under 16 pay half-fare on BritRail, London buses, and the Underground. Many hotels (Trusthouse Forte, for instance) allow children under 16 to share a room with parents without charge, or in a separate room at a reduced rate (25 percent off). Restaurants usually provide children's menus or reduced portions at lower cost.

Qualified baby-sitters are available: Childminders, tel. 935-4386 or 935-9763, 9:15 A.M. to 5:15 P.M. Mondays through Saturdays, is licensed by the Department of Employment to supply nurses, teachers, day nannies, and baby-sitters. Another: Universal Aunts, Ltd., tel. 352-5413.

There are so many things to interest the little blighters that we've listed them in our chapter on "London with Plenty of Time." But the first thing you should do after you arrive is phone Children's London, 246-8007, to see what's currently going on that's intended for kids.

For information on camps, active sport vacations, and hobby holidays for youngsters, check the English Tourist Board's "Activity & Hobby Holidays" guide (c/o Thames Tower, Black's Road, London W6 9E1).

READING MATTER AND THE OTHER MEDIA

In Britain, the media churn out a continuous torrent of information for a highly literate society. Here's a rundown of what slant and content to expect from the various sources:

Newspapers and Magazines

For the most international news daily, there are the *Guardian*, *Telegraph*, and *Times*. Rupert Murdoch's *Times* takes a conservative position on most political matters, even more so than that of the Conservative Party.

Other papers with varying degrees of conservative editorial policies include the *Mail*, *Express*, *Telegram*, *Star*, *Sun*, and *Evening Standard*.

A more liberal editorial viewpoint is found in the *Observer*, the *Manchester Guardian*, and the *Mirror*, which was traditionally Labor's house publication but now is independent. The *Morning Star* is the Communist publication.

For news of cultural events, reviews, and ads of interest to tourists, see the *Guardian*, *Sunday Times*, *Sunday Telegraph*, and, of course, the *International Herald Tribune*. Baseball and other U.S. sports scores are in the *Telegraph*.

Among magazines, *The Economist* and *New Statesman* have liberal views, *The Spectator* is conservative.

Television and Radio

Two of Britain's four TV channels are the government-owned British Broadcasting Company (BBC); the others are Independent Television (ITV) and Channel 4.

TV nightly news programs are generally long on news of British economic and social conditions and police-blotter features, and short on other international news.

You will find enormous diversity on TV, such as series on bird-watching, literary walks (with writers as guides), U.K. trees, architecture of English houses, villages, and towns, and biographies of actors, writers, comics, and composers. There are also movies, sitcoms, and cops-and-robbers shows, both home-grown and imported from the U.S. Some hotels show new movies on closed circuit, plus videotex.

On radio, the vaunted BBC news-on-the-hour throughout the day consists of two minutes of headlines about the immediate British economic crisis, scandal, or horror.

BBC Radio airs an afternoon women's program daily, which presents readings of plays, novels, and poetry—interesting fare for auto travelers between sites.

LEAVING BRITAIN

GETTING TO THE AIRPORT
To Heathrow

Taxi. Your most comfortable and convenient choice. From Kensington it will take 40 minutes or so and cost between £12 ($18) and £20 ($30)—probably about £17 ($26). For three or four persons, this is a bargain. For a single, it's not.

Underground. Probably the most reliable and often the fastest way to Heathrow (no traffic snarls or delays). Trains run on the Piccadilly line (as frequently as every four minutes during rush hours), and the fare is £1.50 ($2.25) from central London. The major drawback is your baggage; if you have only hand luggage, the tube is terrific. If you have one or more heavy bags (and no baggage cart), the stairs to the train and at transfer points can be exhausting. There are escalators and elevators at the terminal. The tube stops at Terminals 3 and 4.

Bus. There are two special bus services to Heathrow. *Flightline 767* starts at Victoria Coach Station, Buckingham Palace Road, and picks up at Eccleston Bridge, at the corner of Kensington and Brompton Roads, and on Kensington High Street opposite the Royal Garden Hotel, and charges £2.75 ($4.13).

Airbus 1 leaves from Victoria Station and stops at Victoria Coach Station, Sloane Street, the Forum Hotel, and Earl's Court on Cromwell Road. *Airbus 2* departs from Paddington Station and stops at Sussex Gardens, the Coburg Hotel on Bayswater Road, and the Kensington Hilton on Holland Park Road. *Airbus 3* starts from Euston Station and stops at Russell Square, Bonnington Hotel–Southampton Row, Marble Arch, the London Hilton at Hyde Park Corner, Prince of Wales Terrace–Kensington High Street, and Novotel Hotel-Hammersmith. Airbus fares are £3, £1.50 for children ($4.50 and $2.25, respectively).

Buses run about every 20 or 30 minutes from 6:30 A.M. to 11:30 P.M. The trip normally takes 45 minutes, barring traffic problems.

Every time we have taxied to the nearest Airbus stop, the hackman has offered to take us to the airport for a reduced rate (last time the quote was £12 or $18). You may want to bargain with your taxi driver for a favorable rate for the trip.

In Terminals 3 and 4 there are plenty of free baggage trolleys to wheel your luggage to the check-in desk. Once cleared, you may go through the passport control (there is a special desk here where you have your VAT refund paper validated and mailed) and security checkpoint to the lounge area. Here you will find newsdealers, bars, cafeterias, and restaurants, as well as first- and business-class lounges.

PERILS & PITFALLS

At the duty-free shop, don't be fooled by the displays or confused by the dollar/pound pricing: There are few bargains—certainly not perfumes or tobacco products. Your best buy, though marginal, may be woolens.

To Gatwick

Taxi. The fare to Gatwick is horrendous. Don't even think about it unless you want to spend £30 ($45) or so.

Flightline 777. This express bus goes from Victoria Coach Station, Buckingham Palace Road, directly to the Gatwick terminal. The fare is £2.75 ($4.13) for the 70-minute trip. Departures are every half hour, beginning at 5:40 A.M. and ending at 10:40 P.M.

BritRail. Express trains to Gatwick leave Victoria Station four times an hour from 5:30 A.M. to 10 P.M. The journey takes about 30 minutes and the fare is £5 ($7.50). (British Caledonian Airways has a check-in facility at Victoria Station, so you can check in your baggage, select your seat, and secure your boarding pass on the spot.)

Gatwick's duty-free shopping is no bargain (see note for Heathrow, above). It's useful only for last-minute purchases or gifts forgotten earlier.

CUSTOMS ON RETURNING HOME
Returning to the United States

OK (items you *can* bring in, duty-free):

Four hundred dollars worth (retail value) of goods you bought abroad; 1 liter of alcoholic beverage; 100 cigars and 200 cigarettes; agricultural products if they are canned, cooked, hermetically sealed, or (as with cheese) do not have raw milk after processing; fish products (such as smoked salmon).

No-no's (items you *cannot* bring in):

Illegal drugs; medicines containing narcotics (without a prescription); toxic substances; liquor-filled candy; absinthe; endangered species, monkeys/primates, their skins or by-products; obscene articles and publications; lottery tickets; copyright-violating books, records, or cassettes; products made by forced labor; firearms and ammunition, without permits; cultural treasures, art, artifacts; most foods, plants, or animals and their products (except as stated above).

The best source of information on all this is the leaflet "Know Before You Go," available free from U.S. Customs Service, Washington, DC 20229, and found at most passport offices.

Returning to Canada

You must declare the following items:

Forty ounces of liquor or wine or 24 bottles/cans (12 oz. each) of beer or ale—for adults; 50 cigars, 200 cigarettes, and two pounds "manufactured tobacco," for adults; up to two days' supply of food products per person; "personal baggage," such as fishing tackle, boats, motors, snowmobiles, etc., camping and sports equipment, radios, TVs, musical instruments, typewriters, cameras, and other goods of a personal nature.

Pets, plants, fruit and vegetable imports require special approval—inquire of Animal Health Division, Food Production and Inspection Branch, Agriculture Canada, Ottawa, Ont. K1A 0Y9

No-no's:

Handguns and firearms with no legitimate sporting use; drugs.

LONDON

LONDON IN A HURRY

London warrants many superlatives. It is Europe's largest, most diverse city, richest in art, architecture, music, theater, and dance. For English-speaking people, it is the most accessible of the world's great cities. Its historic associations and place names strike the sounding brass of memory. It is doubly accessible, with its English-language signs and directions, as well as an admirable transportation system.

In a city as dense as a British Christmas fruitcake with treats, albeit cultural ones, here are our suggestions for the visitor with only one, two, or three days in London.

ITINERARIES IN LONDON

One Day

Westminster Abbey, Horse Guards, Big Ben, Houses of Parliament, Cabinet War Rooms, No. 10 Downing Street, Trafalgar Square, National Gallery, Tower of London, an evening on the South Bank.

Two Days

Buckingham Palace, Changing of the Guard, Queen Victoria Memorial, The Mall, St. James's Palace, Covent Garden, British Museum, St. Paul's Cathedral, Barbican Arts and Conference Centre.

Three Days

South Kensington Museums (Victoria & Albert, Science, Natural History), Harrods, Hyde Park, Museum of London, The City (St. Margaret Lothbury, Bank of England, Stock Exchange, Royal Exchange, Mansion House, St. Stephen Walbrook, Leadenhall Market, George & Vulture Tavern, Lloyd's of London).

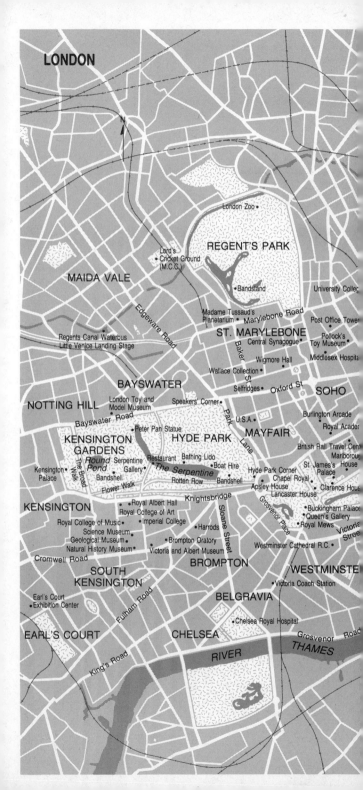

ewish Museum
Percival David
• Foundation of
Chinese Art

BLOOMSBURY

Univ. of London
• British Museum and Library

New Oxford Street

National
Portrait
Gallery

• National Gallery

anada
Charing Cross Pier

Queen Elizabeth Hall and
Purcell Rooms

Horse Guards
Banqueting House
• No. 10 Downing Street
• Cenotaph
e Cabinet   • Westminster Pier
ar Room   River Boats
Houses of Parliament
• Westminster Abbey

mith Square   Lambeth Palace
Lambeth   • Imperial War Museum
Bridge

ate Gallery

Vauxhall
Bridge

Dicken's House
Museum and
Library

HOLBORN

• Gray's Inn

• Lincoln's Inn

Dr. Johnson's House •
Royal Courts of Justice

Fleet Street

Covent Garden   The Temple
• London Transport Museum
Somerset House

National Film Theater
• National Theater
• Hayward Gallery
Royal Festival Hall

• Sadler's Wells

Museum of London •
National Postal Museum

Old Bailey

St. Paul's Cathedral

Blackfriars
Bridge

Gray's Inn Road

BARBICAN

• Wesley's House

Barbican Arts and
• Conference Center

• Petticoat Lane Market

Guildhall•
Bank of England•

Cheapside

Cannon
Street

Stock Exchange
• Royal Exchange

• Monument

Southwark
Bridge

London
Bridge

Tower of London
Tower Pier•

St. Katherine's
Dock

Southwark Cathedral

Tower
Bridge

SOUTHWARK

Tower Bridge Road

LAMBETH

Albert Embankment

**ELEPHANT
AND CASTLE**

SCALE OF MILES

0   1/2 MILE   1 MILE

Westminster Abbey

Try to arrive at Westminster Abbey♛♛♛♛♛ early. Doors open at 8 A.M. to the nave (admission free), but the Royal Chapels (admission charge) open at 10 A.M. Then you will have almost an hour for an Abbey tour before you must make your way a few blocks up Whitehall for the changing of the Horse Guards at 11 A.M. (An alternative is to walk one-half mile along Birdcage Walk to Buckingham Palace for its daily display of regal pomp, the Changing of the Guard♛♛♛♛, which takes place promptly at 11:30 A.M.)

Westminster Abbey is behind the Houses of Parliament, and its entrance is on Broad Sanctuary Street. This magnificent Gothic church, whose architectural cousins are at Amiens and Rheims, is the spiritual heart of Britain (though the Archbishop of Canterbury is the head of the Church of England). The Abbey is a "royal peculiar," under the jurisdiction of a dean and chapter, subject only to the sovereign. This is where the nation crowns, marries, and buries its rulers, the place where it honors and inters many of its heroes. (Sunday services: Holy Communion at 8 and 11:40 A.M., other services at 10:30 A.M., 3 and 6:30 P.M. Evensong Saturdays at 3 P.M., and weekdays—except Wednesdays—at 5 P.M.)

What you see from the street are the latest additions in stone and glass to earlier edifices built on this spot. The first recorded Christian construction was a Benedictine

---

INSIDERS' TIPS

For the first-time visitor, a "get acquainted" tour may give a valuable overview of London. Best bets are (1) the "Official London Sightseeing Bus," London Transport's guided red double-decker that chugs around its illuminating 18-mile circuit, leaving every half hour from Piccadilly Circus, Victoria, Marble Arch, and Baker Street Station (tel. 222-1234), beginning at 10 A.M.; and (2) the "Culture Bus," London Pride's guided all-day coach, which makes more than 20 stops at the city's major cultural sites. You can hop off, visit one (or more), and catch the next Culture Bus on its circuit for a full day for only one fare (tickets bought after 1 P.M. are good the following day). Buses leave from Coventry Street, just off Piccadilly Circus (tel. 629-4999).

monastery a thousand years ago. In 1065, Edward the Confessor built the church that served his palace of Westminster and the monastery attached to it.

William the Conqueror had himself crowned King of England in the Abbey at Christmastime 1066, beginning a coronation tradition that has continued to our own time.

In 1245, the pious Henry III launched an ambitious reconstruction of the Abbey in French Gothic style, completed more than a century later in the 13th-century designs. Major later additions are the towers, designed by Christopher Wren and John Hawksmoor and added in 1740.

As you enter and after your vision adjusts to the soaring height (102 feet) and vastness of the nave, you will see in the pavement before you a marker engraved simply "Remember Winston Churchill."

The Poet's Corner in the south transept is a major attraction for many visitors. Here are the monuments and epitaphs of many of Britain's greatest men of letters, from Chaucer on. You'll see busts of Dryden and Blake, memorials to Browning, Byron, Tennyson, George Eliot, T. S. Eliot, W. H. Auden, Dylan Thomas, and (surprise!) Henry Wadsworth Longfellow. Note also the fine wall paintings of St. Christopher and Doubting Thomas on the end wall. They were uncovered in 1936 and are thought to date from 1280.

Through a gate in the north aisle you will find monuments to General "Chinese" Gordon of Khartoum, political leaders such as Clement Atlee and Ramsay Macdonald, and the social reformers Sidney and Mary Webb. In the north choir aisle are plaques and memorials to men of science, such as Darwin and Newton, and composers like Benjamin Britten and Edward Elgar, along with the tomb of Henry Purcell, who was the Abbey organist as well.

The north transept has memorials and statues of statesmen such as Disraeli, Gladstone, Palmerston, and Pitt, and a grandiose monument to General James Wolfe, who died at the Battle of Quebec.

The Abbey is a veritable who-was-who of British life, but, while caught up in the recognition of famous names from the near and distant past, don't overlook the Abbey's sculptural and architectural splendors.

For pageantry, Henry VII's Chapel ♛ ♛ ♛ ♛ ♛ (finished by his son Henry VIII in 1520) is spectacular, and is enlivened even more by colorful banners of the Knights of the Order of the Bath (originated by Henry VII) that hang here. The chapel is considered the outstanding example of English Perpendicular Gothic, with superb fan-vaulting and lacy windows. Located at the Abbey's eastern end, the central feature is the carved marble Gothic tomb of Henry VII and his queen, Elizabeth of York. Between the door and the altar are buried George II (1683–1760), the last king interred in the Abbey, and his queen, Caroline.

As you leave the chapel, note above you the chantry of Henry V, where his effigy rests on a marble slab. The original silver head and silver-gilt plates that covered the effigy were stolen during Henry VIII's reign. (The head on view is of plastic and dates from 1971.)

The tombs of those polar opposites of the 16th century, Queen Elizabeth I (buried with her half-sister, Mary) and Mary Queen of Scots, are north and south, respectively, of the Henry VII Chapel.

INSIDERS' TIPS

On Wednesday evenings the Abbey is open from 6 to 9:45 P.M. and there are no entry fees.

Among many treasures to look for in the Abbey, note especially:

- A tablet in the apse floor commemorating Oliver Cromwell and three associates, who were buried here, then disinterred (when Charles II was restored), and all but Admiral Blake were beheaded, with their heads displayed at Westminster Hall.
- Edward the Confessor's shrine, behind the High Altar, once a Mecca for worshipers seeking miraculous cures from England's only sainted ruler.
- The sturdy English oak Coronation Chair (1301), used to confirm all British rulers since the reign of Edward II (with the exception of Edward V and Edward VIII who were never crowned). Note the Stone of Scone, the Scottish coronation seat, visible beneath the wood. This was seized in Scotland in 1297 by Edward I, and symbolizes Scotland's union with England.
- The Sanctuary, or High Altar, with some of the most beautiful of the Abbey's tombs. Look for those of Ave-

line, Countess of Lancaster (d. 1273), Edmund Crouchback, her husband (d. 1296), who founded the House of Lancaster, and Aymer de Valence (d. 1324). There is also a Florentine triptych of the Madonna and saints by Bicci de Lorenzo (c. 1450). Anne of Cleves (d. 1557), Henry VIII's fourth wife, is buried below.

Be sure to see the beautiful 13th–14th-century Abbey cloisters, entered from a doorway on the south side of the nave. The northeast part is oldest and best, and as you circle the courtyard you come to the doorway to the historic Chapter House. To enter, you must don felt overshoes to protect the tile pavement.

In this octagonal room, the early House of Commons held meetings beginning in 1376. There are memorials here to Americans James Russell Lowell, poet and U.S. minister to London, and Walter Hines Page, U.S. Ambassador during World War I, along with a Roman sarcophagus and a coffin lid from the 7th-century church that stood on this site.

If you continue along the east cloister walk, you reach the 11th-century Norman Cloister. In the Norman Undercroft is a museum showing the Abbey's history, with effigies of past monarchs, made of plaster, wax, and wood. They were carried in funeral processions through the streets.

When you have more time, pop into St. Margaret's, the tiny church just north of Westminster Abbey. It dates from the 15th century, and has Sir Walter Raleigh's bones under the altar (he was beheaded in the yard) and a window commemorating the betrothal of Catherine of Aragon to Prince Arthur, Henry VIII's older brother. When Arthur died, Henry married her. This is Parliament's parish church and is popular for fashionable weddings (Churchill was married here).

You'll want to move along a few blocks north to Whitehall. The term applies generally to the massive Palladian buildings which form the entire administrative secretariat of the government. You are here not to see the buildings but to witness one of the colorful pageants of British life: the Changing of the Horse Guards ♕ ♕ ♕ ♕.

It is the Household Cavalry who stand sentry duty on horseback at what was once the guardhouse of the vanished Whitehall Palace. Whitehall's government buildings enclose the open yard of Horse Guards Parade.

The ceremony of changing the mounted guards takes place daily at 11 A.M. weekdays and 10 A.M. on Sundays, but is canceled in rainy weather.

Across the street is Banqueting House ♕ ♕ ♕ ♕, built on the site of the original Whitehall Palace. Cardinal Wolsey took over the palace in the 16th century, and Henry VIII seized and enlarged it for a royal palace, which later burned down. Inigo Jones's daring Palladian design—two joined, 55-foot cubes—was built in 1619, using portions of the old palace. This was the first Palladian building erected in London.

Banqueting House's 1635 ceiling is one of Rubens's masterworks, for which he received a princely (at the time) £3,000, plus a knighthood. The work consists of nine allegorical paintings depicting the apotheosis of James I and the glories of his rule. George I later converted the building to a royal chapel, and still later it served as a museum. But it is best remembered as the site of Charles I's execution, in 1649. (You can see the window from which he stepped to the scaffold.) The House has been sumptuously restored to its former glory, and now is a splendid setting for formal receptions and state banquets.

Houses of Parliament

Retrace your steps south now to the Houses of Parliament ♕ ♕ ♕ ♕ ♕, known officially as the Palace of Westminster. The House of Commons is open to the public from 10 A.M. to 5 P.M. daily when Parliament is not in session, and on certain holidays. The House of Lords, at the other end, closes a half-hour earlier. Tours begin at Visitors' Entrance, next to Victoria Tower. (On Tuesdays and Thursdays at 3:15, the Prime Minister answers questions in the House of Commons.)

INSIDERS' TIPS

To hear a debate in the House of Commons is not easy, for there are only 326 seats in the Strangers' Gallery, and you have to queue at St. Stephen's Gate on the west side the day before from 2:30 P.M. (Friday from 9:30 A.M.) for tickets. To arrange in advance to attend a debate, apply to your embassy in London to secure tickets for you.

After a fire in 1834 destroyed the Old Westminster Palace built by Edward the Confessor and his successors, the New Palace of Westminster, i.e., Parliament, was constructed in the Gothic style of Westminster Abbey. It was designed by Sir Charles Barry, who planned the Victoria and Clock towers and Houses of Lords and Commons on either side of a central hall and corridor.

The Clock Tower♔ ♔ ♔ ♔ ♔, with its gigantic 13-ton bell, is widely known as Big Ben. (Actually, the nickname applies to the bell, which took its name from Sir Benjamin Hall, the Commissioner of Works at the time it was inaugurated.) It is to London as the Eiffel Tower is to Paris—the best-known symbol of a great city.

The outside world knows when Parliament is in session by watching the Victoria Tower by day and the Clock Tower at night. A Union Jack flying from the Victoria Tower and a white light in the Clock Tower indicate that one of the Houses is sitting. For statistics collectors, the Clock Tower is 320 feet from pavement to tower-top, and its clock dials are 23 feet in diameter. The Victoria Tower is 323 feet tall.

Your tour may enter through the Victoria Tower, where original copies of all acts of Parliament going back to 1497 are stored. You pass through the Norman Porch, which has busts of prime ministers, and view the Royal Robing Room where the lords' robes are kept and the Queen retires when she opens each session of Parliament. Queen Victoria's 1856 throne is here, as are frescoes of St. George battling the dragon, and King Arthur and his knights in action.

Up the steps is the Royal Gallery, with huge pictures depicting Nelson's death at Trafalgar and (on the other wall) Wellington meeting Blücher after Waterloo in 1815. There are also statues and portraits of assorted British rulers, including Alfred, William the Conqueror, Elizabeth I, and Queen Anne.

In the Peers' Chamber's lavishly decorated Gothic interior, the benches are red, the Lord Chancellor sits on the traditional woolsack, and there is a royal throne from which the sovereign opens each Parliament.

The tour proceeds to the Peers' Lobby, which has coats-of-arms and stained-glass windows, through the central lobby and Commons' Corridor. All of these display paintings of England's history (including the departure of the Pilgrims in 1620).

Members' Lobby, outside the House of Commons, shows the scars of Nazi bombing in 1941, which destroyed the adjoining chamber. Commons agreed to Churchill's proposal that the damage be preserved "as a monument of the ordeal which Westminster has passed through . . . and as a reminder to those who will come centuries after [that] their forebears . . . 'kept the bridge in the brave days of old.' " In the Lobby are statues of Churchill, Lloyd George, and other prime ministers.

Commons was rebuilt to exactly the same size and form as its bombed-out predecessor. By no means roomy, its 45-by-69-foot chamber accommodates 437 M.P.'s on green benches, 15 officials on the floor, and 326 visitors ("strangers"), plus 161 members of the press. The red line separating government and opposition benches is not crossed during a sitting.

Back at the Central Lobby, you descend into St. Stephen's Hall, the first permanent home of the House of Commons, in 1547. St. Stephen's Porch is the entrance to Westminster Hall ♛ ♛ ♛ ♛, the major portion of the original Palace of Westminster to survive the fire of 1834. This historic building, called New Hall when it was built by William II between 1097 and 1099, is nothing short of magnificent, a triumph of medieval engineering. Its beautiful oak hammerbeam ceiling spans without pillar or brace a space similar in size to a football field—a tremendous achievement. Many of England's significant events have taken place in this Hall: the King's Council met here in Norman times; coronation feasts were celebrated here; important trials were held here, including those of Sir Thomas More, Guy Fawkes in the Gunpowder Plot, Charles I, the seven-year trial of Indian empire-builder Warren Hastings, and many others; Cromwell sat in the Coronation Chair here and dismissed Commons. Here too, Britain's rulers and heroes have lain in state before burial. (Churchill's body was here for nearly a week with a round-the-clock vigil of military guards.) The Hall may be visited when Parliament is in recess and mornings when Parliament is not meeting.

The Jewel Tower ♛ ♛ ♛, opposite the Houses of Parliament, was built by Edward III in 1366 as a royal treasury; its medieval miscellany is open to view daily.

The Cabinet War Rooms

Two blocks north on Abingdon Street to King Charles Street, you'll find yourself in the area of government buildings: the Home Office, the Ministry of Housing, and the Foreign and Commonwealth Office. Here, near the Clive Steps, 10 feet underground, beneath the government offices on Great George Street, are the Cabinet War Rooms ♛ ♛ ♛ ♛ (open Tuesday through Sunday), worth a visit by anyone interested in the history of World War II.

In a surprisingly cramped rabbit-warren of spartan rooms was the emergency headquarters that served as the nerve center of the British Empire during the war. Established in the summer of 1938 as war threatened, the War Rooms became operational a week before war was declared in 1939, and were in use until the formal Japanese surrender in 1945. Here the war cabinet, secretariat, and chiefs of staff had protected work spaces. The Joint Planning Staff and Joint Intelligence Committee, who were responsible for preparing and coordinating strategic and operational plans, worked here. And in 1940, when invasion danger was greatest, the Home Forces commander and staff also had rooms here.

The entire place has been restored to its wartime aspect. Most astonishing is the bunkerlike, brick-walled

Cabinet Room, which is nearly filled by a U-shaped table and dominated by a schoolroom-type map of the world. Churchill sat on a large wooden chair in front of the map and presided over more than 100 meetings of the War Cabinet in five years. Above the door, red and green lights indicated whether an air raid was in progress.

The tiny transatlantic telephone room is bare, except for a clock with sets of red and black hands, indicating the times in Washington and London. Churchill telephoned Presidents Roosevelt and Truman from here, and the messages, from August 1943 on, were channeled through a Bell Laboratories scrambler that was too big for the War Rooms. It was installed in the basement of Selfridge's department store in Oxford Street.

In one of the larger rooms (60A), five typists worked for the Joint Planners. Their hand-cranked mimeograph machine is the most modern piece of equipment in the place. The cluttered map room, with its exposed wiring and rough lumber beams and supports, has the look of a hobbyist's improvised garage carpentry shop.

The Prime Minister's room is next door, and it is similarly improvisational in appearance, with wooden supports and helter-skelter electrical wiring. On the side walls are maps of Britain and Europe, and in front is a linoleum-topped double desk with two phones. There is one note of minimal luxury—a carpet covers the floor. At the rear is a single bed with a reading light and a chamberpot. Although he spent only three nights here (during the Blitz in 1940), Churchill delivered several stirring radio broadcasts from this room.

On the wall outside is a hand-lettered sign reading, "There is to be no whistling or undue noise in this passage." One senses that there was not much to whistle about in these quarters.

Aboveground again, you are just a few steps from Downing Street and the Prime Minister's residence, at Number 10 ♛ ♛. This modest Georgian building was originally made available by George II to his P.M., Sir Robert Walpole, in 1732. It is difficult these days to get near enough for a good look, because fear of terrorism has made it necessary for the area to be cordoned off.

Shortly before Whitehall Street opens into Trafalgar Square ♛ ♛ ♛ ♛ you will see on your left the cluster of

Admiralty buildings (the oldest dating from 1725) and Admiralty Arch ♛ ♛.

By now it is probably lunchtime. Great as this area is for sightseeing, it isn't the best locale for treating yourself to a grand lunch. So you may want to hop a taxi for a short drive to Greek Street in Soho and a French lunch at L'Escargot or a Hungarian repast at the Gay Hussar. Then you might meander back south to Trafalgar Square.

Trafalgar Square is one of the finest public spaces in a British city. Here are the fountains and bronze lions guarding the towering column at whose top is the statue of Admiral Horatio Nelson, the victor of the 1805 Battle of Trafalgar. Trafalgar Square is where the action is, a favorite locale for demonstrations and rallies.

Facing the square on the east is James Gibbs's strong but delicate St. Martin-in-the-Fields ♛ ♛ ♛ (1722), which set a style in church construction much copied throughout New England. Looming above the square on the north is the National Gallery.

The National Gallery

The National Gallery ♛ ♛ ♛ ♛ ♛ is deservedly ranked among the outstanding art collections of the world. Its western European works alone number more than 2,000, from the 14th through the 19th centuries. (The Tate Gallery ♛ ♛ ♛ ♛ ♛ takes up where the National leaves off, with the 20th century.)

Among the National Gallery's most famous works are paintings by Leonardo da Vinci, Michelangelo, Titian, van Eyck, Holbein, Rembrandt, Vermeer, El Greco, Velasquez, Goya, and leading British painters from Hogarth and Gainsborough onward.

Art lovers can (and do) spend entire days in the National Gallery, but as your time is limited, we suggest that you next hasten by taxi or Underground (Charing Cross station is one-half block east of Trafalgar Square) to the Tower of London (tube station: Tower Hill), which closes at 5 P.M.

The Tower of London

The "infamous" Tower ♛ ♛ ♛ ♛ ♛ is far more than a dank prison where royal adversaries were tortured before their heads were lopped off. True, it has dungeons, and it served as a prison and execution block, but in addition to its gory history it was a royal mint, armory, and residence. Even as you shudder at the inhumanity of some of its uses in the past, you will enjoy its peerless collection of Crown Jewels, its superb armor collection, its royal chapel and handsome Tudor buildings and courtyards.

The original Tower (the White Tower) at the core of today's complex was built by William the Conqueror in 1078 (probably using stone from Roman city walls), as one of a series of fortresses he established to subjugate a vanquished populace. The White Tower was strengthened and expanded in the 12th to 14th centuries, surrounded by a moat, with outer and inner walls, palace buildings, and not just one tower, but more like 19. The palace buildings were inside the walls until Cromwell ordered them destroyed during the Commonwealth.

As you enter the Tower on the west side, you will meet the Yeoman Warders, dressed in their Tudor *buffetier* ("Beefeater") uniforms. You proceed across two drawbridges over the now drained and grassy moat, through Middle Tower and Byward Tower, where the portcullis can be seen.

Across Tower Green you will see to the west the half-timbered Queen's and Gaoler's Houses and scaffold site next to the royal chapel of St. Peter ad Vincula. On the Green are 6 ravens, whose presence is mandated and protected by the British government because legend has it that the British Empire will end when its ravens leave. (To be on the safe side, the birds' wings are clipped.)

The White Tower and the 17th-century New Armouries exhibit medieval arms and armor, one of Europe's finest collections, formed by the arsenal of Henry VIII. You will see a suit made especially for him, displayed in the belligerent stance of his Holbein portrait.

In the Chapel Royal, a tablet lists some of the many who were executed nearby on the Green, or outside the Tower walls on Tower Hill. Among the best known are Lady Jane Grey and Henry VIII's wives Anne Boleyn and Catherine Howard.

Next to the Chapel Royal is the entrance to the Jewel House, the most popular single stop on the Tower tour.

Dreams of avarice wing through the minds of dazzled spectators as they view the Crown Jewels: the Royal Scep-tre, St. Edward's Crown (used in coronations), the Im-perial State Crown, the Imperial Crown of India, the Queen Elizabeth Crown with its Koh-i-noor Diamond, and many more. Fabulous as the collection is, think of what it would be if *most* of the Crown Jewelry had not been melted down by Cromwell's government.

History tells us that for most who were invited to the Tower, it was not good news. The walls of the many cells carry names and inscriptions carved by famous and in-famous prisoners, among whom were Sir Thomas More, Edward V, Elizabeth I, Henry VI, James I of Scotland, and, in our own time, Rudolf Hess, the Nazi who parachuted into Britain during World War II.

Outside the Gaoler's House on Tower Green is the scaffold site, with a brass plate marking the spot where the condemned were executed. Keep an eye peeled for the Yeoman Gaoler, who occasionally appears, clad in his traditional uniform, flourishing his executioner's axe.

While dwelling on things macabre, be sure to inspect "Traitor's Gate" where prisoners entered and their bodies unceremoniously exited. The infamous "Bloody Tower" was built by Richard II. In it the Little Princes were allegedly murdered in 1483, and Sir Walter Raleigh most certainly spent 13 years, during which he wrote his *History of the World.*

When the Beefeaters lock you out of the Tower at 5 P.M., you may want to enjoy the Thames view from Tower Bridge 👑 👑 👑 or take a riverboat from Tower Pier to Westminster, to see the heart of the London waterfront and the magnificent view 👑 👑 👑 👑 👑 of Big Ben and the Houses of Parliament from the river.

For your evening, head to the South Bank complex, where you are bound to find something that appeals to you. Your easiest transportation will be a taxi or the Underground from St. Paul's station to Waterloo station. About three blocks north of Waterloo Road is the con-stellation of contemporary buildings that have made this an international arts center.

The complex includes the Royal Festival Hall, Queen Elizabeth Hall, and Purcell Room for concerts, the Nation-

INSIDERS' TIPS

For first-rate pretheater concerts, free, pause in the vast foyer of the National Theatre. Every evening and before Saturday matinees, Britain's young musicians play for audiences waiting for curtain time, as well as passersby simply interested in a free concert. The printed performance schedule is available in advance from Tourist Information Offices, or by writing National Theatre Mailing List, FREEPOST, London SE1 7BR. Information by phone: 928-2033.

al Film Theatre for motion pictures, Hayward Gallery for art exhibits, and the three stages of the National Theatre for live theater: Olivier, Cottesloe, and Lyttleton.

Inside the complex are bars, buffets, and cafeterias where you can buy snacks or a light supper. You also may enjoy strolling along the river terrace for views of the Thames and the London skyline. (The paved area near the National Film Theatre is a favorite for skateboard virtuosi.)

PERILS & PITFALLS

The National Theatre presents plays in repertory on a rotating schedule. Be sure to check the schedule of performances (schedules are widely available at tourist information offices and hotel desks) to make sure the play you want is on for the date you have available. Tickets can be reserved by phone (see Insiders' Information for London— Theaters and Concert Halls, page 159).

LONDON THE SECOND DAY

In our one-day itinerary we suggested beginning at Westminster Abbey. We are leading you back to the same general neighborhood, more or less, today. Your prime goal this morning is to see one of London's spectaculars, the Changing of the Guard 👑 👑 👑 👑 in the forecourt of Buckingham Palace 👑 👑, the Queen's residence. The ceremony takes place promptly at 11:30 A.M., and crowds gather early.

Even so, you'll have time beforehand to inspect the building's somewhat bland if not pompous exterior, which dates from a 1913 remodeling. The original 1703 building belonged to the Duke of Buckingham, who sold it to George III in 1761. John Nash redecorated the interiors magnificently, and Queen Victoria was the first ruler to make this an official residence. You won't get to peek inside, unless invited by the Queen.

You might walk around the south corner to see if the Queen's Gallery ♛ ♛ ♛ is open (or phone 930-4832 and ask). This, formerly Buckingham Palace's chapel, is from time to time a showcase for art from royal collections. If you have an interest in carriages and horses, visit the Royal Mews on Buckingham Palace Road. There are vintage motorcars, carriages, and horses to be seen, usually Wednesdays and Thursdays, from 2 to 4 P.M.

Turn now past Queens Gardens circle and the Queen Victoria Memorial and stroll down one of London's finest avenues, the Mall. Fronting on Green Park, the first building on your left is Lancaster House, which was built in 1827 for the Duke of York, and is now used for government receptions (open weekends). Next comes the Queen Mother's home, Clarence House. It was built in 1825 for the Duke of Clarence, who became William IV. Adjoining it is St. James's Palace ♛ ♛, which was originally built by Henry VIII. Only the 19th-century restoration is visible (note the uniformed sentry). New ambassadors present their credentials here, and from 1699 until Victoria's accession in 1837, this was the official seat of the British court.

Across Marlborough Gate Street is Marlborough House ♛ ♛, designed by Sir Christopher Wren (much altered later) as a "town house." It was the home of the Prince of Wales in the 19th century and is sometimes open to view. Beside it is the Queen's Chapel, a 1627 Inigo Jones design.

At this point you might be ready for a change of pace, so head toward Covent Garden ♛ ♛ ♛ ♛ for its nonstop action, open-air market, unusual shops, and wide selection of pubs and restaurants. (It is a half-mile walk or a quick trip via the tube from Embankment or Charing Cross stations to Covent Garden.)

The name supposedly stems from the 16th-century "convent garden" of the abbey of St. Peter's, Westminster. The monks sold their surplus vegetables here, and the tradition of merchandising they started continues today.

During the Reformation the monastic lands were confiscated, and this area of the city was developed by the Duke of Bedford, who hired Inigo Jones to design a square. Jones, a classicist, derived his 1631 design from the Piazza d'Arme in the Italian city of Livorno. A tiny market on the square expanded by 1671 into a great and famous marketplace.

St. Paul's Church♛♛ on the square was also Inigo Jones's work, for the Duke of Bedford, who wanted no costly frills. "You shall have the handsomest barn in England," Jones assured him. It was here that Punch's Puppet Show was first performed (and witnessed by Samuel Pepys in 1662).

Thus began a Covent Garden theatrical tradition that still lives. There has been at least one theater in the area since 1733. David Garrick, the famous 18th-century actor, lived at 27 Southampton Street nearby, as a plaque over the door reveals. St. Paul's is considered the "actors' church," and many a famous thespian is buried here.

The Royal Opera House in Convent Garden is home base of the world-renowned Royal Ballet, and served as the launching pad for Benjamin Britten's and William Walton's operas. Outside the Opera House, Professor Henry Higgins met the cockney flower seller Eliza Doolittle in Shaw's *Pygmalion* (which was the basis for the musical *My Fair Lady*).

Today's Covent Garden has changed form and become "gentrified" since the produce market moved south of the Thames in 1974. The 19th-century neoclassical yellow brick building where the fruit and veggie merchants used to vie for trade has become, since 1980, a spacious two-story mall enclosed by a high arched skylight. Eliza Doolittle's flower market is now the London Transport Museum, with exhibits recounting the history of the Underground and the trams, trains, and buses.

Covent Garden's reopening brought a rejuvenated spirit of youthful insouciance that is evident in the open market stalls, trendy boutiques, craft shops, and the entire neighborhood.

The new Covent Garden's cultural vitality is apparent also in alfresco concerts and impromptu performances by mimes, jugglers, and mountebanks, in street-theater productions in St. Paul's Church, and in jazz and pop music concerts on its porch at lunchtime during the summer. Activity continues into the night, when pubs, wine bars, and discos in the area accelerate the tempo.

The area, with its lively, kaleidoscopic qualities, is a perfect place to have lunch. You may opt for a quick, inexpensive meal at one of the fast-food places in the Garden itself. For something different, try Calabash in the Africa Center, or Poon's for Cantonese *dim sum*, both nearby on King Street. If you want to lunch in style, the chic Neal Street Restaurant is also handy on the street for which it is named, and where you can easily be sidetracked by the many intriguing shops.

Boswell's, at 8 Russell Street, a good coffee stop, is on the site where James Boswell was introduced to Dr. Samuel Johnson more than 200 years ago. Brahms & Liszt, on Russell Street, is a wine bar with jazz, not classical, music. The cozy old (1623) Lamb & Flag pub on Rose Street is an actors' favorite.

INSIDERS' TIPS

Occasionally there are "Covent Garden Proms" in which several hundred tickets to performances of the Royal Opera Company and/or the Royal Ballet are available at giveaway prices. They are made available one hour before curtain time on the day of the performance, at the Foyer Box Office, Royal Opera House, Covent Garden; tel. 240-1066.

Keep in mind that Covent Garden is conveniently located to reach many other activities. It is bordered on the north by bookshop-rich High Holborn, and Shaftesbury Avenue's theater row. On the east and south are more West End theaters in Drury Lane (where Nell Gwynn sold oranges before she became an actress and Charles II's mistress), Aldwych, and the Strand.

The British Museum

Almost straight north is one of the world's most remarkable treasure houses, the British Library and Museum♛♛♛♛♛ at Great Russell and Bloomsbury streets. It is, in fact, far more than either a library or a museum.

Founded in 1753, it is in a gargantuan 1847 building (designed by Sir Robert Smirke) that houses a national library of millions of works of art, documents, publications, and books. In addition, the Museum has some 8 million permanent exhibits and fields numerous special shows.

By (copyright) law, the Library has a copy of every publication produced in Britain since the Magna Carta (a copy of which is on display). The range of the Library's holdings includes medieval manuscripts, music, first folios of Shakespeare's plays, ships' logs (that of Nelson's *Victory*, among many), first drafts of many famous literary works, and postage stamps. Drawings and prints from the 15th century onward constitute an unparalleled collection.

Since its opening the Library has been a major resource for countless authors and politicians. Karl Marx did his research here and frequented the Museum Tavern across the street (another good lunch bet). It is reported that Marx and Metternich, the Chancellor of the Austro-Hungarian Empire, once collided on the library steps and denounced each other for Europe's political troubles.

The most visited treasures of the British Museum are undoubtedly the Elgin Marbles, those eloquent sculptures brought from the Parthenon in Athens in 1801 and 1802 by Lord Elgin (they're in rooms 8 and 9 of the Duveen Gallery). The Rosetta Stone, which proved to be the key to deciphering ancient Egyptian hieroglyphics, is another prime attraction.

Other museum "hits" include the following:

- The Egyptian art collection (note the delicacy of the tomb and mummy painting). If you have children in tow, the mummies win hands-down in fascination.
- The unequaled Assyrian art and sculpture exhibits.
- The Oriental art (especially Chinese ceramics) collection—one of the best in the West.
- Three thousand sophisticated, beautiful African bronzes brought back by the 1897 Benin punitive expedition. It changed the world's view of black artistic accomplishments.
- Roman, Anglo-Saxon, and other British objects of memorable quality and historic significance, such as the Sutton Hoo find, the treasure from a 7th-century Anglo-Saxon burial site.

The above list only hints at the riches in the Library and the Museum. Obviously you could spend days in the building (regulations require visitors to leave by 5 P.M. weekdays and 6 P.M. Sundays).

Not far away is Sir John Soane's Museum ♛ ♛ ♛ ♛ (closed Sundays and Mondays) at 13 Lincoln's Inn Fields (tel. 405-2107). It shines as the delightful expression of Britain's great neoclassical architect. With innovative design, Soane admirably showed his collection of paintings and classical antiquities. The house is an idiosyncratic wonder, just as he left it.

But onward now, in order to reach St. Paul's Cathedral in time to look around before it closes at 6 P.M. Your simplest transportation will be by taxi or Underground, from the Tottenham Court Station at the corner of New Oxford Street, to the St. Paul's station.

INSIDERS' TIPS

Other excellent portions of the British Museum's collections are displayed at the Natural History Museum ♛ ♛ ♛ (plants, minerals, animal kingdom) on Cromwell Road, and the Museum of Mankind ♛ ♛ ♛ ♛ (ethnic and cultural exhibits) in Burlington Gardens.

St. Paul's Cathedral

You emerge on Newgate Street, and the entrance to St. Paul's Cathedral ♛ ♛ ♛ ♛ ♛ is only a short block south. From such close range you cannot see and therefore cannot sense the inspiration given during World War II by St. Paul's profile, looming above a city skyline often illuminated by eruptions of flame and billowing smoke, pierced by searchlights and laced by tracer bullets and shell explosions. Until the advent of high-rise buildings, St. Paul's dominated London's skyline.

There is evidence that a wooden church existed on this patch of ground as early as A.D. 604. In the 11th century, a Gothic St. Paul's Cathedral was built. One of Europe's largest, the church was almost 600 feet long, with a spire reaching nearly 500 feet. By 1600 it was neglected and sadly in need of repair. Inigo Jones worked on the west portico in 1634, but the building was all but destroyed in the Great Fire of 1666.

Christopher Wren proposed renovating the Cathedral as a cornerstone in his ambitious plans for rebuilding London. His design called for a neoclassical building with a dome rather than a spire. Wren's early designs were rejected (models of them are displayed in the Cathedral trophy room) until the present plan was approved. Building began in 1675, and Wren's son placed the final stone in the lantern in 1708 when Wren was too infirm to do so himself. The Cathedral was completed in 1711.

Called Wren's masterpiece, St. Paul's is laid out like a conventional English cathedral. Its nave has aisles on either side, with a choir and high altar beyond the transepts. There are small chapels, and towers flank the entrance. The major innovation is the dome, which Wren placed above the crossing of nave and transepts. The building is roomy, even vast, but Wren's genius makes the exterior lyrically rhythmical and the interior appealing and gentle, never overpowering.

Inside, when you look up, you see an inner dome that barely reaches the height of the lowest rim of the outer dome. A massive amount of stonework above the inner dome supports the outer one, which is sheathed in lead. Major interior features include the 19th-century ceiling mosaics and the Whispering Gallery at the base of the inner dome, 100 feet above the floor. Any sound on one side of the dome is heard perfectly on the other side.

PERILS & PITFALLS

It's a strenuous climb to the Whispering Gallery up the staircase next to the south transept. Hours for the dome, crypt, and treasury are 10 A.M. to 4:15 P.M. weekdays, and 10 to 11 A.M. Saturdays; tel. 248-2705.

The choir is adorned with some of Grinling Gibbons's finest woodcarvings of angels, leaves, and fruit. World War II bombs destroyed the Victorian high altar and baldachino, but they were replaced in 1958, working from Wren's sketches. In the apse is a new Jesus Chapel dedicated to American military personnel who were stationed in Britain and died in World War II.

In a south-side chapel, look for the 1631 statue of poet

John Donne, who was dean of the Cathedral. Around each pier in the crossing are memorial statues, those of Samuel Johnson and Joshua Reynolds among them.

In the south transept is a monument to Horatio Nelson, and in the crypt below, Nelson's body is in a black marble sarcophagus made in Italy much earlier and originally intended for another tenant, Cardinal Wolsey. The stairway to the crypt is opposite Nelson's monument.

There are scores of memorials and tombs in the crypt, including one for Lawrence of Arabia, and a massive juggernaut made of melted cannonballs used to bring Wellington's body to its final rest. Fittingly, Christopher Wren is buried here, and the simple stone marking his grave reads in Latin, "If you seek my monument, look around you."

INSIDERS' TIPS

For sheer contrast, you might like to see one of London's earliest surviving churches. It's the hauntingly simple St. Bartholomew the Great ♛ ♛ ♛ ♛, a Norman church of 1123, located a short distance north of St. Paul's, at the corner of Little Britain and Cloth Fair streets. Awesomely evocative.

The Barbican

As an evening option, we heartily recommend theater at the Barbican Centre. It is located on Beech Street, a short walk from St. Paul's.

Built by the City of London on a site that was bombed out in World War II, the Barbican's formidable exterior looks like a cavernous concrete bunker. Inside is something else: a handsome art gallery, half a dozen exhibition areas, a hall for major concerts, and two excellent theaters for live performances and two for cinema.

The Barbican Theatre is the Royal Shakespeare Company's home, and you can expect to find at least one Shakespeare play in repertory, alternating with a modern work. Barbican Hall offers concerts by the Philharmonia, the London Philharmonic, the Royal Philharmonic, and smaller groups such as the English Baroque Orchestra, the Guarneri Trio, and outstanding soloists.

There are also occasional concerts by current pop music stars. And, for the pleasure of visitors, there are free exhibits of arts and crafts as well as occasional foyer events—which might include such assorted artists as the British Wind Quintet, the Carrig Irish folk singers, the Zigeuner Gypsy musicians, the Veena Concert Orchestra, and Dave Cliff's modern jazz quartet. Something is happening here daily.

For information on what's playing at the Barbican, when, and at what prices, the monthly "Barbican Centre Diary" is the definitive reference. For information by phone, call 638-4141, extension 218/365. Recorded information: 628-2205 or 628-9760.

A THIRD DAY IN LONDON
South Kensington Museums

If you have concluded your one- and two-day itineraries, we recommend that you begin your third day with a look at the extraordinary cultural concentration clustered along Cromwell Road in South Kensington. In a way, the whole group owes its being to Prince Albert, Queen Victoria's husband and consort, for he fostered plans for what became this complex of museums and colleges.

From the proceeds of the enormously successful Great Exhibition of 1851, a South Kensington Museum was built. Originally it included both science and the arts, but quickly outgrew the space, and science was moved to its own building nearby. Growth of the fine and applied arts collection led to the creation of the present huge Victoria and Albert Museum, which Edward VII opened in 1909.

The V&A ♛ ♛ ♛ ♛ ♛ has accurately been called "the national attic." But what an attic! It's the only one of its kind, and the extent and quality of its riches cannot easily be grasped. Nevertheless, for starters, visit the Museum Shop and use the postcards and publications as an index to the Museum's exhibits. For guidance, try *100 Things to See in the Victoria and Albert Museum* and/or the *Brief Guide*.

Your own interests will dictate what to see, but here are some strong contenders:
- Indian art and sculpture, including miniatures from Rajasthan, Mogul paintings from the Clive collection, and

Gandhara Greco-Roman figures.

- Splendid Italian Renaissance sculpture, but the major treasure is the series of 9 full-size watercolor cartoons that Raphael painted for the Sistine Chapel tapestries.
- Ceramics, from Italian Majolica to English Wedgwood—a V&A specialty.
- Furniture, especially French 17th-century and English from Tudor through Victorian times, displayed in authentic room settings. Notable are the artistry of Robert Adam and Chippendale, as well as the famous eleven-foot-square "Great Bed of Ware" mentioned in *Twelfth Night* (minus the eight-at-a-time that it reputedly slept).
- Rooms of furnishings produced by William Morris and his Pre-Raphaelite associates, including the Green Dining Room and a complete Morris interior, with a gold-and-silvered piano.
- Rugs, tapestries, embroideries, and a wide range of textiles from many lands.
- Excellent paintings by British artists, especially Constable.
- Outstanding European wooden sculpture, much of it from churches, from the 14th century onward.
- Costumes, including the typical dress of different eras, engagingly presented.

Don't miss the "New Acquisitions" room, where you will see displays of recently arrived items, often surprising delights.

Across Exhibition Road from the V&A is the British Museum of Natural History ♕ ♕ ♕, a century old in 1981. The main doorway originally had Adam standing at the peak, lording it over the birds and beasts that decorate the façade. Some say he was pushed off, others that he was blown away by World War II bombs. Anyway, he has not reappeared and has been little missed.

The Museum, looking for all the world like a German Romanesque cathedral, was intended to display the grand design and wonders of God's Creation. Its first director, Sir Richard Owen, had specified that he wanted "space for seventy whales" an extravagant request that appalled his Victorian supporters.

Owen didn't get all the space he wanted, or the 70

whales. He did, however, wind up with a grand new building and a collection that has grown into one of the world's
largest and finest. From dinosaurs to dolphins, from emus
to elephants, from ants to antelope, if its a form of animal
life, you're likely to see it here. Everything to do with the
earth, its rocks and minerals, is displayed in the Geologi-
cal Museum section. (Plants are at the Kew Garden
museum.)

Next door is the Science Museum ♛ ♛ ♛ ♛. The building was cloned from the Natural History Museum in the
1930s and is noted for its superb collection of Industrial
Revolution artifacts. No wonder. Britain was the hotbed of
industrial development, and here you can see James Watt's
steam engine, Arkwright's spinning mill, navigation instruments, locomotives and autos, and a plethora of other
seminal devices.

Display and explanatory aids for the exhibits are of a
high order. Not all exhibits are from the far-gone past, for
the museum also features contemporary subjects ranging
from microchips, fiber optics, and lasers to space exploration, and video recording. Popular phenomena, such as the
special effects used in films like *Star Wars*, have made
memorable special exhibits.

To help you choose from the museum's enormous
menu, pick up a copy of *Fifty Things to See* at the front
desk.

From any of these South Kensington museums, it is
less than a mile to the fashionable Knightsbridge area and
one of London's key attractions: Harrods Department
Store.

Knightsbridge takes its name from the legendary clash
of two knights on a bridge over the West Bourne river in
ancient times. It was a green and rural area where
Londoners escaped the Plague or the crush of the city
(Samuel Pepys picnicked here in 1666), and where nobles
had country retreats. The French Revolution's refugees
flooded in and opened shops, mixing Gallic goods and
panache, which attracted Londoners.

Lord Grosvenor, who owned much of the land, built
fashionable homes in the adjacent Belgravia section, and
with the international success of the Great Exhibition of
1851 nearby, Knightsbridge blossomed. Today it is one of
London's major shopping areas, anchored by Harrods. Just

a few dozen yards to the east is Jaguar- and Porsche-filled Sloane Street, home ground of Britain's female yuppies, the so-called Sloane Rangers, and their male counterparts, "Hooray Henrys."

Harrods

Harrods began in 1849 as Henry Charles Harrod's tiny grocery on Brompton Road, an area notorious for highway robberies. Harrods' pink Victorian palace now occupies a square block, is Europe's largest department store, and not only sells every kind of merchandise imaginable, but provides services seldom found in stores.

You won't be out of place in Harrods; 40 percent of their sales are to overseas customers. Whatever you want, you'll probably find it. There are 230 departments (34 of them for fashion items). In addition to the expected goods, Harrods sells real estate, vacations, and, in its famous white-tiled Food Halls, meats, cheeses, fresh-baked bread and pastries, and other cooked and raw foodstuffs, plain and fancy.

You seldom expect a store to operate a bank and tourist-information desk, to sell insurance, pets, and theater tickets, or to check customers' luggage and baby-sit their pets, repair shoes and lighters, and arrange funerals. Harrods does all of the above, and more. It also operates London's last subscription library and a pharmacy, photo studio, dry cleaner, and jewelry appraiser. Its hairdressers shear men, women, and children.

If you are hungry, Harrods can cope; it has seven restaurants and four bars, each with a distinct character. Among them are the fast-food West Side Express on the ground floor, the quickie Health Juice Bar on the lower ground floor, the fancy Georgian Restaurant on the fourth floor, and the self-service Dress Circle on the first floor.

Harrods' eat-as-much-as-you-like Grand Buffet Tea in the fourth-floor Georgian Restaurant is justly famous. It threatens the weak-willed sweets maven with literally dozens of different exquisitely crafted cakes, tarts, pastries, puddings, trifles, fruit concoctions, ices, and yet-to-be-labeled desserts for a set price that includes tea and allows repeat trips. Though kids love it, they are out-numbered 20-to-one by adults at this high-calorie extravaganza.

One of our own favorite havens at Harrods is the Green Man Pub, reached via stairs in the ground-floor men's clothing department on the Basil Street side. This is a good, quick lunch stop for shoppers. The ales are fresh and the pub food well prepared and inexpensive; service by friendly waitresses is prompt.

For most visitors, Harrods is a high point of a London visit. It's a place where you can easily spend a day, not to mention all your available cash. Harrods is surrounded by intriguing small streets, lanes, and mews with galleries, boutiques, and restaurants. For a different kind of lunch, try Ménage à Trois (see Insiders' Information for London—Where to Eat, page 140), where there are no main courses, you just mix and match a variety of inventive starters.

INSIDERS' TIPS

Harrods' semiannual sales—the first Friday in January and first Friday in July—are international events, advertised in American newspapers, and draw hordes of shoppers from home and abroad, intent on taking advantage of markdowns of 50 percent or more. Experienced shoppers advise waiting until after 3 P.M. on the first day, when the crowds may have thinned.

Hyde Park

But you have other places to see, and one of these is Britain's most famous park. There are 80 parks within 7 miles of Piccadilly Circus, but Hyde Park ♛ ♛ ♛ is surely the best known. Head straight north from Harrods.

The most direct route takes you through Edinburgh Gate to the welcome greenery of the park that Charles I opened to the public in 1625. Once the property of Westminster monks, it was seized by Henry VIII in 1536 and turned into a royal preserve for hunting wild boar and bulls. Today the bulls are gone, but the wild bores are at Speakers' Corner, especially on Saturdays and Sundays.

If you turned straight east, you would arrive at Hyde Park Corner, with its 20-foot, muscular bronze Achilles statue dedicated to the Duke of Wellington. Across the street is Apsley House, the Duke's home and now a museum of his belongings and art collection.

Instead, continue north and you will come to *le route du roi* to Kensington Palace, more than a mile to the west. This soft sand road or bridle path for fashionable riders is better known today as Rotten Row. It was along this road that, in Georgian days, the "swells" drove their carriages or landaus to see and be seen. You may see cavalry horses from the Knightsbridge Barracks, at the southern edge of the Park, being exercised here. It is from these barracks that the Horse Guards set out for Whitehall every morning at 10:30.

At one point Rotten Row nearly touches the southeast tip of that misnamed lake, the Serpentine. In 1730 Caroline, George II's queen, ordered the West Bourne stream and local springs harnessed to form this boomerang-shaped lake, which soon became a favorite place for boating and swimming—and for suicides as well. (Shelley's first wife, Harriet, was one of them. She drowned herself in the Serpentine in 1816.) If you've a mind to cool off, the Lido, or bathing beach, is on the south side of the Serpentine. On a sunny, hot day the entire lake seems to be alive with rented boats, swimmers, and ducks.

Follow the east end of the lake north to Serpentine Road. If you turn west, you may stroll along the north side of the lake to the boat-hire pavilion and onward to the beautifully proportioned 1826 bridge designed by George Rennie. There are fine views from here of London's high-rise buildings beyond the Park to the east and south, and of the grassy banks and landscape of the Park itself.

Across the lake to the west, the Park changes its name and character to Kensington Gardens ♛ ♛ ♛, the surroundings of Kensington Palace ♛ ♛ ♛. Christopher Wren designed the building for William and Mary, and it has been a royal residence ever since. In it are formal flower gardens, shrubbery, and an orangery.

If you look southwest, you will see the frenetically eclectic and sentimental 1876 Victorian memorial to Prince Albert. Opposite it is the cavernous Albert Hall, another memorial to the prince. It is in almost constant use for concerts, rallies, beauty contests, boxing, and the famed Promenade Concerts.

East of the white-railed bridge and gas lamps, the rivulet leading out of the lake leads you to the tranquil Dell, a green nook with a small waterfall and a mighty Cornish stone megalith, placed there in 1861.

Marble Arch

To the northeast are Marble Arch and Speakers' Corner, where anyone can speak his mind, even if it's absent. John Nash designed the Arch as a formal entranceway to Buckingham Palace, but it was moved here in 1851. By the end of the Edwardian era it was clearly a bottleneck, and so traffic was routed around rather than through it.

Extending due west from Marble Arch, within the Park, is the north range of the Ring, an avenue that was a popular track for carriages and riders in the 17th century. As late as 1856, a Frenchman was startled to see the ornate carriages "with powdered footmen and rustic herds of cows, sheep and goats with elegant ladies trailing silks and laces among them. . . ." Not only a social center, the Ring was used to test carriages and their equipment. In that process, Oliver Cromwell fell here and was dragged by his horses in 1654. (As if that were not injurious enough, a gun exploded in his pocket.)

The site of Marble Arch lives in English history as Tyburn, where scaffolds stood to dispatch condemned prisoners. Tumbrels brought them by St. Sepulchre's, where they received flowers, to St. Giles, where they were given beer. The wretches would be carried along Oxford Street, and upon arrival at Tyburn, prayers preceded a noose around the neck, after which the cart was driven out from under them, providing the avid audience with a thrill a minute.

Promoters built bleachers and sold tickets to the executions and reaped the profits. These were substantial when a popular highwayman like Jack Sheppard was strung up. His demise was a gala event in 1724, drawing some 200,000 spectators. It was at Tyburn that the exhumed bodies of Cromwell and his colleagues, Ireton and Bradshaw, were displayed after Charles II's Restoration. Public floggings and tortures, and the executions of pickpockets, forgers, robbers, rebels, and traitors continued here until 1783. Today the mayhem is unauthorized, random, and vehicular.

London Museum

Leave the leafy greenery and relentless torrent of London traffic now for the London Museum ♛ ♛ ♛ ♛ (closed Mondays).

Take a taxi or the Underground at the Marble Arch station to Barbican station (on Sundays when Barbican station is closed, go to St. Paul's station). Walk south on Aldersgate Street to London Wall Street (aptly named for the wall that once enclosed the old city). You are now in the oldest section of London, called the City. Here 5,000 people live and 500,000 people work, flooding in each workday from 8 to 10 A.M. and ebbing out between 4 and 6 P.M.

This commercial and financial capital of Britain was devastated by bombs during World War II. The remarkable London Museum is in a postwar building that is part of the Barbican redevelopment complex constructed on the ashes.

As such, the museum is a model of what the latest and best exhibition techniques can do to re-create other eras. You will see historic objects and re-creations of events dramatically presented, and also hear the voices and sounds of the time and place you are viewing.

On display is a visual/aural biography of a great city presented chronologically, from its prehistoric, Roman, Saxon, and Viking beginnings onward. Be warned that the Museum is large and can absorb hours of fascinated viewing if you have that much time to spare.

Among the discoveries to be made are these:

■ A gorgeous, gilded baroque bonbon—the Lord Mayor's Coach, which you may have seen on TV in its annual trip from Guildhall to the Law Courts for the Lord Mayor's ceremonial installation.

■ A Roman temple of Mithras 1,900 years old, uncovered in 1954 during excavations for a new building. Among items displayed are fine marble heads of Mithras, the sun god, and Serapis, god of the underworld.

- An intricate and beautiful art deco elevator from Self-ridge's department store.

- The 17th-century stock hidden by a jeweler who had a well-to-do clientele. Called the Cheapside Hoard after the area where it was found, it includes gem-studded brooches, pins, necklaces, and rings, and finely-worked crosses, belts, and chains.

- A diorama of the London fire of 1666, which destroyed more than four-fifths of the city, with crimson light flickering wickedly over the model skyline.

Wind up your viewing and head south on Aldersgate to Gresham Street, which you can follow east by Goldsmith's Hall ♛ ♛, on your right on Foster Lane, to the ancient and impressive Guildhall. It's behind St. Lawrence Jewry Church (a Wren building restored after World War II bombing) on flagstone-paved Guildhall Yard. "Jewry" refers to the money-lender Jews who were exiled to this area by Edward I, and who lived here until 1290.

INSIDERS' TIPS

On only 10 days each year (2 each in March, April, June, July, and October), Goldsmith's Hall opens its doors to visitors. The fortunate few who manage to secure free tickets have a guided tour of the sumptuous interiors and historic gold and silver pieces and treasures in the Exhibition Room. Also, if you visit on one of the two March days, you can witness the "Trial of the Pyx," which began in medieval times. It is the annual analysis of batches of current British coins, to see if they measure up to specifications. Tickets are distributed only by the City of London Information Centre, tel. 606-3030.

Guildhall ♛ ♛ ♛, the Hall of the Corporation of the City of London, has been the center of city government for a millennium. The original 1411 building was all but destroyed in the Great Fire and World War II bombings. The 4-story façade, with its prominent coat of arms and pinnacles, was installed in 1789. You step through the original stone entrance porch into the great Gothic Hall (restored), where banners and shields of the city companies (guilds) hang. It is used for ceremonies, receptions, the election of sheriffs, and the annual Lord Mayor's banquet, a re-creation of a medieval feast.

There are 84 guilds, such as the Company of Thames Watermen and Lightermen; Clothworkers; Vintners and Dyers; and, most recently (1964), the Worshipful Company of Scientific Instrument Makers. The original ancient organizations were societies to pay *gild* (Saxon for "money"). Some 500 years ago they developed into craft unions and standard-setting agencies, and were given the privilege of wearing ceremonial robes or livery. In their medieval finery, members congregate here each Michaelmas (September 29) and elect two aldermen to the post of sheriff. Each Lord Mayor is a guild member, liveryman, former alderman, and former sheriff.

Rich in history, Guildhall recalls such events as Lord Mayor Dick Whittington receiving Henry V after his victory at Agincourt. (Whittington was elected mayor 4 times, and became wealthy using his catboats to carry goods.) It was also the site of historic trials, such as the one in 1553 in which Lady Jane Grey and her husband were condemned.

Also within the Guildhall is a library that holds rare folios of Shakespeare's plays and a deed signed by the poet, along with priceless maps and city memorabilia. The Guildhall Art Gallery features loan exhibitions in addition to its permanent collection, which began in 1670.

The City

Now for a walk in the City, London's financial district. You'll spot some of its more tradition-bound denizens—jobbers and brokers—by their bowler hats, black suits, and umbrellas or "brollies." Occasionally you will spy a "bill broker" in a top hat. These are directors of discount houses, who visit their clients and customers in person, disdaining the telephone.

Take time, in leaving Guildhall and heading east on Lothbury (that is its full name—not Lothbury *Street*), to duck into St. Margaret Lothbury Church ♛ ♛ ♛ on the left.

It is one of the finest of Christopher Wren's 53 post-London-fire churches. Rebuilt by Wren in 1686, its interior houses furnishings from other now-vanished churches. The spread-eagle great screen and elaborately carved pulpit are extraordinary, as are the font carvings. The church's sumptuousness is appropriate, for this is the parish church of the Bank of England, "the Old Lady of Threadneedle Street" ♛ ♛, across the street. She is, certainly, a lady with a heart of gold. Her vaults hold Britain's bullion.

For 25 years, starting in 1782, Sir John Soane labored to design and construct a splendid Bank of England building. Unfortunately, it was largely obliterated by pedestrian changes made in this century. Look for remnants of Soane's sensitive handiwork in the ground-level walls on Princes and Threadneedle streets.

For more color, go into the Threadneedle Street entrance hall and see the Bank's famed messengers in their top hats, red waistcoats, and pink tailcoats. The men in crimson-and-gold gowns are the gatekeepers.

When the Bank faced a run in 1745 during the panic caused by the advance of Bonnie Prince Charlie's army, it knew what to do. Not only did it pay each depositor with the smallest coins available, one by one at a maddeningly slow pace, but it made sure that the queue included a liberal number of Bank employees, who promptly turned in the money after they withdrew it.

Across the street is the Royal Exchange ♛ ♛ ♛, established by Sir Thomas Gresham and opened by Queen Elizabeth in 1565. The original burned in 1666, as did the second one (whose cornerstone was laid by King Charles II) in 1838. The building you see was finished in 1844, and its weather vane bears the great (11 feet long) gilded grasshopper—Gresham's crest—from the second exchange. Inside the building you will find a glass roof over what was once an open courtyard surrounded by arcades. Nowadays, special art exhibitions take place here from time to time.

Just behind the Royal Exchange is a pedestrian street, Freeman's Court, with a statue of George Peabody, the American whose London brokerage firm made him a multimillionaire. He spent millions on London slum clearance and low-rent housing and was buried in Westminster Abbey (later, his body was shipped home to Massachusetts).

Across Threadneedle Street from the Royal Exchange and east of the Bank of England is the Stock Exchange. Its modern tower belies the organization's 17th-century origins, in which rascals tossed out of the Royal Exchange for stock-jobbing regrouped in Change Alley. Their numbers grew, and early in the 19th century their descendants erected their own building, predecessor of the current one. Visitors are welcome to watch the action♛♛ from the gallery during Exchange trading hours, 9:45 A.M. to 3:15 P.M.

Facing the Bank of England from the south side of the 8-street intersection is the 1753 Mansion House♛♛ of George Dance the Elder. This Palladian building is the Lord Mayor of London's residence. In addition to the private rooms and state rooms, there is a 90-foot-long Egyptian Hall and (perhaps unique in modern official residences) a jail! You can't visit without an invitation—or an arrest.

Just behind Mansion House is St. Stephen Walbrook Church♛♛♛, where Christopher Wren tested his ideas for St. Paul's Cathedral. The exterior is not compelling, but the interior is a baroque masterpiece, ambitious, intricate, rhythmic, with fine carvings and a decorated dome. It is ironic that the great 18th-century architect Sir John Vanbrugh, master of ponderous stately buildings (Castle Howard, Blenheim) is buried here, surrounded by Wren's airy delicacy.

Have a quick look down Lombard Street, which extends southeast from Mansion House. Its Continental aspect is a delight, created by the flowery windowboxes and shingles, or street signs, that are similar to the medieval banners that once hung here over the offices of Italian moneylenders.

Today's signs are logos of current and former banks (merged into still others). Some of them are a golden cat playing a fiddle (National Commercial Bank of Scotland); a golden thistle (Alexander's Discount Company); a golden anchor (Glyn Mills); 3 golden crowns (Coutts); a black horse on a red shield (Lloyd's); and a black spread-eagle (Barclays).

At No. 16 Lombard Street there was a coffee house run by Edward Lloyd, where, in 1689, merchants who dared to insure ships and their cargoes gathered. Lloyd encouraged their business by publishing a news sheet that still exists as London's oldest daily newspaper. This was the informal beginning of Lloyd's of London. By 1771 the insurers had organized, and in 1796 they moved into the Royal Exchange building, where they remained until they built their own headquarters just down the way, at Leadenhall Street.

You'll see a bridge over Lime Street joining this with Lloyd's avant-garde building♛ ♛. Now you can visit the "Room" (as it's called) where the underwriters in their pews are polled by a red-robed Caller as brokers mill about signing up insurers on each policy. Open Monday–Friday; 10 A.M.–2:30 P.M.; free.

Your visit to the City would be incomplete without a look-in at its most historic pub, the George & Vulture in St. Michael's Alley, off Cornhill Street. Chaucer is said to have frequented the George, as did Ben Franklin during his London days. The George traces its origins to 1150, but the Great Fire caused an amalgamation with a tavern called the Live Vulture. The pub, with its high-backed stalls and horse boxes, is headquarters of the local Pickwick Club, appropriately, for Dickens was a pub patron. Pickwick pudding is a specialty here; genial service (especially at lunchtime) is not.

You'll find the Bank Underground station at the Bank of England–Mansion House intersection. It's below that peculiar equestrian bronze statue of Wellington, the Iron Duke, placidly riding bootless and without stirrups, clad in a Roman toga. He knew how to travel light.

LONDON WITH PLENTY OF TIME

Lucky you, if you have the luxury of time to savor and explore this most fascinating of cities. In our suggestions for visitors with limited time, we included places we would recommend as among the most important to see.

If you have time, there are many other possibilities; London caters to specialized interests.

A wonderful way to explore the city is to walk it, alone or in a group walking tour. There are delightful ones, usually led by specialists (some are museum docents, some are teachers) who know, love, and are enthusiastic about their subjects. They often impart facts and gossip that give you insights that make the city come alive.

The typical tour is organized on a theme. The group usually assembles at a specified time and tube station or well-marked meeting place. The tour leader identifies him/herself, collects the modest fee (£2 or $3, or less), and you're off!

Among the perennially popular tours are "Sherlock Holmes's London," "Haunted London: A Ghost Walk," "Shakespeare's London," "Dickens's London," "A Journey Through Tudor and Stuart London," and "The 1660s, Great Plague and Great Fire." A number of tours focus on specific sections such as Kensington, the City, Bloomsbury, and Chelsea. The variety is prodigious.

You will find information about walking tours at all tourist information offices and by checking schedules and listings in *What's On and Where to Go in London,* or *Time Out,* the weekly entertainment guide magazines, or the Monday edition of the London *Times;* or phone Victoria Station's Tourist Information Centre (730-3488).

Come with us on a walking tour we recently took of Dickens's London. Our guide, a youthful lawyer and Dickens enthusiast, meets us at the Aldgate tube station. Our first stop is Doctor's Commons and the Aldgate pump, referred to in *Nicholas Nickleby.* "One pump serviced a lot of people," our guide points out. And since the water was often polluted, cholera, typhoid, and typhus often resulted. "In the last ten years of the 19th century, 60,000 to 70,000 people a year died in London—more than from the Great Plague!"

At Carter's Lane, the guide points out where you get marriage licenses. The next stop is the site where Blackfriars Priory—founded in 1278—once stood and where Shakespeare and Burbage acted. St. Bride's Church on Fleet Street, with its "wedding cake" steeple, is just visible on the horizon. We trek onward down Pilgrim Street, from which pilgrims set out for Canterbury, huddled together for protection.

On we stroll, past the Victorian George pub, with its red awning, to the huge, stone Edwardian Central Criminal Courts building, on the site of old Newgate Prison. It was built as an extension of the Old Bailey of Dickens's time, whose slogan was "Defend the children of the poor and punish the wrongdoer." Outside the Old Bailey, scaffolds were erected for executions (as many as 20 in a day until the last public one in 1868). Dickens rented the second-floor window of the Magpie & Stump tavern, across from the prison, so he could observe and write about these "gallows events."

We assemble in a nearby courtyard. "We're now standing in what was Fleet Prison," says our guide, explaining that the Fleet River became so polluted in the 18th century that it was covered over. "Unfrocked clergy, loose women, and debtors were imprisoned here," he continues, "including Mr. Pickwick." Until 1840 it was legal for prisoners to be married through the grated windows of the prison.

We scoot under Holborn Viaduct and up Shoe Lane to Saffron Lane, associated with Fagin in *Oliver Twist*. At the Fleet Lane end, we are told, "hot" goods were sold, and as one proceeded north, "the more nefarious it became." Bill Sikes had his headquarters in the West Smithfield district, an area of "nasty Victorian warehouses—much the same today."

We turn up Cock Lane (once London's only walk licensed for prostitutes) to Giltspur Street to see the gold cherub (called Fat Boy) of 1680 high on a red brick building. It marks where the Great Fire ended. To the northwest is Pie Corner, where an old pub, the Fortune of War, stood until 1910. It was the center and warehouse of "resurrectionists"—professional body snatchers—who dug their merchandise in the graveyard of St. Sepulchre Church, close by, and sold the cadavers to surgeons from St. Bartholomew's Hospital down the road.

We cross West Smithfield in front of St. Bartholomew's Hospital, which dates from the 12th century and was founded by Henry I's courtier, Rahere. On the striking gateway is a statue not of Rahere, but of Henry VIII. Our guide points out the Church of St. Bartholomew the Great, one of London's oldest, with its beautiful Gothic gate and half-timbered Tudor building above it.

Across the way is the low-slung Smithfield Market (still going strong) with its Victorian red brick and blue iron arcades. This was the site of Ben Jonson's play *Bartholomew Fair*. Next we see the late 17th- or early 18th-century Hall of the Worshipful Company of Cutlers, one of the City's livery companies.

Soon we reach Warwick Square, behind old Newgate Prison. In Dickens's day this was the gateway to the Press

Yard, so named because, according to our guide, "here lead weights were slowly heaped on prisoners until they confessed . . . or died." Then, as a fitting coda, we are at Ave Maria Lane, Amen Court, and Amen Corner, where our temporary band disperses with thanks to the informative guide.

Several groups (one hesitates to call them companies, for they're not organized that formally) of highly qualified guides have been conducting such tours for a decade or more. Among the best known are London Walks (772-2763), Streets of London (882-3414), Citisights of London (241-0323), Exciting Walks in London (624-9981), Tragical History Tours (639-5165), and Discovering London (0277-213-704).

For do-it-yourself walks guided by recorded talks, there are "Tours by Tape," which include guidebooks as part of the package. These can be purchased at Victoria Station's Tourist Information Centre.

Museums and Galleries

For art lovers, London has world-class galleries and smaller ones with special collections. Among those not to be missed (in addition to the ones mentioned in earlier pages) are the following:

The Tate Gallery♔ ♔ ♔ ♔ ♔ On the Thames at Millbank (821-1313 or 821-7128). Officially the National Collection of British Art from the 16th through the 19th century, the Tate has phenomenal riches in the paintings of J. M. W. Turner, William Blake, William Hogarth, George Stubbs, and John Constable. Its modern collection

---

INSIDERS' TIPS

The Tate Restaurant (*not* its coffee shop) has one of London's best-selected lists of exceptionally fine wines at unbelievably modest prices (because it buys and warehouses abroad itself). Open from noon to 3 P.M. Monday through Saturday, the Restaurant is so crowded that reservations are advisable. (If you select your wine in advance, it will be opened appropriately before your appointed arrival.) Tel. 821-1313.

is strong in well-known examples of Futurism, Dadaism, Surrealism, postwar Abstract Expressionism, and Pop, Minimal, and Conceptual period works. Represented are major artists from Cézanne and Van Gogh to Picasso, Matisse, Klee, and current painters and sculptors. Open Monday through Saturday, from 10 A.M. to 6 P.M., and on Sunday from 2 to 6 P.M.

The Wallace Collection♛♛♛♛♛ Manchester Square (935-0687). This extraordinary collection of the Hertfords in their (much remodeled) London home has outstanding French 17th-century and 18th-century works and excellent examples of famous Flemish, Dutch, British, and Italian masters. The arms, armor, china, and furniture collections are also superb. Open Monday through Saturday, 10 A.M. to 5 P.M., and Sunday from 2 to 5 P.M.

Courtauld Institute Galleries♛♛♛♛ Woburn Square (580-1015). This is home to Impressionist and Post-Impressionist paintings, plus many fine old masters. Open Monday through Saturday, 10 A.M. to 1 P.M., and Sunday from 2 to 5 P.M.

National Portrait Gallery♛♛♛♛ Behind the National Gallery, St Martin's Place (930-1552). As a catalog of the rogues, rakes, and royals who have paraded through British history from Tudor times to the present, this would be fascination enough, but the Gallery also displays many portraits of distinction, from Holbein to Hockney. Open Monday through Saturday, 10 A.M. to 6 P.M., and Sunday from 2 to 6 P.M.

Collections with first-rate works, but perhaps narrower in scope, are Apsley House♛♛♛ at Hyde Park Corner (499-5676); Royal Academy of Arts♛♛, Burlington House, Piccadilly (734-3471); and for historic ritual antiques, the Jewish Museum♛, Woburn House, Tavistock Square (388-4525).

For changing exhibitions of contemporary art, Serpentine Gallery (run by Britain's Arts Council), Kensington Gardens (402-6075); Hayward Gallery, South Bank (928-3144); Whitechapel Art Gallery, Whitechapel High Street (377-0107); Barbican Gallery, Silk Street (628-2295); ICA, Nash House, The Mall (930-3647); and National Theatre's Foyer, South Bank (928-2252).

For fine handicrafts and the latest in modern design of furniture and objects for home and office, the Crafts Council Gallery♛ ♛ ♛, 12 Waterloo Place, lower Regent Street (930-4811), is an outstanding showcase.

If you are particularly interested in stately homes and their interiors and furnishings, you should, by all means, see these in addition to those mentioned earlier.

Kensington Palace State Apartments♛ ♛ ♛ Kensington Gardens (937-9561). This 1689 Jacobean country mansion was redesigned by Wren, with later additions, for William III and Mary. Queen Victoria was born and brought up here. The Court Dress Collection spans 200 years. Open daily.

Apsley House♛ ♛ ♛ Hyde Park Corner (499-5676). An elaborate house given to the Duke of Wellington by a grateful nation, it is a display case of 19th-century taste in the china, silver, and plate showered on the Duke. More appealing to moderns are the many excellent surprises in the art collection. (And check out that wild, gigantic nude of Napoleon by Canova!) Closed Mondays and Fridays.

Geffrye Museum♛ ♛ ♛ Kingsland Road (739-8368). In 18th-century almshouses around a courtyard are period rooms from Elizabethan to Art Deco. (Jane Austen's writing table is here, also.) Closed Mondays.

Leighton House Art Gallery and Museum♛ ♛ 12 Holland Park Road, Kensington (602-3316). A High Victorian interior and Lord Leighton's paintings play second fiddle to the influential Arab Hall, a fanciful rendering of an Alhambra-esque *sala*. Closed Sundays.

Linley Sambourne House♛ ♛ 18 Stafford Terrace (994-1019). The home of *Punch* magazine's political cartoonist Edward Linley Sambourne (d. 1910), the house is a "must" if you want to see how Victorian/Edwardian Londoners really lived at the turn of the century. Closed Mondays, Tuesdays, Thursdays, Saturdays.

Marble Hill House♛ ♛ Richmond Road, Twickenham (892-5115). Built for George II's mistress, the house became home to George IV's morganatic wife, Mrs. Fitzherbert. Visit it for the 18th-century furnishings. Closed Fridays.

If you would like to visit the homes of famous people, we suggest these: Carlyle's House♛ ♛, 24 Cheyne Row, Chelsea (352-7087); Chiswick House♛ ♛ ♛, where Edward VII lived as Prince of Wales, Burlington Lane (995-0508); Marlborough House♛ ♛ ♛, designed by Wren, with chapel by Inigo Jones, Pall Mall (930-9249); Dr. Samuel Johnson's House♛♛, Gough Square (353-3745); Hogarth's House♛♛, Hogarth Lane, Great West Road (994-6757); Wesley's Chapel and House♛♛, where Charles and John Wesley lived and preached, City Road (253-2262); Freud Museum, the famous psychoanalyst's last home, 20 Maresfield Gardens, Camden.

PERILS & PITFALLS

Charles Dickens House at 48 Doughty Street, where he lived from 1837 to 1839, is always on the list of authors' houses to visit. He wrote books such as *Nicholas Nickleby* and *Oliver Twist* here, and his desk is on view along with manuscripts, letters, pictures, and memorabilia. Nevertheless, we find the house and its displays singularly unrewarding. Its collection of authentic Dickens material is overweighted with such items as "the window frame through which Bill Sikes escaped."

If last resting places of the famous intrigue you, consider a visit to Highgate Cemetery, Swains Lane, N6, where you will find Karl Marx, George Eliot, Christina Rossetti, and Michael Faraday; Bunhill Fields, City Road, where nonconformists William Blake, John Bunyan, Daniel Defoe, and others are buried. Kensal Green (Kensal Green station on the Underground) has Thackeray, Trollope, Leigh Hunt, and the engineering Brunels.

If parks and gardens are your special interest, London has more than its share of excellent ones, in addition to those mentioned earlier: Royal Botanic Gardens, Kew♛♛♛♛; John Nash's splendid Regent's Park and Queen Mary's Garden♛♛♛♛; Hampstead Heath♛♛♛; Syon Park♛♛♛; Wimbledon Common♛♛♛; Chelsea Physic Garden♛♛♛; Holland Park♛♛♛; Museum of Garden History♛♛♛; St. James Park♛♛; Green Park♛♛; Richmond Park♛♛; Victoria Embankment Gardens♛♛ (where you will find "Cleopatra's Needle," the ancient Egyptian obelisk).

If you revel in blood and gore and enjoy the macabre, especially when it's historical, be sure to visit these: Madame Tussaud's♛♛♛, Marylebone Road (935-6861); London Dungeon♛, 28-34 Tooley Street (403-0606). Note: The Dungeon experience is *not* for the faint of heart, the young and tender, or the suggestible. For the martial-minded, add the extremely well-presented National Army Museum♔♔♔♔, Royal Hospital Road, Chelsea (730-0717); and the Imperial War Museum♔♔♔, Lambeth Road (746-8922).

Children's London

There are many London treats for children: The Science Museum (children's section and others)♔♔♔♔♔, Exhibition Road (589-3456); London Zoo in Regent's Park♔♔♔; Madame Tussaud's and Planetarium♔♔♔, Marylebone Road (935-6861); London Toy and Model Museum♔♔, 23 Craven Hill (262-7905); London Transport Museum♔♔♔, Covent Garden (379-6344); Pollock's Toy Museum♔♔, 1 Scala Street (636-3452); Bethnal Green Museum of Childhood♔♔, Cambridge Heath Road (980-2415); London Brass Rubbing Centre, St. James's Church Hall, Piccadilly (437-6023); and Guinness World of Records, Trocadero, Piccadilly (439-7331).

In addition, there are theaters devoted to productions for children. The playbills change, of course, so you will have to check theater listings in the weekly entertainment magazines, or phone for current information. Here are some of them: Cockpit Theatre, Gateforth Street (402-5081); Little Angel Marionette Theatre, 14 Dagmar Passage, Islington (226-1787); Polka Children's Theatre, 240 The Broadway (543-4888); National Youth Theatre, 34 York Way (837-0118); Unicorn Theatre for Children, Arts Theatre, Great Newport Street (836-3334); Young Vic Theatre, 66 The Cut (928-6363).

Note also that there are backstage tours of the National Theatre on the South Bank; tel. 633-0880.

More Special Interests

If you fancy markets, London has plenty for you to enjoy: Berwick and Rupert streets between Shaftesbury Avenue and Oxford Street in Soho, for fruit and vegetables; Leather Lane in the crowded diamond district at Hatton Garden; Petticoat Lane, Middlesex Street, probably London's most famous market; Portobello Road, also famous, changing from a general market weekdays to predominantly antiques and attic gleanings on Saturdays. (Watch out for pickpockets.)

Avid shoppers will find maximum opportunities in these streets and areas: Oxford Street, both east and west, especially from Oxford Circus to Marble Arch; stately Regent Street; Bond Street, both Old and New; Knightsbridge, Brompton and Fulham Roads; Kensington High Street; King's Road; Covent Garden; Piccadilly and Burlington Arcade.

Tottenham Court Road has furniture, radios, and electronic gear; Charing Cross Road is the book and music store street; Kensington Church Street for antiques and trendy clothes. For more specifics, see the "Shopping" section.

Little known to most visitors are the delights of canal boat cruising in London. Gaily decorated and traditionally outfitted canal boats take small groups on trips that run an hour and a half. (You can walk the towpath if you prefer.) Every May there is a two-day "Canalway Cavalcade" of the decorated and illuminated boats at Little Venice.

Regent's Park Canal goes along the edge of the Park and by the Zoo to Little Venice. The other is the Grand Union Canal west from Little Venice through what Len Deighton calls a voyage through remaining, grotty elements of Dickens's London. Some boats serve lunch or dinner en route.

The Regent's Park Canal trip on the *Jason* or *Serpens* leaves from Little Venice opposite 60 Bloomfield Road (286-3428). There are lunch and dinner trips on the floating restaurant *The Lace Plate*. *Jenny Wren* and the *My Fair Lady* restaurant boat leave from 250 Camden High Street (485-6210). *Regent's Canal Waterbus* leaves from near Warwick Avenue Underground in Little Venice (200-0200).

If boats are a major interest of yours, you will want to see the variety collected at St. Katharine's Dock near Tower Hill. This is where the Historic Ships Collection is kept. It consists of the lightship *Nore* and the Royal Research Ship *Discovery*, plus a Thames spritsail barge. Also here are modern yachts in the marina. Opposite the Tower is HMS *Belfast*, an 11,500-ton cruiser that now is a floating naval museum. It is reached via the London Bridge Underground stop or ferry from Tower Pier.

Thames River cruises are offered by many boats leaving from three piers. Summer cruise offerings are as follows: From Charing Cross Pier (839-3312), Festival Pier (930-0971), and Westminster Pier (930-4097), boats leave every half hour in summer to the Tower of London and Greenwich. From Tower Pier (488-0344), there are additional trips to Greenwich and Westminster. From Westminster Pier there are also cruises to Richmond, Kew, and Hampton Court, and evening cruises past Parliament and the Tower of London, plus circular cruises to London Bridge and return (839-4869), and luncheon cruises to Greenwich (839-2349). Ask about cruises (they start at 9 P.M.) to see the floodlit bridges, Parliament, and the London skyline from Tower Bridge to Chelsea Bridge.

If ancient and unusual instruments, European and exotic, fascinate you, by all means visit the Museum of Instruments at the Royal College of Music, Prince Consort Road (589-3643).

Ethnic art and cultures are exhibited in London at the Museum of Mankind ♕ ♕ ♕ ♕, part of the British Museum, Burlington Gardens (437-2224); Commonwealth Institute ♕ ♕ ♕, Kensington High Street (603-4535), shows arts and culture of each Commonwealth country and has programs of music and dance; Horniman Museum ♕ ♕, London Road, Forest Hill, has ethnographic collections.

Theater buffs will enjoy the Theatre Museum in the Flower Market, Covent Garden; Bear Gardens Museum of the Shakespearean Stage, 1 Bear Gardens, Bankside (928-6342), on the site of the 16th-century bear-baiting arena.

Architecture in its infinite varieties is a major London attraction. We have named many of the city's architectural masterpieces in previous pages and should mention, at the very least, some others that will please you.

Westminster Cathedral ♕ ♕ ♕, Victoria Street, is Byzantine in design, was completed in 1903, and is Britain's major Roman Catholic church.

Brompton Oratory ♕ ♕ ♕, Brompton Square, is a vast baroque building completed in 1884. It was designed by H. Gribble for the Catholic order of St. Philip Neri, which was brought to Britain by Cardinal Newman.

EXCURSIONS FROM LONDON

Herewith, our selection from scores of delightful destinations around London. Each of these you can visit, enjoy and return to central London within a day—many in half a day. We begin our selection east of London, moving clockwise around the city.

Greenwich, the "time town" east of London on the Thames, is not just a Royal Observatory, but a panoply of ships, splendid architecture, science, and history.

At the Greenwich Pier are the famed 1870 *Cutty Sark* clipper ship ♛ ♛ ♛ (in drydock) and the tiny *Gipsy Moth IV* ♛ ♛ in which Sir Francis Chichester solo-sailed around the world in 1967.

It's a short walk to the Royal Naval College ♛ ♛ ♛, now in the old 1664–1698 Greenwich Hospital buildings, designed by Wren, Vanbrugh, Webb, and Hawksmoor, and built on the site of the 1426 Placentia Palace where Henry VIII, Mary Queen of Scots, and Elizabeth I were born and Anne Boleyn's death warrant was signed. Especially notable: the 1789 chapel ♛ ♛ ♛ and 1703 "Painted Hall" with its frescoed ceiling.

Up (Admiral) Romney Road is the 1637 National Maritime Museum ♛ ♛ ♛ (formerly the Queen's House), a magnet for the nautically inclined. It is a major architectural landmark, for with it Inigo Jones launched the Palladian style in Britain. Inside: British naval history, with Nelson memorabilia, uniforms, and a "history of shipbuilding" section.

Greenwich Park climbs the hill above the Museum to the original home of the 1675 Old Royal Observatory ♛ ♛ ♛ in Wren-designed Flamsteed House. (The Observatory today is actually in Sussex.) The 0° Greenwich Meridian from which all east and west navigation measurements are made, goes directly through the house. Antique navigation instruments are on display; there are planetarium shows in the South Building. At 1 P.M., watch the time ball drop from the turret. It signals ships to set their chronometers to Greenwich Mean Time.

Greenwich can be reached by tour boat or hydrofoil from Tower Pier, and by train from Charing Cross Station.

Another excursion choice, southwest of Greenwich, is West Dulwich, with London's first public art gallery

PERILS & PITFALLS

Unless you have time to burn, do not take the bus to or from Greenwich. It's a lengthy, wearying journey through London's less attractive areas.

(1814), the Dulwich College Picture Gallery ♛ ♛ ♛, which was designed by the inventive Sir John Soane and displays an art collection (Rubens, Van Dyck, Rembrandt, Tiepolo, many others) fit for a king. In fact it was assembled in 1795 for a Polish king who lost his kingdom. The collection, therefore, was never delivered and the art dealer left it to the College.

West Dulwich is reachable by BritRail trains from Victoria Station in 11 minutes; the Gallery is a short walk through the Georgian village.

Still farther south of the Thames is Knole ♛ ♛ ♛ ♛ ♛, the 1456 manor house in the ancient village of Sevenoaks, now a popular commuting town.

One of the grandest of stately homes, Knole was given by Elizabeth I to the Earl of Dorset and still belongs to the original family, the Sackvilles. If you have time for only one stately home, let this be your choice.

The house, in rambling Tudor style, contains 365 rooms and 52 stairways. It is lavishly decorated and stuffed with treasures. Among these are portraits by Van Dyck, Gainsborough, Romney, and Reynolds; spectacular Louis XIV silver furniture in the King's Room; and fine porcelain, rare rugs, and tapestries. Vita Sackville-West was Virginia Woolf's closest friend, and a first edition of Woolf's *Orlando* is one of Knole's more modest gems.

Sevenoaks is reachable by train from Charing Cross and Waterloo East stations (4 departures per hour).

Nearby are two other points of interest, if you wish to make a day of it, or if you are driving into Kent.

Only a few miles west is the village of Westerham. General Wolfe, the victor of the 1759 Battle of Quebec against the French, lived here as a youth. His Quebec House ♛ contains memorabilia.

Westerham's other famous resident was Winston Churchill. His home, Chartwell ♛ ♛ ♛, is in a wooded area 2 miles south of the village. Outside are his gardens and a lake. His studio, paintings, maps, uniforms, and mementos are seen throughout the large brick manor house.

Chartwell and Quebec House can be reached on Green Line motorcoach tours.

A short distance south of Chartwell at Edenbridge is Hever Castle ♛ ♛ ♛, family home of Anne Boleyn. This brick 13th-century moated castle with drawbridge was rebuilt after 1903 by William Waldorf Astor. Its Edwardian interiors are beautifully paneled and carved. There is a range of Tudor-style buildings attached. The lavish Italian formal gardens have topiaries, fountains, and marble sculptures Astor collected in Italy.

Across the road from the Castle is St. Peter's Church, with the tomb of Sir Thomas Bullen, Anne Boleyn's father. You can do a brass rubbing of it for a modest fee.

Hever can be reached by hourly trains from Victoria Station (it's a mile and a quarter to the Castle) and by coach tours.

Less than 6 miles south of London's Chelsea section is Wimbledon, best known for its annual international lawn tennis tournaments, first played in 1877. There is also a Lawn Tennis Museum ♛ in the town. Both are at the All England Tennis Ground.

To relieve your tennis eyestrain, visit Eagle House (1613) in the High Street, and the 1817 windmill in Wimbledon's green and leafy 1,000-acre Common. There are the remains of Caesar's circular fortress, from his 55 B.C. invasion. The Common was a favorite dueling ground until 1840.

Wimbledon can be reached by train from Waterloo Station or by tube on the District Line.

Across the road, so to speak, northwest of Wimbledon, is Richmond, an upscale village-within-London, named after Henry VII's palace, which was a favorite house of Elizabeth I; she died there in 1603. The Gatehouse ♛ ♛, beside the vast 2,400-acre Richmond Park Green, remains, as do the elegant houses of courtiers; see Georgian houses on Maids of Honour Row ♛ ♛ (where the Princess of Wales's maids lived in 1724).

A major Richmond treat is 17th-century Ham House ♛ ♛ ♛, a magnificent redbrick building overlooking the Thames. Now a National Trust property, it is furnished with items borrowed from the Victoria and Albert Museum that display the harmonious baroque Restoration taste of the Duke of Lauderdale, a minister to Charles II. The Peter Lely portraits and superbly restored 17th-century kitchen are noteworthy.

Richmond can be reached by District Line Underground and BritRail trains from Victoria Station.

All visitors to Britain should know about the National Trust, because it owns so many of the places you will want to see. It is a private, nonprofit organization dedicated to preserving Britain's heritage. A century old, it is the nation's third-largest landowner—after the state and crown.

The National Trust owns and maintains 84 stately homes, 105 gardens, 24 castles, 22 villages, 11 barns, 17 dovecotes, and more than a thousand farms (500,000 acres of land), plus 500 miles of coastline. In recent years it has welcomed visitors at the rate of some 7 million per year through its properties.

INSIDERS' TIPS

"Open to View" tickets are available (adults, $23; children under 16, $11.50), which permit you to visit hundreds of National Trust properties an unlimited number of times during a one-month period. The ticket also entitles you to a 10-percent discount on goods sold in their shops. These tickets are sold at British Rail offices abroad.

Hampton Court Palace

A bit farther west along the Thames is Hampton Court Palace 🏅🏅🏅🏅🏅, a not-to-be-missed, spectacular leap into the past.

The epitome of a Tudor palace, Hampton Court was originally built in 1514 by one of England's wealthiest men, Cardinal Wolsey (his annual income was over £100,000), who staffed it with 500 servants to maintain its 280 rooms. The palace was so extravagant that his enviously smoldering sovereign, Henry VIII, asked how a private citizen could have such a home. "In order to present it to his Sovereign," was Wolsey's tactful reply. Done! Henry accepted it as a "gift" in 1526.

Though Charles I lived in it as king and as prisoner, and William and Mary greatly extended it, Hampton Court will always be associated with Anne Boleyn, who lived here during her brief reign as one of Henry VIII's queens. In her day the standard approach was by boat on the Thames, hence the tower clock tells not only time and important astrological conjunctions (did they warn Anne?) but the time of high water at London Bridge.

The Royal Apartments in the Wren wing display 3,000 weapons and serve as an art gallery. (Only one of the 500 paintings was totally destroyed in a lamentable 1986 fire in apartments above the galleries.) Among many outstanding works to be seen are those by Duccio, Titian, Tintoretto, and other Italians of the 16th to 18th centuries, and by Cranach, Holbein, Breughel, and 17th-century Flemish painters. The entranceway to the building has 1707 wall and ceiling murals by Antonio Verrio.

Monumental is the word for the nine canvases of *The Triumph of Caesar* by Mantegna, displayed in the separate Lower Orangery building. They have a curious history that began when Mantegna painted them for the Gonzaga family of Mantua.

Much later the paintings were bought by England's Charles I, and suffered a near-disastrous "restoration" by Verrio. In the 1960s and 1970s, the curator of the Queen's pictures, Sir Anthony Blunt, had them restored superbly, and today they are priceless treasures. (Blunt's devotion to art, it developed, was greater than his loyalty to his country; he was the long-sought "fourth man" in the Burgess-Maclean-Philby Soviet spy ring.)

Hampton Court's gardens are among the world's finest and include Henry VIII's tennis court, French-style formal gardens, a baffling maze (often filled with scores of "lost" people screaming directions to one another), a 1769 Black Hamburgh "Great Grape Vine" more than 100 feet long, and an orangery.

Hampton Court is reached easily by BritRail from Victoria Station or by the frequent bus tours offered by many coach companies.

Near the Thames south bank is Runnymede ♛, which consists of open fields near Egham—but what important fields! Here King John set his seal to the Magna Carta in 1215. In the field at the base of Cooper's Hill is a 1957 memorial given by the American Bar Association "to commemorate Magna Carta, symbol of freedom under law."

Halfway up the hill is a touching memorial to John F. Kennedy.

Runnymede is included on many coach tours.

While you're weighing destinations southwest of London, consider Winchester, England's ancient capital. It's a bit over 50 miles from London but well worth the journey, for this small town is one of England's gems.

Winchester was important in Roman times as a major city, and was the capital of Anglo-Saxons, Danes, and Normans. Its rulers included such kings as Alfred the Great, Canute, Edward the Confessor, and William the Conqueror (who made it co-capital with London and was crowned in both).

Many of England's kings and queens were married and buried here. Winchester reached its zenith in the 12th century, as many of its buildings attest, and excavation of the Roman forum continues next to the cathedral.

You will enjoy Winchester Cathedral ♛ ♛ ♛ ♛ ♛, Europe's longest medieval church, not for its length but for its richness in architecture and treasures. The building was begun in 1079 and consecrated in 1093, giving it rare unity of design. The richness of the See and the opportunities for embellishment have made its interior a veritable museum of Norman and Gothic architecture.

Deserving your special attention are a splendid 12th-century font depicting St. Nicholas's miracles; 13th-century wall paintings of Christ's life; the oldest (1305) and some believe the finest choir stalls in Britain; the chair used by Queen Mary for her marriage (here) to Philip of Spain; the Norman crypt; and fine tombs almost beyond count. These include the burial places of kings Canute and William Rufus, St. Swithin, Jane Austen, and Izaak Walton. In the Cathedral's treasury is a glorious opus, the 12th-century Winchester Bible with its matchless illuminations.

Include in your visit the famous boys' school, Winchester College ♛ ♛ ♛ ♛, founded in 1382 by William of Wykeham. See the chapel, dining hall, cloisters, and chantry.

The town still has a medieval look and feel, you will find, if you walk High Street to the West Gate and up Castle Hill to the Great Hall ♛ ♛ ♛ of William the Conqueror's castle, where Raleigh stood trial in 1603. The purported "Round Table" of King Arthur hangs at the end of the Hall (it dates from 1400 or earlier). A walk along Southgate Street takes you into the 18th century, and a visit to the 12th-century Hospital of St. Cross ♔ ♔ ♔, with its red- or black-gowned brethren, is not to be missed.

Think about Winchester when you read Keats's "Ode to Autumn," which he wrote here in 1819.

Winchester is easily reached by road on the M3 or rail: 1 hour and 5 minutes from Waterloo Station.

Kew Gardens

Returning to destinations still west of London but closer to the city, consider the justly famous Kew Gardens ♔ ♔ ♔ ♔ and Kew Palace ♔ ♔ ♔. Officially the Royal Botanic Gardens, Kew's 288 acres show British gardening at its finest. The Palm and Succulent Houses are full of rare plants, and there is a 1761 pagoda and an idyllic lakeside walk.

Kew's roster of 45,000 exotic plants is unmatched. Among the practical achievements of this famous garden is that it nursed and transplanted rubber, banana, coffee, and quinine to create entire industries in alien lands.

A high point for many visitors is the very Dutch, all-brick 1631 Kew Palace, where George III and Queen Charlotte lived in the early 19th century. It is truly petite—only 50 by 70 feet—with an unusually homey quality, chock-full of family mementos and toys like the king's fishing tackle and princesses' fans.

Kew can be reached via District Line Underground (to Kew Gardens station).

West of Kew Gardens is Syon House ♔ ♔ ♔, which began as a convent in the 15th century. Henry VIII locked Catherine Howard away here preceding her execution, but the place is no prison. On the contrary, the interior is a tour de force by Robert Adam, who redecorated it sumptuously during the 1760s. (Adam was to walls and ceilings as Wedgwood was to porcelains.) There are also portraits by Gainsborough and Reynolds, Lely and Van Dyck, and a 6-acre rose garden considered one of Britain's finest.

Syon House is reached by two trains per hour from Waterloo Station.

Less than 2 miles north, close to the M4 motorway, is Osterley Park House ♛ ♛ ♛. Originally an Elizabethan banker's (Sir Thomas Gresham, who established the London Royal Exchange) house of 1576, Osterley was transformed by Robert Adam from 1760 to 1780 into a superb neoclassical palace set in a spacious, wooded park.

The beautifully integrated rooms and furniture show Adam in top form. Osterley and Syon have profoundly influenced interior decoration for two centuries. See also the Elizabethan stables and Adam's orangery and greenhouse.

Osterley can be reached by Underground on the Metropolitan Line.

Windsor

Almost due west is Windsor ♛ ♛ ♛, site of William the Conqueror's fortress, around which grew the present castle and town of 31,000.

The town has much to offer: cobbled streets, many Georgian houses, clusters of tea rooms and antiques shops. It boasts a guildhall by Wren (with a fine painting collection), a splendid Brunel-designed railway station with a tableau by Madame Tussaud's of Queen Victoria's Diamond Jubilee. The Queen's carriages and horses are on exhibition, too. It all makes a delightful walkabout.

Each June, Ascot Week—the horse-racing event of the year—is held at the racetrack in the village adjoining Windsor Great Park. Thousands descend on Windsor during this season, which opens with a typically impressive royal procession through the Park, led by the Queen.

Windsor Castle ♛ ♛ ♛ ♛ ♛ is said to be the world's largest inhabited castle. Surely it has notched a record in its 900 years of use by England's rulers. Nothing of the Norman tower remains, but every king has added something.

A highlight is the 15th–16th-century St. George's Chapel ♛ ♛ ♛ ♛ ♛, burial place of monarchs (including Henry VIII and Charles I). It is a peak achievement of English Gothic Perpendicular. Begun by Edward IV, the Chapel dazzles with its rich vaulting and the ensigns and coats of arms of the Knights of the Garter since 1348. Eye-catchers are the Art Nouveau Duke of Clarence and bare-breasted Princess Charlotte of Wales monuments.

The State Apartments display works by Memling, Dürer, Holbein, Canaletto, Clouet, Rubens (his *St. George and the Dragon* includes impressions of London and idealizations of Charles I and his queen) and several of Van Dyck's best. Selections from Windsor's famous print collection are on exhibit.

Also to be visited are the timber-and-brick horseshoe cloisters, kitchens, barracks, armor, furniture, porcelain, and the much-loved Queen's Doll House. Don't miss the view from the top of the Round Tower across the Thames to Eton. (Note: the castle, or parts of it, are subject to closing for security reasons at any time.)

The Windsor Festival (last two weeks in September) features outstanding musical groups playing classical music in the Waterloo Chamber and St. George's Chapel.

Eton College ♛ ♛ ♛ ♛, the prestigious boys' school, is across the river from Windsor. Founded in 1440 by Henry VI, primarily for the education of poor youths, today it has 1,200 pupils, only 70 of them "poor" or scholarship youths. Eton numbers 20 prime ministers among its Old Boys.

Both the School Yard and Lower School are 15th-century, and the walls of the 1694 Upper School are adorned with pupils' names (Shelley, Gladstone, Walpole, Fox) carved in the desks and panels. Henry VI's chapel (much restored) has been incorporated in the church and contains a splendid roof and remarkable 15th-century wall paintings that were rediscovered only in the 19th century. The great gatehouse with Lupton's Tower dates from the early 16th century. Visit also the dining hall of 1450 and library of 1729 (which contains priceless manuscripts).

Windsor and Eton are reached by trains (two per hour) from Waterloo Station, and from Paddington with a change at Slough, and by Green Line buses (three per hour) from Victoria Coach Station, Eccleston Bridge.

A short distance farther along the Thames is Cliveden ♛ ♛ ♛, once the manor house of Lord and Lady (Nancy) Astor and the "Cliveden Set," who were notorious for pro-appeasement views of Hitler and Mussolini in the

1930s, and for sex scandals and the Profumo affair of the 1960s.

The Italian palazzo mansion, stableyard, and clock tower were designed by House of Commons architect Sir Charles Barry, in 1850. The interior was redone by the Astors in the 1890s and redone again in 1986 when it was turned into a luxury hotel (see Insiders' Information, page 135). Its most striking features are a baronial wood-paneled entrance hall with a French 16th-century fireplace flanked by Sargent's larger-than-life, full-length portrait of Nancy Astor; a dining room with paneling from Chateau d'Asnieres; and "his and hers" library-sitting rooms.

Formal gardens punctuated with Italian sculptures skirt the house and sweeping grounds (designed by Capability Brown), which follow the river. This is a National Trust property, and certain rooms are open to view on certain days.

Cliveden can be reached by BritRail from Paddington to Taplow Station; a taxi is required from there.

Continuing clockwise around London, north of the city is the Royal Air Force Museum ♛ ♛, which gives a quick survey of British military aviation history. Pride of place belongs to the aircraft used in the Battle of Britain and World War II.

The RAF Museum can be reached via the Northern Line Underground to the Colindale station.

Kenwood House ♛ ♛ ♛ ♛ in Hampstead Heath is a 17th-century building superbly remodeled in 1769 by Robert Adam. Among its treasures are excellent examples of Adam's decorative work (the library is a standout), plus a collection of major art works (the Iveagh Bequest) that includes paintings by Vermeer, Rembrandt, Hals, Boucher, Guardi, and other 17th- and 18th-century artists. As if that were not enough, the grounds are splendid, designed by Humphrey Repton in the 18th century.

Kenwood can be reached via the Northern Line Underground to Golders Green station, then bus or taxi.

St. Albans

St. Albans ♛ ♛ ♛, some 20 miles north of the Thames, has several compelling attractions. The Romans built a city—Verulamium—here, and in Christian times the town grew up around the shrine of England's first martyr.

St. Albans Abbey ♛♛♛ is a largely Norman and early English Gothic church, all that remains of a once-powerful Benedictine monastery. When whitewash was removed in 1877, excellent 13th- and 14th-century murals were discovered. The church tower is built largely of brick from the Roman ruins.

Aficionados of things Roman will beeline to the Verulamium Museum ♛♛♛ to see mosaics and artifacts from the Roman city. Nearby are the Roman hypocaust, theater, walls, and sections of the Roman metropolis sacked by Boadicea in A.D. 61.

Also in St. Albans is the Saxon Church of St. Michael ♛♛, begun in the 10th century. Note the effigy of Francis Bacon, seated (d. 1626), and fine 14th-century brasses.

In St. Albans's ancient center are a 1412 clock tower, many ancient buildings—especially on "French Row" ♛♛—and the Fleurs de Lys Inn ♛♛ where French King John was supposedly held prisoner after capture at Poitiers.

St. Albans can be reached by train from St. Pancras Station in 19 minutes.

Beyond St. Albans, 42 miles north of London, is Woburn Abbey ♛♛♛♛, 8 ½ miles northwest of Dunstable. This 17th-century mansion has been the home of the Dukes of Bedford for 300 years. It exhibits three floors of superb art (Rembrandt, Velasquez, Canaletto, Van Dyck, Cuyp, Teniers, Reynolds, and many more), plus French and English furniture, silver, and china. On premises: a unique antiques center of 40 shops rescued from demolition. There is also a 3,000-acre Deer Park landscaped by Humphrey Repton.

Woburn is reached via bus tours, booked through Cityrama (720-6663), Frames Rickard (837-3111), and Green Line (668-7261).

Almost due north of central London is Hatfield House ♛♛♛♛, the grandiose redbrick manor built by Robert Cecil, Earl of Salisbury, in James I's reign. It is an atmospheric, evocative Elizabethan/Jacobean building, with a regal Great Hall, Italianate staircase, and Long Gallery.

Hatfield's catalog of treasures is lengthy. Highlights include two famous portraits of Elizabeth I; pictures by Lawrence, Reynolds, Romney, and others; tapestries, furniture, stained glass, and oddments such as a hat, stockings, and gloves of Elizabeth I, who lived as a child at the royal palace on the site.

Don't miss the gardens and the surviving wing of the 1497 Royal Palace of Hatfield ♥ ♥. (Cecil used the rest of it to build his new Hatfield House.) The National Collection of Model Soldiers and various special exhibitions are on the premises.

Hatfield House can be reached by trains from Kings Cross Station to Hatfield Station, directly opposite the main entrance.

In handsome Lloyd Park, northeast of central London in the suburb of Walthamstow, the William Morris Gallery ♥ ♥ ♥ is installed in an attractive Georgian house where the poet-artist-craftsman spent his youth. It's a museum of Morris's life and the Arts and Crafts movement. On display are furniture, textiles, metalwork, and ceramics produced by Morris, Rossetti, Burne-Jones, Voysey, and William de Morgan, and *fin de siècle* works by the Welsh artist Sir Frank Branwyn and others.

Lloyd Park can be reached by Victoria Underground Line to the Walthamstow station.

Also accessible are the homes of two writers that may interest you:

Ayot St. Lawrence, or Shaw's Corner ♥ ♥ ♥, in the Hertfordshire hills north of London. A sturdy brick house on a corner of a country road, where playwright George Bernard Shaw lived from 1906 to 1950, it is kept as it was when he died: hat on the peg, typewriter at the ready, pens and books as he left them.

Ayot St. Lawrence is reachable by car, 3 miles northwest of Welwyn Garden City, one mile northeast of Wheathamstead.

Keats' House ♥ ♥ in Hampstead Heath was new in 1815. The poet John Keats lived here from 1818 to 1820 and wrote "Ode to a Nightingale" in the garden. On display are his letters, books, and personal memorabilia.

Hampstead Heath can be reached via the Northern Line Underground to Belsize Park or Hampstead station.

INSIDERS' TIPS

"Super value" tickets, combining travel and admission to many attractions in the London area, are offered at offices of Green Line, Eccleston Bridge, London SW1, and London Visitor & Convention Bureau offices.

From your hotel desk or London Transport Travel and Tourist Centres (such as those at Heathrow Airport, Piccadilly Circus, 12 Regent Street, and Victoria Station), pick up a free Central London map, the leaflet called *Day Trips Around London,* and BritRail's *Days Away From London.* The English Tourist Board publishes a valuable booklet, *A Day Out of London.* These are packed with basic information about destinations and special fare breaks.

Also, London Transport offers a variety of "London Explorer Tickets" in 1-, 3-, 4-, or 7-day forms at appropriate prices that represent substantial savings. They allow virtually unlimited travel on the tube and red buses serving the London suburbs as well as central London. You can buy them at any Underground station.

Gourmet Getaway

This isn't the name of a tour, but it is our idea of a pleasant sojourn in the country. Some of England's very best restaurants are within a short ride of central London in tranquil countryside or small villages untroubled by tour buses. These are among the best possible choices:

- Waterside Inn♛♛♛♛♛, Bray-on-Thames, Ferry Road (near Windsor); tel. (0628) 20691. One of the Roux Brothers' triumphs in a Renoir setting.
- Marryat Room♛♛♛, Chewton Glen Hotel, New Milton; tel. (04252) 5341. A lovely country hotel backdrop for exuberantly good food.
- Le Manoir♛♛♛♛♛, Le Manoir aux Quat' Saisons Hotel, Church Road, Great Milton; tel. (084-46) 8881. A park and garden setting for exceptional cuisine.

For day-tripping from London you have several public transportation alternatives:

- The Underground—10 tube lines and 268 stations.
- British Rail network—quick and efficient, especially on the short runs near London.

■ Coach lines serving popular tourist destinations in the area are London Transport, National Express, and Green Line. Their major terminal is Victoria Coach Station, Buckingham Palace Road, London SW1. These lines offer package tours. For information, phone London Transport at 222-1234; National Express at 730-0202; Green Line at 668-7261 (if no answer, try 222-1234, 834-6563, or 730-0202).

For information about how to reach a specific destination from where you are now, you can speak to a live human respondent at the Underground and Bus telephone inquiry desk, 222-1234.

INSIDERS' INFORMATION FOR LONDON
(Area Code 01)
WHERE TO STAY

Berkeley ♛ ♛ ♛ ♛ ♛
Wilton Pl. SW1X 7RL. Tel. 235-6000.
2 persons in twin, $150.
An opulent oasis with Knightsbridge convenience. 160 rooms, 2 restaurants, bar, indoor swimming pool, sauna. Known for quiet chic, attentive service, splendid rooms.

Claridge's ♛ ♛ ♛ ♛ ♛
Brook St. W14 2JQ. Tel. 629-8860.
2 persons in twin, $225–263.
Mayfair landmark, blend of neoclassical and Art Deco styles. 205 rooms, 2 restaurants, bar. Renowned for helpful staff, spacious rooms and suites. Favorite pad of Spain's King Juan Carlos and other royals.

Connaught ♛ ♛ ♛ ♛ ♛
Carlos Pl. W1Y 6AL. Tel. 499-7070.
2 persons in twin, $176–200.
So discreet in its handy Mayfair location, there's no sign in front. 90 rooms, superb restaurant, bar. Quiet elegance, like dignified private club, flawless service.

Dorchester ♛ ♛ ♛ ♛ ♛
Park Lane W1A 2HJ. Tel. 629-8888.
2 persons in twin, $248–266.
Central location, luxurious rooms, friendly and helpful staff. 280 rooms, 2 outstanding restaurants (The Terrace;

Grill Room), bar. Currently owned by Sultan of Brunei, service regal but unpretentious.

The Ritz ♛♛♛♛♛
Piccadilly W1V 9DG. Tel. 493-8181.
2 persons in twin, $210–270.
Grande Olde Dame still glitters in handy Piccadilly location. 128 rooms, many suites, deluxe restaurant, bar, cabaret, garden. Splendor in the glass, marble, and gilded accoutrements. Impressive decor.

Large ♛♛♛♛ *Hotels*

Britannia Inter-Continental ♛♛♛♛
Grosvenor Sq. W1A 3AN. Tel. 629-9400.
2 persons in twin, $158–225.
Handsome edifice diagonally across square from U.S. Embassy. 356 rooms, restaurant, 2 bars, pub, café, coffee shop. Well-done public areas, attractive rooms and suites. Lively scene.

Grosvenor House ♛♛♛♛
Park Lane W1A 3AA. Tel. 499-6363.
2 persons in twin, $195–248.
Sir Edwin Lutyens–designed building, Mayfair convenience. 475 rooms, 160 apts., restaurant, bar, health club, indoor swimming pool, sauna, gym. Crown Club executive floor, many business services.

Hyatt Carlton Tower ♛♛♛♛
Cadogan Pl. SW1. Tel. 235-5411.
2 persons in twin, $150 up.
Modern high-rise overlooking Cadogan Gardens. 217 rooms, elegant restaurant (Chelsea Room), 2 bars, tennis, garden. Comfortable and convenient. Helpful staff.

Inn on the Park ♛♛♛♛
Hamilton Pl., Park Lane W1A 1AZ. Tel. 499-0888.
2 persons in twin, $248.
Hyde Park overlook from this modern hotel with traditional interiors. 228 rooms, restaurant, banqueting rooms, bar, garden. Understated elegance in public and private rooms, king-size beds, amenities galore.

Inter-Continental ♛♛♛♛
1 Hamilton Pl., Hyde Park Corner W1V 0QY. Tel. 409-3131.

2 persons in twin, $218.
Modern (1975) hotel stands conveniently at bustling Hyde Park Corner. 500 rooms, superb restaurant (Le Soufflé), coffee shop, 2 bars, sauna, disco. Favorite with business travelers for comfortable rooms, many amenities.

London Hilton on Park Lane ♛ ♛ ♛ ♛
22 Park Lane W1A 2HH. Tel. 493-8000.
2 persons in twin, $266.
Modern building, handy to shopping, theater, and London's center. 503 rooms, 2 restaurants, bar, disco, 4 floors of spacious, super-service executive suites and lounges. Great views of Green and St. James's parks and city from upper floors and Roof restaurant.

London Marriott ♛ ♛ ♛ ♛
Grosvenor Sq. W1A 4AW. Tel. 493-1232.
2 persons in twin, $158.
Modern hotel in handy Mayfair location, facing Grosvenor Square. 229 rooms, 2 restaurants, bar, conference facilities. More subdued than usual Marriott decor, handsome public areas, large rooms.

May Fair Inter-Continental ♛ ♛ ♛ ♛
Stratton St. W1A 2AN. Tel. 629-7777.
2 persons in twin, $195–225.
A Mayfair standby since 1927, handy to shops and restaurants. 322 rooms, restaurant, 2 bars, coffee shop, theater, and cinema. Spacious rooms, some with Jacuzzis, faultless service and maintenance.

Meridien Piccadilly ♛ ♛ ♛ ♛
Piccadilly W1V 0BH. Tel. 734-8000.
2 persons in twin, $218–240.
Large hotel right on lively Piccadilly, handy to theater district. 290 rooms, 3 restaurants, bar, gym, squash, indoor swimming pool, sauna, nightclub. $24-million glamorously glitzy facelift brought back high-ceilinged elegance of old Piccadilly Hotel. Helpful staff.

Savoy ♛ ♛ ♛ ♛
Strand WC2R 0EU. Tel. 836-4343.
2 persons in twin, $150 up.
A Strand landmark since Richard D'Oyly Carte opening late 19th century. 202 rooms, restaurant in the Grand Tradition, bar. Ask for room with Thames view. Spacious, gracious, the Savoy wears age well.

Small ♛ ♛ ♛ ♛ Hotels

Brown's ♛ ♛ ♛ ♛
Dover St. W1A 4SW. Tel. 493-6020.
2 persons in twin, $198–210.
Venerable favorite, convenient to Piccadilly and Bond
Street. 130 rooms, elegant restaurant, bar, writing room.
As quiet and comfortable as when Rudyard Kipling made it
his London "home."

Capital ♛ ♛ ♛ ♛
22 Basil St. SW3 1AT. Tel. 589-5171.
2 persons in twin, $180–210.
Handy location near Harrods. 60 rooms, excellent restaurant, bar. High standards of courtesy and service, elegant
decor.

Goring ♛ ♛ ♛ ♛
15 Beeston Pl., Grosvenor Gardens SW1W 0JW. Tel. 834-
8211.
2 persons in twin, $147.
Individual attention, family-run, quiet, roomy, traditional
hotel. 90 rooms, restaurant, bar, gardens. Exquisitely decorated public areas, comfortable rooms and suites.

Hyde Park ♛ ♛ ♛ ♛
Knightsbridge SW1Y 7LA. Tel. 235-2000.
2 persons in twin, $203–248.
Imposing redbrick Victorian hotel across from Harrods
and Hyde Park. 180 rooms, restaurant, bar. Ample rooms
combine period antiques (four-posters) with all modern
comfort. Magnificently refurbished in great style.

Stafford ♛ ♛ ♛ ♛
St. James's Place SW1A 1NJ. Tel. 493-0111.
2 persons in twin, $165–187.
18th-century hotel is discretion itself, tucked into secluded street off Piccadilly. 62 rooms, restaurant, bar,
garden. "Best service in London," some say. Edwardian
elegance; private, pretty rooms.

Basil Street ♛ ♛ ♛
Basil St., Knightsbridge SW3 1AH. Tel. 581-3311.
2 persons in twin, $87–130.
A find. Even the façade is handsome in this 1910 Knightsbridge jewel. 103 rooms, restaurant, bar. Edwardian-*cum-*

oriental elegance. Ask about Parrot Club, a haven for solo women travelers.

Cadogan Thistle ♛ ♛ ♛

Sloane St. SW1. Tel. 235-7141.

2 persons in twin, $158–188.

Lillie Langtry's Edwardian charmer overlooking gardens near Sloane Ranger action. 69 rooms, restaurant, bar, gardens. Turret Rooms where Oscar Wilde stayed; lounges, handsome decor, oak paneling, 18th-century French furniture.

Duke's ♛ ♛ ♛

35 St. James's Pl. SW1A 1NY. Tel. 491-4840.

2 persons in twin, $218–240.

Discreet Edwardian redbrick building at end of mews near Piccadilly. 51 rooms, restaurant, bar, courtyard. Stylishly refurbished recently, but retains quiet 19th-century elegance, superb service.

Westbury ♛ ♛ ♛

New Bond St. W1A 4UH. Tel. 629-7755.

2 persons in twin, $161–180.

This post–World War II hotel is one of London's most popular. Great for shoppers. 256 rooms, restaurants, bar. Quietly conservative in decor, attractive lounges.

Blakes ♛ ♛

33 Roland Gardens SW7 3PF. Tel. 270-6701.

2 persons in twin, $203–225.

5-story attached Victorian townhouses close to Fulham Road shopping. 50 rooms, restaurant, bar, sauna, patio. Lobby redecorated with offbeat oriental flair, some guest rooms spacious, others modest.

Cavendish ♛ ♛

Jermyn St. SW1Y 6JF. Tel. 930-2111.

2 persons in twin, $144.

Modern hotel with historic site and name, convenient to Piccadilly. 253 rooms, 2 restaurants, Edwardian bar adds nostalgic touch. Airy, modern rooms.

Chesterfield ♛ ♛

35 Charles St. W1X 8LX. Tel. 491-2622.

2 persons in twin, $158–165.

Former Georgian home of Lord Chesterfield in Mayfair center. 85 rooms, restaurant, bar. The lobby is the star here, furnished with flair. Rooms compact but clean, service good.

Durrants ♛ ♛
George St., W1H 6BJ. Tel. 935-8131.
2 persons in twin, $68–120.
Regency-era building in interesting neighborhood. 104 rooms, restaurant, bar. Clubby ambience, attractive rooms, all modern conveniences.

Marlborough Crest ♛ ♛
Bloomsbury St., WC1B 3QD. Tel. 636-5601.
2 persons in twin, $131.
Totally refurbished old hotel near theater district, British Museum. 169 rooms, restaurant, brasserie, bar. Handsome period look to interior, large public areas, compact rooms, comfortable amenities.

The Mountbatten ♛ ♛
Covent Garden, WC2H 9HO. Tel. 836-4300.
2 persons in twin, $164–186.
Old hotel lavishly restored, in Covent Garden area. 120 rooms, restaurant, bar. Public areas handsomely decorated, guest rooms more mundane, but very comfortable.

Ebury Court ♛
26 Ebury St., SW1. Tel. 730-8147.
2 persons in twin, $81–96 (incl. English breakfast). Small hotel close to Victoria Station. 38 rooms, restaurant, bar. Tidy, homey ambience, with cheerful public rooms, friendly staff.

Royal Horseguards Thistle ♛
2 Whitehall Ct., SW1A 2EJ. Tel. 839-3400.
2 persons in twin, $90–150.
Once French-chateau-like apartment house, facing Thames. 284 rooms, coffee shop, bar, terrace. Handy for sightseeing. Modernized, vestiges of character remain.

Wilbraham ♛
Wilbraham Place, Sloane St. SW1 X9AE. Tel. 730-8296.
2 persons in twin, $57–86.
Belgravian townhouse near Sloane Square. 50 rooms, restaurant, bar. Snug, men's-club ambience, good service, a budget "sleeper."

WHERE TO EAT

Le Gavroche ♛ ♛ ♛ ♛ ♛
43 Upper Brook St., W1. Tel. 408-0881.
Average dinner: $75.

A total experience—superb food, wines, staff, ambience. Classical French all the way.

La Tante Claire ♛ ♛ ♛ ♛ ♛

68 Royal Hospital Rd., SW3. Tel. 352-6045.

Average dinner: $65.

Exquisite, subtle food in a setting to match. Superior *nouvelle* cooking by a master, Pierre Koffmann. Outstanding wine list.

Capital Hotel ♛ ♛ ♛ ♛

22-24 Basil St. SW3. Tel. 589-5171.

Average dinner: $30–45.

Refined French cuisine in relaxed setting. Fine wine list.

Chez Nico ♛ ♛ ♛ ♛

129 Queenstown Rd. Battersea SW8. Tel. 720-6960.

Average dinner: $30–40.

Uneven, but when the chef is "on," food is among Britain's best, most inspired.

Connaught ♛ ♛ ♛ ♛

Connaught Hotel, 16 Carlos Pl. W1. Tel. 499-7070.

Average dinner: $58–65.

Traditional French/English menu at its best in gentlemen's-club-like setting. Knowledgeable service.

Le Soufflé ♛ ♛ ♛ ♛

Inter-Continental Hotel, 1 Hamilton Pl., Hyde Park Corner W1V 0QY. Tel. 409-3131.

Average dinner: $40–50.

Superior French food, flawless and friendly service, plush decor make this a winner. Don't forget the unbelievable soufflés. Excellent wine list.

The Terrace ♛ ♛ ♛ ♛

Dorchester Hotel, 5 Park Lane W1. Tel. 629-8888.

Average dinner: $55.

Chef Anton Mosimann continues his magic here and in hotel's Grill Room. If you're not too hungry, go with the master's *cuisine naturelle*, a lighter rendering of French classics. Don't miss Mosimann's bread pudding, a rare wonder. Fine wine list.

Bombay Brasserie ♛ ♛ ♛

Bailey's Hotel, Courtfield Close, 140 Gloucester Rd. SW7. Tel. 370-4040.

Average dinner: $18–30.

Luxurious, nostalgia-for-colonial-In'ja setting, grand Indian dishes.

Chelsea Room♛♛♛
Hyatt Carlton Tower Hotel, 2 Cadogan Pl. SW1. Tel. 235-5411.
Average dinner: $70
French style, at its best in various fish dishes. Fine wine list.

Hilaire♛♛♛
68 Old Brompton Rd. SW7. Tel. 584-8993.
Average dinner: $25–36.
Prix fixe lunch menu is among the best buys in the city. Imaginative food, cramped quarters.

Interlude♛♛♛
7-8 Bow St. WC2. Tel. 379-6473.
Average dinner: $28–35.
Formerly Interlude de Tabaillau. Changed ownership, but still tops, and chic too. Exquisite French food. Handy to opera and theaters. Fine wine list.

Neal Street♛♛♛
26 Neal St. WC2. Tel. 836-8368.
Average dinner: $40.
Where the trendies go, but exquisite food nonetheless. Decor by artist David Hockney is coolly elegant.

L'Arlequin♛♛
123 Queenstown Rd. SW8. Tel. 622-0555.
Average dinner: $20–55.
A small, fastidious French gem. Go for the fish specialties.

Brown's Hotel♛♛
Dover St. W1. Tel. 493-6020.
Average dinner: $40–55.
Nouvelle cuisine expertise in a traditional, wood-paneled setting.

Gay Hussar♛♛
2 Greek St. W1. Tel. 437-0973.
Average dinner: $20–30.
Long-time favorite with politicos and journalists for its consistently reliable Hungarian classics. Oh, that *foie gras!*

Lane's♛♛
Inn on the Park, Hamilton Pl., Park Lane W1. Tel. 499-0888.
Average dinner: $40–45.
After-theater supper menu is a winner. Light food, skillfully prepared and served in an airy, attractive setting. Fine wine list.

Ma Cuisine ♛ ♛
113 Walton St. SW3. Tel. 584-7585.
Average dinner: $30–35.
Tiny, bistro-like, unpretentious, in the French mode.

Ninety Park Lane ♛ ♛
Grosvenor House, 90 Park Lane W1. Tel. 499-6363.
Average dinner: $36–75.
Some spectacular dishes in a posh setting to match. Fine wine list.

Red Fort ♛ ♛
77 Dean St. W1. Tel. 437-2525.
Average dinner: $18–25.
Handsome, understated decor matches first-rate Indian food. Good value.

Rue St. Jacques ♛ ♛
5 Charlotte St. W1. Tel. 637-0222.
Average dinner: $30–45.
Imaginative modern French cuisine on the expensive side, but some splendid dishes, such as the many marinated fish ones.

Shezan ♛ ♛
16-22 Cheval Pl. SW7. Tel. 589-7918.
Average dinner: $40.
Elegant backdrop for excellent Pakistani dishes. Service can be slow.

Chiang Mai ♛
48 Frith St. W1V 5TE. Tel. 437-7444.
Average dinner: $25–28.
Tiny place with tempting Thai dishes and gentle Thai service.

Gavvers ♛
61 Lower Sloane St. SW1. Tel. 730-5983.
Average dinner: $27–38.
Popular with Londoners, despite crowded tables. Robust French country dishes (among others) compensate.

Greenhouse ♛
27A Hay's Mews W1. Tel. 499-3331.
Average dinner: $27–30.
Hard to find, but worth it. French-English menu expertly translated.

Hard Rock Cafe ♛
150 Old Park Lane W1. Tel. 629-0382.
Average meal: $18.

Burgers and Budweiser, can you believe? But fun just to see what's trendy with young Londoners. Long queues, no reservations, so go off-hours.

Inigo Jones ♛
14 Garrick St. WC2. Tel. 836-6456.
Average dinner: $35–60.
Theater district standby, with new chef and much more interesting food.

Justin de Blank Cafe ♛
General Trading Company, Sloane St. SW1. Tel. 730-6400.
Average meal: $6–10.
A great breakfast or lunch stop for homemade pastries, light dishes.

Langan's Brasserie ♛
Stratton St. W1. Tel. 493-6437.
Average dinner: $30.
Fast-moving, trendy place with stylish 1920s decor, 1980s food fashions, i.e., spinach soufflé with anchovy sauce.

The Last Days of the Raj ♛
22 Drury Lane. WC2. Tel. 836-1628.
Average dinner: $15–25.
Reliable Indian dishes, convenient to theaters.

Ménage à Trois ♛
15 Beauchamp Pl. SW3. Tel. 584-9350.
Average meal: $15–20.
Mix-and-match starters and desserts. Imaginative, light-hearted food. Fine wine list.

Meridiana ♛
169 Fulham Rd. SW3. Tel. 589-8815.
Average dinner: $18–20.
Attractive setting for stylish Italian fare, good wine list.

Poons of Covent Garden ♛
41 King St. WC2. Tel. 240-1743.
Average meal: $25.
A Chinese standby, at its best for a *dim sum* lunch.

Rules ♛
35 Maiden Lane WC2. Tel. 836-5314.
Average dinner: $15–18.
Go for Edwardian nostalgia, more than the food, in this famous 19th-century theatrical district favorite.

San Frediano ♛
62 Fulham Rd. SW3. Tel. 584-8375.
Average dinner: $25–30.

Fine Italian fare with flair; a Sloane Ranger hangout.
Tate Gallery Restaurant ♛
Millbank SW1. Tel. 834-6754.
Average lunch: $26. Lunch only. (Do not confuse with the café.)
Authentic historic English dishes (some Elizabethan), superlative wine list, and moderate prices.
Tiger Lee ♛
251 Old Brompton Rd. SW5 9HP. Tel. 370-2323.
Average dinner: $40–45.
Stylish, Frenchified renderings of Chinese cuisine, one of the best Chinese restaurants in London.
Waltons of Walton Street ♛
121 Walton St. SW3. Tel. 584-0204.
Average dinner: $25–65.
Elegant ambience for festive occasions. Food can be super, but inconsistent.
Woodlands ♛
77 Marylebone Lane. W1. Tel. 902-9869.
Average dinner: $15–18.
Nothing fancy to look at, but commendable southern Indian vegetarian food.

Afternoon Tea—Really Special Places:

Basil Street Hotel, Basil St., Knightsbridge SW3. Tel. 581-3311.

Brown's Hotel, Dover St. W1. Tel. 493-6020.

Cavendish (The Gallery), Jermyn St. SW1. Tel. 930-2111.

Dorchester Hotel (Promenade), Park Lane W1. Tel. 629-8888.

Fortnum & Mason, 181 Piccadilly. W1. Tel. 734-8040. Still going strong, tasty as ever.

Grosvenor House (Park Lounge), Park Lane W1. Tel. 499-9563.

Harrods (Georgian Restaurant), Knightsbridge SW1. Tel. 730-1234. Gargantuan buffet of sweets. Great value, but always a long queue.

Hyde Park Hotel (Park Room), Knightsbridge SW1. Tel. 235-2000

Maison Sagne, 105 Marylebone High St. W1. Tel. 935-6240. Old-fashioned tea shop, cakes baked on premises.

Richoux, 41A South Audley St. W1. Tel. 629-5228.

The Ritz Hotel (Palm Court), Piccadilly W1. Tel. 493-8181. So popular, reservations are a must.

Savoy Hotel (Thames Foyer), Savoy Hill, The Strand WC2. Tel. 836-4343.

Selfridge's, 400 Oxford St. W1. Tel. 629-1234.

Waldorf Hotel, Aldwych WC2. Tel. 836-2400.

Pubs

Admiral Codrington, 17 Mossop St. SW8. Tel. 589-4603. Toby mugs and minimal decor, but popular with Sloane Rangers.

PERILS & PITFALLS

Some attractive pubs are located in areas you should not walk in alone, late at night. We've flagged these "Taxi."

The Anchor, 1 Bankside, Southwark SE1. Tel. 407-1577. On site of Globe Theatre; fine river views. Taxi.

Angel, 101 Bermondsey Wall East, Rotherhithe SE16. Tel. 237-3608. Samuel Pepys and Captain Cook were customers; great river views from the terrace. Taxi.

Antelope, 22 Eaton Terr. SW1. Tel. 730-3169. A haven for real ale and reporters.

The Barley Mow, 82 Duke St. W1. Tel. 629-5604. Hogarth prints and piano music.

The Blue Posts, 6 Bennett St. SW1. Tel. 493-3350.

Bull's Head, 1 King St. EC1. Tel. 253-1789.

Bunch of Grapes, 207 Brompton Rd. SW3. Tel. 589-4944. Handy to Harrods.

The Chequers Tavern, 16 Duke St. SW1. Tel. 930-4007.

The Dove, 19 Upper Mall, Hammersmith W6. Tel. 748-5405.

El Vino, 47 Fleet St. EC4. Tel. 353-6786. Ancient citadel of journalists; "proper attire" required.

Enterprise, 35 Walton St. SW3. Tel. 584-8858. Close to Harrods.

The George Inn, 77 Borough High St. SE1. Tel. 407-2056. London's last galleried inn, from 1677; National Trust.

The Goat, 3 Stafford St. W1. Tel. 629-0966. Clock collection.

Goose & Firkin, 47 Borough Rd., Southwark SE1. Tel. 403-3590. Real ale.

Green Man, (in Harrods), Knightsbridge SW1. Tel. 730-1234. Shoppers' delight; good luncheon value.

The Grenadier, 18 Wilton Row SW1. Tel. 235-3074. Sloane Ranger heaven.

Hereford Arms, 127 Gloucester Rd. SW7. Tel. 370-4988. Real ale.

King's Head, 115 Upper St. N1. Tel. 226-1916. Fringe Theatre pub, entry fee covers dinner and show, Mon.–Sat.

Kings Head and Eight Bells, 50 Cheyne Walk SW3. Tel. 352-0711. Venerable 400-year-old pub with literary associations; overlooks the Thames.

Lamb, 94 Lamb's Conduit St. WC1. Tel. 405-5692. A favorite of Bloomsburyites Lytton Strachey and Maynard Keynes.

Lamb & Flag Tavern, 33 Rose St. WC2. Tel. 836-4108. A long-time actors' hangout; Covent Garden's oldest pub (since 1623).

Mayflower, 117 Rotherhithe St. SE16. Tel. 237-1898. Close to Pilgrim departure spot. Appealing dining room with exposed beams. Taxi.

Museum Tavern, 49 Great Russell St. WC1. Tel. 242-8987. Karl Marx's "local" when doing his British Museum research across the street.

Nag's Head, 10 James St. WC2. Tel. 836-4678. Theatrical posters.

Old Bell Tavern, 95 Fleet St. EC4. Tel. 353-3796. Next to St. Bride's Church, where carolers congregate at Christmas.

Prince Regent, 71 Marylebone High St. W1. Tel. 935-2018.

Prospect of Whitby, 57 Wapping Wall E1. Tel. 481-1095. 600 years young. Taxi.

The Queen's Elm, 241 Fulham Rd., SW3. Tel. 352-9157. "Local" for Chelsea artists and writers.

Railway Tavern, Liverpool St., EC2. Tel. 283-3509. Railroad decor, models, logos.

The Red Lion, 23 Crown Passage, Pall Mall SW1. Tel. 930-8067. One of the oldest licensed pubs.

The Red Lion, 2 Duke of York St. SW1. Tel. 930-2030. High Victorian.

Shepherd's Tavern, 50 Hereford St. W1. Tel. 499-3017. Behind the Hilton; 300 years old.

Spaniards, Spaniards Lane, Hampstead Heath NW3. Tel. 455-3276. Delightful rear garden.

Star and Garter, 62 Poland St. W1. Tel. 437-1208.

Sun in Splendour, 7 Portobello Rd. W11. Tel. 727-6345.

Surprise, 6 Christchurch Terr. SW3. Tel. 352-0455.

Ye Olde Cock Tavern, 22 Fleet St. EC4. Tel. 353-3454. Dickens bar upstairs has mementos.

Wine Bars

Les Amis du Vin, 11 Hanover Pl. WC2. Tel. 379-3444.

Brahms and Liszt, 19 Russell St. WC2. Tel. 240-3661. One of the oldest, still going strong.

The City Flogger, 120 Fenchurch St. EC3. Tel. 623-3251. Aimed at ad agency traffic.

Cork & Bottle, 44-46 Cranbourn St. WC2. Tel. 734-7807.

Draycott's, 114 Draycott Ave. SW3. Tel. 584-5359.

The Ebury, 139 Ebury St. SW1W. Tel. 730-5447.

Lautrec, 31 Eastcheap EC3. Tel. 623-1477.

Loose Box, 136 Brompton Rd. SW3. Tel. 584-9280. An upstairs-downstairs favorite with Harrods' shoppers.

Motcombs, 26 Motcomb St. SW1. Tel. 235-6382.

Mother Bunch's Wine House, Arches F&G, Old Seacoal Lane EC4. Tel. 236-5317.

Palookaville, 13a James St. WC2. Tel. 240-5857. Live jazz and restaurant too.

Penny's Place, 6 King St., Covent Garden WC2. Tel. 836-4553.

Shampers, 4 Kingly St. W1. Tel. 437-1692.

Solange's, 11 St. Martin's Ct. WC2. Tel. 240-0245.

PERILS & PITFALLS

One of London's oldest pubs, Olde Cheshire Cheese, may have fed Samuel Johnson in the 18th century. Today it is a madhouse at mealtime, offering a mass feed for tourists. Any original character is lost in the clatter and clutter.

Shopping

Bond Street Area

Asprey & Co., 165–169 New Bond St. For gifts, silver, jewelry, china, antique furniture.

Beale & Inman Ltd., 131–133 New Bond St. Men's and women's clothes.

Benson & Hedges, 13 Old Bond St. Besides pipes and cigarettes, men's clothing, leather goods, B&H gold-packaged chocolates.

Blade's, 8 Burlington Gardens. English tailoring and fabrics.

Brown's, 24–27 S. Molton St. Stylish clothes, attractive blouses.

Butler & Wilson, 20 S. Molton St. Antique and original modern costume jewelry, unique blown-glass jewelry.

Charbonnel et Walker, 28 Old Bond St. Handmade chocolates, favored by the Royal Family.

Colefax & Fowler, 39 Brook St. Old prints, fabrics, the "English country look," everything needed to achieve it is here.

Courtenay, 22 Brook St. Satisfy your lust for luxurious lingerie here.

Crombie, 118 New Bond St. Jewelry.

David Berk, 46–50 Burlington Arcade. Cashmere heaven.

E. Tessier, 26 New Bond St. Jewelry and silver.

Ferragam, 24 Old Bond St. Stylish shoes.

Frank Smythson Ltd., 53 New Bond St. "Stationers to Queen Elizabeth."

Gerald Austin, 37 New Bond St. Men's clothes.

Gieves & Hawkes, 1 Savile Row. The epitome of the custom-tailoring tradition.

Halcyon Days, 14 Brook St. Great traditional gifts, such as enameled clocks, antique boxes.

Herbie Frogg, 125 New Bond St. Men's clothes with a modish look.

Hobbs, 47 S. Molton St. Fine-quality women's shoes.

H. R. Higgins Ltd., 42 S. Molton St. Coffee specialists.

Ireland House Shop, 150 New Bond St. Everything's coming up Irish here—nubbly tweeds, Aran sweaters, Waterford crystal.

Loewe, 25 Old Bond St. High-fashion Spanish leather and accessories.

Louis Vuitton, New Bond St. Quality leather goods.

Mallet & Son, 40 New Bond St. Antique fine furniture, complete room settings.

Marlborough Rare Books Ltd., 35 Old Bond St.

Next, 10 S. Molton St. (also 62 S. Molton St.) Trendy men's and women's clothes.

Noble Jones, 12–14 Burlington Arcade. Notable for woolens and cashmeres.

N. Peal Ltd., 37 Burlington Arcade (men's shop at 54 Burlington Arcade). Top-flight woolens and cashmeres.

Nutters, 35A Savile Row. Stylish, correct men's clothing.

P. & D. Colnaghi, 14 Old Bond St. Old Masters, other art.

Pratesi, 73 New Bond St. Italian bed and table linens fit for a king.

Prestat's, S. Molton St. Prestigious chocolate truffles.

Ralph Lauren, 143 New Bond St. Fashion-conscious men's clothing.

Sac Frères, 45 Old Bond St. Specialists in amber from all over.

Sotheby's, 34–35 New Bond St. The famous auction house.

Thomas Agnew & Sons Ltd., 43 Old Bond St. Old Master prints, modern English paintings.

Tommy Nutter, 18–19 Savile Row. Fine woolens.

W. Bill Ltd., 93 New Bond St., 28 Old Bond St. Classic and trendy clothes in wool, cashmere, and tweed. Note the women's cashmere capes.

Chelsea/Pimlico

Butler & Wilson, 189 Fulham Rd. A happy mix of real Art Nouveau *objets* and fun fakeries.

Chelsea Cobbler, 164 Fulham Rd. A favorite with Sloane Rangers for ballgowns, wedding dresses, Victoriana.

Colefax & Fowler Chintz Shop, 149 Ebury St.

David Mellor, 4 Sloane Sq. Known for stunning tableware and functional kitchen equipment.

Divertimenti, 139–141 Fulham Rd. Everything you need in modern tableware and kitchen equipment.

The General Trading Company (Mayfair) Ltd., 144 Sloane St. All-purpose gift store with imported goodies.

Gordon Lowes Ltd., 173–174 Sloane St. Loden coats and other classics.

Habitat, 206 King's Rd. Everything for interiors.

Laura Ashley, 157 Fulham Rd. Fabulous fabrics with that special flowery look.

Lunn Antiques, 86 New King's Rd., Parsons Green.

Oggetti, 133 Fulham Rd. High-tech home accessories.

Parrots, 56 Fulham Rd. Imaginative gifts for all ages.

The Penguin Bookshop, 157 King's Rd.

Peter Jones, Sloane Sq. Good value department store.

The Poster Shop, 168 Fulham St. Vast selection.

Rodier, 15 Sloane St. Social London shops here for dressy women's clothes.

Soleiado, 171 Fulham Rd. British home to the famous Provençal fabrics.

Covent Garden Area

Bertram Rota, 30 Long Acre. First editions, rare and antique books are the house specialty.

British Crafts Centre, 43 Earlham St. Handsome changing exhibits, high-quality handicrafts.

The Cartoon Gallery, 56 Earlham St. A collector's heaven. Buttons too.

Coppershop, 48 Neal St. and Shorts Gardens. Copper, copper every*ware*, in decorative and cooking utensil forms.

Covent Garden General Store, 111 Long Acre.

David Mellor, 26 James St. Great modern home accessories.

Dress Circle, 57 Monmouth St. Theatrical memorabilia: posters, records, tapes.

Edward Stanford Ltd., 12 Long Acre. Books, maps.

Glasshouse, 65 Long Acre. Watch glass blown, then buy it as it cools.

The Hat Shop, 58 Neal St. Mad hats, glad hats, great trendy and old-time hats.

Hills, 15 Henrietta St. Rent-a-tux and other men's formal wear.

Hobbs, Covent Garden Market. Nifty clothes and shoes.

Hobbs & Co., 3 Garrick St. Wide choice of cheeses, other deli items.

The Kite Shop, 69 Neal St. Every imaginable identified flying object.

Land & Burr, 35 Neal St. Great clothes.

Les Amis Gourmands, 30 James St., Covent Garden. Gourmet foods, sandwiches, and a basement café.

Monsoon, Covent Garden Market. For separates and informal gear.

Neal Street East, 5 Neal St. Oriental foods, goods, and books; offbeat tea selection.

Paul Smith, 43 Floral St. Clothes for trend-watching men.

Penhaligon, 41 Wellington St. The place for uncommon scents—bath oils, soaps, and pomades too, all handsomely packaged.

Pollock's Toy Theatres, 1 Scala St., also 44 Covent Garden Market. Toy theaters, toys, games.

Post Card Gallery, 32 Neal St.

The Poster Shop, 28 James St. Covent Garden. Voluminous selection of art, modern, and trendy posters.

Ray Man Eastern Musical Instruments, 64 Neal St. Kotos, sitars, tablas, and other oriental instruments.

S. Fisher, 18 Covent Garden Market. Fine men's clothes.

The Tea House, 15A Neal St. A tea lover's nirvana, stocked with tea and all the necessary tea equipment.

Theatre Zoo, 21 Earlham St.

W. & G. Foyles, 119/125 Charing Cross Rd. Famous comprehensive bookstore, a source for *almost* everything.

The Warehouse, 39 Neal St.

Westaway & Westaway, 62–65 Great Russell St. Fine values in Scottish woolens, cashmeres, sweaters, scarves, skirts, kilts, gloves, hats.

Knightsbridge

Austin Reed, 163–169 Brompton Rd. Handsome clothes and accessories for women.

Bruce Oldfield, 27 Beauchamp Pl. Elegant clothes.

Caroline Charles, 11 Beauchamp Pl. Designer fashions for women.

Charles Jourdan, 47 Brompton Rd. High-style, quality shoes and ready-to-wear.

Chinacraft, 1 and 3 Beauchamp Pl. Look for Spode, Wedgwood, Royal Doulton, other big-name English china.

Cibi, 49 Beauchamp Pl. *Haute couture* leather and suede ensembles.

Deliss, 41 Beauchamp Pl. For shoes custom-made within days.

Dragons, 23 Walton St. Custom-made, hand-painted furniture for kiddies and adults.

Eric Van Peterson, 117 Walton St. Famous for antique watches and original Art Deco jewelry.

Graff Diamonds, 55 Brompton Rd. *The* place for rare diamonds and gems.

Harrods, 87–135 Brompton Rd. London's finest department store; 230 fabulous departments. Don't miss the cheese selection in the Food Halls.

Harvey Nichols, 75 Brompton Rd. 7 floors of fashionable men's and women's clothing, home furnishings.

Jaeger, 96 Brompton Rd. Classic cashmeres, casual clothes, and more.

John Boyd, 91 Walton St. Women's hatter supreme to Britain's royals.

Justin de Blank Hygienic Bakery, 46 Walton St. A favorite for deli goods, teas, cakes, croissants, cookies.

Kanga, 8 Beauchamp Pl. Original and cute designer clothes for women. Fabulous floral patterns.

Kutchinsky, 73 Brompton Rd. Once jewelers to the Bavarian Court; specialists in rare and splendiferous gems.

The Map House, 54 Beauchamp Pl. Framed prints and maps, antique globes.

Marose, 103 Brompton Rd. France's top *parfumerie* in London.

Merola, 178 Walton St. Maria Merola's old and new costume jewelry.

Monogrammed Linen Shop, 168 Walton St. A quality selection.

Monsoon, 52 Beauchamp Pl. A favorite for sports clothes, separates, and Indian designs.

Moussie, 198 Walton St. Popular for hand-knits and blouses.

Reject China Shop, 33–34 and 56–57 Beauchamp Pl. Good prices on name-brand bone china and stoneware "seconds"; branches all over Britain.

Saville-Edells, Walton and Hasker Sts. Lalique crystal, Herend porcelain, other unusual gifts.

Scandinavian Shop, 170 Brompton Rd. Great for Norwegian sweaters and other Nordic woolies.

The Scotch House, 2 Brompton Rd. Everything you've always wanted in Scottish woolens, knitwear, more than 300 tartans.

Scruples, 26 Beauchamp Pl. High-quality women's clothing.

Oxford and Regent Street Area

Aquascutum, 100 Regent St. One of Britain's great names for men's and women's clothing, especially rain-gear and woolens.

Debenhams, Oxford St. Super prices in off-the-rack men's ready-to-wear, shirts.

Garrard & Co., Ltd., 112 Regent St. Crown jewelers to European royalty, including Queen Elizabeth.

Gray's Antique Market, Gray's Mews, Davies St. Huge quality-antiques selection in 100 or more stalls.

Hamleys, 188–196 Regent St. One of the world's greatest toy stores; dig those toy soldier collections.

The Irish Shop, 11 Duke St. Not all green, but all Irish clothing.

Liberty, 210 Regent St. Home of the Liberty fabrics, scarves, and ties.

Mappin & Webb, 170 Regent St. Celebrated silver-smiths and jewelers to the Royal Family since 1774.

Marks & Spencer, 458 Oxford St. Flagship store, excellent values, huge selections. Branches all over the U.K.

Selfridge's, Oxford St. The old, established London department store.

Wedgwood, 34 Wigmore St.

PERILS & PITFALLS

Carnaby Street, off Regent Street, is long past its prime. All you'll find along this once-trendy enclave is glitzy, over-priced sleaze. Don't even bother to look.

Piccadilly Area

Alfred Dunhill, 30 Duke St. Now with men's clothes and luggage, as well as all smoking accessories.

Alfred Snooker, Jermyn St. Excellent value in British woolens, cashmeres, and Shetlands.

Arthur Davidson Ltd., Jermyn and Duke Sts. Known for quality antiques.

Astley's, 109 Jermyn St. Delightful pipe shop with Victorian ambience, oak paneling.

Bates, Jermyn St. Called "the gentleman's hatter," with infinite variety, from top hat to tweed cap.

British Design Centre, 28 Haymarket. The best in British design; a "must" stop if you want the latest; good book selection, too.

Burberry's, 18 Haymarket. Get that famous traditional raincoat here at the main store.

Cesar, 103 Jermyn St. Elegant shoes in unique designs.

Christie's, 8 King St., St. James's. The auction house.

Christie's Contemporary Art, 8 Dover St. Changing exhibits of new works.

Coleridge, 192 Piccadilly. Note the beautiful iridescent glassware.

Czech & Speake, 39C Jermyn St. Your stop for elegant, unusual bath fixtures and toiletries.

David Hicks, 101 Jermyn St. Handsome English interior design.

Demas, 31 Burlington Arcade. Known for its antique jewelry.

Floris Ltd., 89 Jermyn St. *The* place for superior scented soaps, fine toilet goods, perfume flasks.

Fortnum & Mason, 181 Piccadilly. The Queen's deli, with top drawer foodstuffs and teas. The Fountain is a splendid quick lunch or tea spot.

George F. Trumper, 9 Curzon St. In-the-know men's hairdresser; also men's perfumes, fine-quality toiletries.

Harvey & Gore, 4 Burlington Gardens. Known for fine jewelry since 1723.

Harvie & Hudson, 97 Jermyn St. Look for top-drawer men's clothes, custom & ready-made shirts.

Hatchards, 187 Piccadilly. Books and more books crammed into every cranny.

Hawes & Curtis, 23 Jermyn St. Regal shirtmaker, also sells silk dressing gowns and cashmere socks.

Henry Poole & Co., 15 Savile Row. Oldest and largest Savile Row custom tailor, with immense fabric selection.

Hilditch & Key, 37, 73, and 87 Jermyn St. Noted for men's shirts, ties, clothes, women's custom-tailored shirts.

H. Huntsman & Sons Ltd., 11 Savile Row. One of London's oldest and top custom tailors; famous for riding and hunting clothes.

Ivan's & Trumper's Men's Hairdressers, 20 Jermyn St. Barber to the elite.

James Lock & Co., Ltd., 6 St. James's St. 200-year old hat shop, with custom-made and ready-to-wear men's head garb.

Kilgour, French & Stanbury, 33A Dover St. Top prices for top men's tailoring.

Lillywhites, Piccadilly Circus. If it's sports gear you want, here's the place for it.

London Brass Rubbing Centre, St. James's Church, Piccadilly.

Lord, 41 and 66 Burlington Arcade. Here's another place for custom-made shirts; also fine leather, ties, sweaters.

N. Peal, 54 Burlington Arcade. Sweaters *par excellence.*

Paul Longmire, 12 Bury St. Here's the place for engraved, enameled cufflinks and other jewelry.

Paxton & Whitfield, 93 Jermyn St. One of London's choicest cheese selections; pricey but fine quality.

The Pewter Shop, 18 Burlington Arcade.

Richard Ogden, 28–29 Burlington Arcade. A stop on your jewelry hunt.

St. James's Pharmacy, 92 Jermyn St.

Simpson's of Piccadilly, 203 Piccadilly. Block-long department store, traditional style.

Spink & Son, King Street, St. James's. Western world's oldest fine-art dealers (1666); known for English paintings, silver, jewelry, oriental and Islamic art, coins.

Swaine, Adeney, Brigg & Sons Ltd., 185 Piccadilly. *The* best umbrellas, walking sticks, and comprehensive hunting and riding gear.

Tricker's, Jermyn St. For choice custom riding boots and shoes.

Turnbull & Asser, 71 Jermyn St. Finest quality custom-made shirts, especially elegant silks, also suits.

Ultimo, Francesco and Uno, 55 Jermyn St. The ultimate in stylish men's wear in Continental mode.

Worcester, 30 Curzon St.

Markets and Arcades

Alfie's Antique Market, 13–25 Church St., Marylebone NW8.

Antiquarius, 135 and 141 Kings Rd. SW1. Open weekdays; numerous stalls with jewelry, Art Deco *objets,* fine furniture.

Bermondsey, Between Tower Bridge Rd. and Bermondsey St. SE1. Antiques street market, also known as Caledonian, open Friday morning until noon.

Camden Passage, Islington High Street N1. Street market. Early attic flea market; Wednesdays and Saturdays.

Chelsea Antiques Market, 253 Kings Rd. SW1. Open daily.

Hampstead Antiques Emporium, 12 Heath St., Hampstead Heath. 20 dealers.

Petticoat Lane, Middlesex St. E1. The historic and still operating market.

Portobello Market, Portobello Rd. W11. All day Saturday you can fight your way through the crowds to browse and bargain among the trash and treasures in this street market. Few real bargains can be found.

Silver Vaults, Chancery Lane WC2. Open daily; arcadelike building crammed with silver shops, old, new, real, less so.

Auction Houses

Look for listings of upcoming sales in the *Times* Tuesdays and Sundays.

Bonhams, Montpelier Galleries, Montpelier St., Knightsbridge SW7. Tel. 584-9161. Also Old Chelsea Galleries, 75–81 Burnaby St., Chelsea SW7. Tel. 352-0466. 7 auctions a week, late-night viewings on Tuesdays. Long established (since 1793), known for art, silver, furniture, jewelry.

Christie's, 8 King St. SW1. Tel. 839-9060.

Christie's South Kensington, 85 Old Brompton Rd. SW7. Tel. 581-2231. This 1766 firm specializes in medium-price items and new collectibles.

Hodgeson's Room, 115 Chancery Lane WC2. Tel. 405-7238. Mostly books.

Harrods, Arundel Terr., Barnes SW13. Tel. 748-2739.

Phillips, 7 Blenheim Street, New Bond St. W1. Tel. 629-6602.

Phillips Marylebone, Hayes Place NW1. Tel. 723-1118.

Phillips West 2, 10 Salem Rd. W2. Tel. 221-5303. Third-largest auctioneer in the world.

Sotheby's, 34 New Bond St. W1. Tel. 493-8080.

Nightlife

Gambling

The paperwork takes two days. Arrange through your hotel hall porter or take your passport in person, 48 hours ahead of time, to the club where you wish to gamble. You will become a "member," and after the necessary formalities you may then gamble. Clubs are located at the Ritz Hotel, Carlton House Terrace, Park Lane Casino.

Cabarets and Nightclubs

Boulogne, 27 Gerrard St. W1. Tel. 437-3186. Victorian decor, dancing to live band; cabaret shows at 11 P.M. and 1:30 A.M., Monday through Saturday.

Concordia Notte, 29 Craven Rd. W2. Tel. 402-4985. Guitarists and quartet play for sheiks, starlets—and you. Dancing too. From 8 P.M., Monday through Saturday.

Fantasia, 34 Eversholt St. NW1. Tel. 388-6787. Live bouzouki, dancing, cabaret. Nightly.

Stringfellows, 16 Upper St. Martin's Lane WC2. Tel. 240-5534.

Tiberio, 22 Queen St. W1. Tel. 629-3561. Live quartet, dancing, and "I spy" the celebrities and royals who flock here. Monday through Saturday.

Medieval Banquets

Beefeater, St. Katharine's Dock. E1. Tel. 408-1001. Tower Hill tube station. £23.50, £25.50 Saturdays.

Caledonian, Hanover St., W1. Tel. 408-1001. £23.50, £25.50 Saturdays.

Elizabethan Banquets, Old Palace, Hatfield, Hertfordshire. Tel. Hatfield 62055. Tuesday, Thursday, Friday, Saturday.

Tudor Rooms 1520 A.D., 80–81 St. Martin's Lane, WC2. Tel. 240-3978. Daily.

Private Clubs

Les Ambassadeurs, 5 Hamilton Pl. W1. Tel. 499-6555. Located in a Baron Rothschild mansion; dignified setting; requires letter of introduction from a member or from secretary of an affiliated club.

Annabel's, 44 Berkeley Sq. W1. Tel. 629-3558. This noisy disco-club shares basement with Clermont. Visits organized through a member.

Chelsea Arts Club, 143 Old Church St. SW3. Tel. 352-

0973. Visitors admitted with a member only; no exchange privileges.

Clermont, 44 Berkeley Sq. W1. Tel. 493-5587. Gaming club in a Palladian town house (circa 1742), with good kitchen, fine wine list. Arrangements through members only.

Harry's Bar, 26 S. Audley St. W1. Tel. 408-0844. Visitors admitted with member, or by hotel arrangement.

Theaters and Concert Halls

Adelphi, Strand WC2. Tel. 836-7611/2. Charing Cross tube station. Musicals.

Albery, St. Martin's Lane WC2. Tel. 836-3878. Leicester Sq. tube.

Aldwych, Aldwych WC2. Tel. 836-6404/0641. Holborn tube.

Ambassadors, West St., Cambridge Circus WC2. Tel. 836-6111. Leicester Sq. tube.

Apollo, Shaftesbury Ave. W1. Tel. 437-2663. Piccadilly Circus tube.

Apollo Victoria, 17 Wilton Rd. SW1. Tel. 828-8665. Victoria tube. Musicals.

Astoria, Charing Cross Rd. WC2. Tel. 437-6564. Tottenham Court Rd. tube. Musicals.

Barbican Hall, Barbican Centre, Silk St. EC2. Tel. 638-8891. Barbican/Moorgate tube. Concerts.

Barbican Theatre, Barbican Centre, Silk St. EC2. Tel. 638-8891 or 628-8795. Barbican/Moorgate tube. Royal Shakespeare Company in repertory.

Coliseum, St. Martin's Lane WC2. Tel. 836-3161. Leicester Sq./Charing Cross tube. English National Opera, also ballet.

Comedy, Panton St. SW1. Tel. 930-2578. Piccadilly Circus tube.

Cottesloe, National Theatre, South Bank SE1. Tel. 928-2252. Waterloo tube. National Theatre in repertory.

Criterion, Piccadilly Circus W1. Tel. 930-3216. Piccadilly Circus tube.

Dominion, Tottenham Court Rd. W1. Tottenham Court Rd. tube. Musicals.

Donmar Warehouse, Earlham St., Covent Garden WC2. Tel. 240-8230. Covent Garden tube.

Drury Lane (Theatre Royal), Catherine St. WC2. Tel. 836-8108. Covent Garden tube. Musicals.

Duchess, Catherine St. WC2. Tel. 836-8243. Covent Garden tube.

Duke of York's, 104 St. Martin's Lane WC2. Tel. 836-5122. Leicester Sq. tube. (For Fringe theatre bookings too.)

Fortune, Russell St. WC2. Tel. 836-2238. Covent Garden tube.

Garrick, Charing Cross Rd. WC2. Tel. 836-4601. Leicester Sq. tube.

Globe, Shaftesbury Ave. W1. Tel. 437-1592. Piccadilly Circus tube.

Haymarket (Theatre Royal), Haymarket SW1. Tel. 930-9832. Piccadilly Circus tube.

Her Majesty's, Haymarket SW1. Tel. 930-4025/6606. Piccadilly Circus tube.

Lyric, Shaftesbury Ave. W1. Tel. 437-3686/7. Piccadilly Circus tube. Musicals.

Lyric, King St., Hammersmith W6. Tel. 741-2311. Hammersmith tube. Fringe theatre.

Lyttleton, National Theatre, South Bank SE1. Tel. 928-2252. Waterloo tube. National Theatre in repertory.

Mayfair, Stratton St. W1. Tel. 629-3036. Green Park tube.

Mermaid, Puddledock, Blackfriars EC4. Tel. 236-5568. Blackfriars tube.

New London, Drury Lane WC2. Tel. 405-0072. Holborn tube. Musicals.

Old Vic, Waterloo Rd. SE1. Tel. 928-7616. Waterloo tube.

Olivier, National Theatre, South Bank SE1. Tel. 928-2252. Waterloo tube. National Theatre in repertory.

Palace, Shaftesbury Ave. W1. Tel. 437-6834. Leicester Sq. tube. Musicals.

Palladium, Argyll St. W1. Tel. 437-7373. Oxford Circus tube. Concerts.

Phoenix, Charing Cross Rd. WC2. Tel. 836-2294. Tottenham Court Rd. tube. Musicals.

Piccadilly, Denman St. W1. Tel. 437-4506. Piccadilly Circus tube. Musicals.

Prince Edward, Old Compton St. W1. Tel. 734-8951. Leicester Sq. tube. Musicals.

Prince of Wales, Coventry St. W1. Tel. 930-8681. Piccadilly Circus tube. Musicals.

Queen Elizabeth Hall, SE1. Tel. 928-3191. Waterloo tube. Concerts.

Queens, Shaftesbury Ave. W1. Tel. 734-1166/0261/0120. Piccadilly Circus tube.

Royal Albert Hall, Kensington Gore SW7. Tel. 589-8212. S. Kensington tube. Major symphony, pop, and rock concerts, big events.

Royal Festival Hall, Belvedere Rd. SE1. Tel. 928-3002 or 928-3191. Waterloo tube. Major symphony concerts, big events.

Royal Court, Sloane Sq. SW1. Tel. 730-1857. Sloane Sq. tube. Experimental plays.

Royal Opera House, Bow St., Covent Garden WC2. Tel. 240-1066 or 240-1911. Covent Garden tube. Home of Royal Opera and Royal Ballet.

Sadler's Wells, Rosebery Ave. EC1. Tel. 278-8916. Angel tube. Musicals.

Savoy, Strand WC2. Tel. 379-6219 or 836-0749. Charing Cross tube.

Shaftesbury, Shaftesbury Ave. WC2. Tel. 379-5399. Tottenham Court Rd. tube.

St. Martin's, West St., Cambridge Circus WC2. Tel. 836-1443. Leicester Sq. tube.

Strand, Aldwych WC2. Tel. 836-2660. Charing Cross tube. Musicals.

Vaudeville, Strand WC2. Tel. 836-9987 or 836-5645. Charing Cross tube.

Victoria Palace, Victoria St. SW1. Tel. 834-1317 or 828-4735. Victoria tube. Musicals.

Whitehall, Whitehall SW1. Tel. 930-7765 or 839-4455. Trafalgar Sq. tube.

Wigmore Hall, 36 Wigmore St. W1. Tel. 935-2141. Bond St. tube. Recitals, chamber and orchestral works.

Wyndham's, Charing Cross Rd. WC2. Tel. 836-3028. Leicester Sq. tube.

The Young Vic, 66 The Cut SW1. Tel. 928-6363. Waterloo tube. Fringe theater.

Music Halls

Aba Daba, 328 Gray's Inn Rd. WC1. Tel. 722-5395. Shows Thursday, Friday, and Saturday nights.

Bee and Bustle, West End Lane NW6. Tel. 794-9077. Alternate Sundays only.

The Players, Villiers Street WC2. Tel. 839-1134. The only full-time English music hall extant.

Offbeat London

Heaven, Underneath the Arches, Villiers St. WC2, Charing Cross. Busiest and most spectacular gay club, huge dance floor, spectator gallery, snack bar, shop, 14-screen video lounge. Tues., Wed., Fri., Sat., 10 P.M. to 3 A.M. Mixed male/female crowd, all ages.

Brief Encounter, St. Martins Lane, WC2. Mostly men, but women welcome.

Rock Garden, corner of King and James streets, Covent Garden, WC2. 8 P.M. to 2 or 3 A.M., depending on day, till midnight on Sun. Typical group: Cold Pharaohs, a punk group.

USEFUL ADDRESSES AND TELEPHONE NUMBERS

INSIDERS' TIPS

It's surprising what you can accomplish by telephone these days. Here are some *London* numbers to use for information that may be interesting, if not vital, to you (look in the "General Information" section of other city phone books for local numbers):

Air travel conditions and info	246-8033
Bedtime story (6 P.M. onward)	246-8000
Brain teasers (answered tomorrow)	246-8050
Business news	246-8026
"Dial an Exhibition" info	730-0977
Events for children in London	246-8007
Events of the day, London	246-8041
Rail travel conditions and info	246-8030
Recipe of the day (Monday–Friday)	246-8071
Road travel conditions and info	246-8031
Sea travel conditions and info	246-8032
Sports roundup	246-8020

Emergency Telephone Numbers

999	Police, fire department, or ambulance (operator will ask which of these you want; ambulance will take you to the nearest hospital emergency room)

The following are all London numbers:

954-7373	Breakdown service, Automobile Association, Fanum House, 5 New Coventry St., WC2
839-7050	Breakdown service, Royal Automobile Club, 83 Pall Mall, SW1
584-1008	Dentist referral service
624-8000	Drugstore, open 24 hours a day. Bliss Chemist, 54 Willesden Lane, NW6
402-4323	Emergency contact-lens replacement
142	Information, London telephone system
192	Information, telephones outside London
246-8021	Road and rail conditions, Metropolitan London area
123	Time check
246-8091	Weather report, London area

Travel Information Offices

730-3400	British Travel Authority (BTA) new one-stop Travel Centre supermarket where you can make rail, air, coach, rental car, or tour accommodations and theater bookings, find free literature, change money, and buy travel books. Open 9 A.M.–6:30 P.M. daily, 10 A.M.–4 P.M. Sunday at 4 Lower Regent Street (two blocks south of Piccadilly Circus), SW1.
(0293) 288-22	Airport—Gatwick
759-4321	Airport—Heathrow
(0582) 360-61	Airport—Luton
(0279) 502-380	Airport—Stansted

370-4255	Air Terminal, West London
278-2477	BritRail info for northeast England
387-7070	BritRail info for northwest England, Midlands, and North Wales
262-6767	BritRail info for west England and South Wales
928-5100	BritRail info for southeast and south England
606-3030	City of London Information Centre, St. Paul's Churchyard, EC4
730-3488	London Tourist Board, 26 Grosvenor Gardens, SW1
222-1234	London Transport 24-hour information service
730-3488	National Tourist Information Centre, forecourt, Victoria Station, SW1 (7 days a week, 9 A.M.– 8:30 P.M.)
222-3232	Pub Information Center (any queries about which pubs have what features—even ghosts!)

Embassies and Consulates (in London)

PERILS & PITFALLS

DON'T expect the prodigal-son treatment from the U.S. Embassy consular section if you've lost your passport, money, driver's license, or other valuables. Report any loss to the police first (insurance companies insist on such reports), then the consulate. They will do their best to help you—but take a number and get in line. Lost traveler's checks are redeemed by the issuing company, not the consulate. And there are lost property offices at British Rail stations.

If you're arrested, do call the consulate in your embassy for advice and help; see number below.

Australia: Australia House, The Strand, WC2. Tel. 438-8000

Canada: Canada House, Trafalgar Square, SW1. Tel. 629-9492

Ireland: 17 Grosvenor Place, SW1. Tel. 235-2171

New Zealand: 80 Haymarket, SW1. Tel. 930-8422

United States of America: 24 Grosvenor Square, W1. Tel. 499-9000

WEST TO OXFORD, THE COTSWOLDS, AND STRATFORD

Oxford is an excellent starting point for exploration west of London. From there you can make a loop into the Cotswolds, north to Stratford-upon-Avon and Warwick. This entire area is so rich a plum pudding of thatch-roofed stone houses and villages, gardens, stately homes and history, you could spend a month and not digest it all. But in a week you'll at least taste the essence and see some highpoints.

Oxford's history stretches back to 879, when King Alfred established a mint here. Its fame as an education center began, many believe, when King Henry II ordered English students to return from Paris in 1167. By the 13th century the first colleges were already established. Today there are 35 colleges, each with its own green velvet quadrangle(s), superb halls, chapels, and traditions. The university world coexists with the industrial, commercial city Oxford has become.

PERILS & PITFALLS

Oxford's traffic is congested. Park your car as soon as possible in a designated car park (parking lot) and bus to the city center, from which walking distances to major sites are relatively short.

For the visitor, Oxford University spreads a feast of the finest English architecture, art, and sculpture. On a brief visit there isn't time for all the colleges, but these are especially rewarding: Christ Church, Magdalen, Merton, New College, and St. John's. Most colleges admit visitors to selected areas—usually the chapel, hall, quadrangle, gallery, and library—at specified times.

Begin at Magdalen (pronounced *maudlin*) College ♛♛♛♛ on the Cherwell River—known for the aristocratic and royal pedigrees of many of its alumni, as much as for its 15th-century Gothic tower ♛ ♛ ♛ ♛, which dominates the city's skyline and the beauty of the Gothic chapel ♛ ♛ ♛ ♛.

Another landmark is the Bodleian Library ♛ ♛ ♛ on Radcliffe Street, which takes its name from Sir Thomas Bodley. He spent the final years of his life restoring the library, after its works had been all but destroyed during Henry VIII's Reformation. Bodley, one of Elizabeth I's diplomats, endowed the library in 1611. The Bodleian today has more than 3 million volumes. "The Bod's" Upper Exhibition Room displays priceless books, such as Caxton's 1481 *Mirror of the World*, the first illustrated book printed in England, and Persian illuminated manuscripts.

Nearby, the Museum of the History of Science ♛ ♛, in the old Ashmolean building, exhibits a diverse collection of fascinating scientific paraphernalia ranging from ancient astrolabes and microscopes to photographic, X-ray, and surgical apparatus to Einstein's blackboard.

Across the street to the south the Ashmolean Museum ♛ ♛ ♛ ♛ ♛, named after Elias Ashmole, an astrologer and antiquarian, is a treasure house of art, said to be Europe's first public museum.

"Stuffy," critics call the displays, but no one disputes the quality of its excellent Egyptian, Greek, and Roman sculpture, Asian ceramics and bronzes, Italian Renaissance paintings, works by Flemish, French Impressionist, and Pre-Raphaelite artists, and one of the finest print collections in Britain.

Among Oxford's other major sights is the Sheldonian Theatre ♛ ♛ ♛. It was designed by Christopher Wren, at the time an Oxford professor of astronomy. His semicircular theater (named after its donor, Archbishop Sheldon of Canterbury), intended for university ceremonies such as commencements, was completed in 1669. Notice the wall

---

INSIDERS' TIPS

Guided tours of Oxford, at 10:45 A.M. and 2:15 P.M. daily from Easter through mid-November, depart from the Oxford Information Centre, across from Town Hall on St. Aldate's street. The information-rich tours take about 2 hours and are led by well-informed, often witty guides. The price is modest.

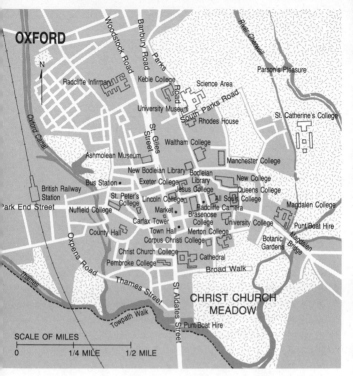

and railing on the south side, whose pillars are topped by titanic stone heads of famous philosophers.

Go north to New College ♛ ♛ ♛ ♛, whose quadrangle is an example of 14th-century planning; all the necessities of education were concentrated in one harmonious block. The college's luscious gardens incorporate part of the 13th-century town wall.

West on St. Giles Street is St. John's College ♛ ♛ ♛, which boasts the most beautiful grounds and gardens. Up the street, whose name changes to St. Aldate's, is Christ Church ♛ ♛ ♛, the largest college. Its octagonal "Tom Tower" ♛ ♛ ♛ ♛, designed by Christopher Wren, still tolls its curfew at 9:05 P.M. daily. The 101 peals of the seven-ton bell (cast in 1680) roll out across the city, signifying the original enrollment of 101 students. The College was founded by Cardinal Wolsey in the 15th century. Both Henry VIII and Charles I banqueted here.

Christ Church's intricately carved cathedral ♛ ♛ ♛ (England's smallest) was originally the church of an Augustinian priory. The college's Picture Gallery, by Canterbury Gate, shows Italian 14th- to 18th-century paintings, some Van Dykes, and a room displaying Old Master drawings. (For a glimpse of Lewis Carroll and other Old Boys, visit the 16th-century dining hall, where their portraits hang.)

Just off High Street is Merton College ♛ ♛ ♛. Its "Mob Quad" quadrangle is Oxford's oldest (completed 1311), with a notable library dating back to 1379; the chapel is a Gothic extravaganza completed in 1451. In the college's Max Beerbohm Room, the satirist's drawings are on display. (Before visiting Oxford, read Beerbohm's *Zuleika Dobson*, the great classic book on life at the university.)

In a city so profuse with sights, the Norman cathedral ♛ ♛ ♛, originally the church of a 12th-century Augustinian priory, is often passed by in favor of the colleges. This deserves a look, though, for its 15th-century vault, monuments, brasses, and 14th–17th-century stained glass.

As you would expect in a university town, Oxford has several fine restaurants and numerous pubs. (See Insiders' Information—Oxford, page 179.) Take time to refresh yourself at one, such as the old Turf Tavern, whose crowded, low-ceilinged, smoky rooms, outdoor patios, hot wassail, and home-cooked pub grub attract SRO crowds. It's a good place for glimpsing collegiate life, English-style.

Woodstock ♛ ♛ ♛, 8 miles north of Oxford, is a bustling town with appealing tea rooms, hotels, and pubs, but best known for Blenheim Palace ♛ ♛ ♛ ♛ ♛. This baroque masterpiece, created by Sir John Vanbrugh, was a gift to John Churchill, first Duke of Marlborough, by a grateful monarch after his victory over the French in the Battle of Blenheim in 1704. The Palace replaced the Old Manor where the Black Prince was born and young Princess Elizabeth was imprisoned. The Duke was Winston Churchill's ancestor, and Churchill's modest grave can be visited in the Bladon churchyard, just a mile outside Woodstock.

There's nothing modest about Blenheim, however; it's a testament to an age of conspicuous consumption. "If you've got it, flaunt it"—and the John Churchills really did.

A stroll along Park Street takes you by the stocks, the 16th–17th-century Fletcher's House (now the County Museum), and "Chaucer's House," which belonged to the writer's son, who became Speaker of the House of Commons. Park Street leads to the triumphal arch entrance to

Blenheim, whose sweeping, free-form grounds were laid out by Capability Brown, with exquisite formal gardens by Achille du Chene.

PERILS & PITFALLS

Come early. When tourist buses arrive, the crowds can be immense and the Blenheim tours hurried and unsatisfying.

In the monumental Italianate palace are displayed tapestries of the Duke's victories, as well as paintings, sculpture (many carvings by Grinling Gibbons), and furniture in grandiose halls, staterooms, and staircases. In one of the simplest rooms on view, Winston Churchill was born, and you will see his letters, books, photos, and belongings.

THE COTSWOLDS

From Oxford it's just 20 miles west on A40 to the Cotswolds, a cluster of rounded hills (wolds) that rise near Bristol and continue 50 miles northeast, ending at Chipping Campden. The area is a magnet for visitors in search of the picturesque. They find it in tiny villages and hamlets, in gabled and dormered, honey-colored 16th- and 17th-century buildings made of the local limestone, and in tranquil churches, tidy gardens, clipped hedges, and pristine lawns.

Within an area 20 by 50 miles, you'll discover many a serene spot. You will also find jam-ups in one-street villages when carloads of tourists stop for antique-shopping or photographing. Yet for the walker, the Cotswolds are ideal. The sense of timelessness seems real.

INSIDERS' TIPS

For suggested itineraries and helpful, detailed walks, consult *The National Trust Book of Long Walks* (Harmony Books) or *Walker's Britain* (Pan Books).

Enter the Cotswolds at Burford, on the eastern edge. A thriving wool town as early as 1100, Burford is often called "the gateway to the Cotswolds." Many of the town's stone and gabled houses are pre-16th-century, especially along High and Sheep streets, Priory and Lawrence lanes. On High Street you'll see a grammar school founded in 1571 and also St. John the Baptist Church, restored over the protests of the artist William Morris in 1876. The vicar told Morris, "This Church, Sir, is mine and, if I choose to, I shall stand on my head in it." Appalled, Morris straightaway founded the Society for the Protection of Ancient Buildings.

INSIDERS' TIPS

Churches are often the Cotswolds' hidden treasures. Funded by wealthy farmers and wool merchants in the era when wool was fluffy white gold, many churches contain unexpected "finds," such as Fairford Church's stained-glass scenes of animal-faced imps gleefully prodding the Damned (all female) into the abyss of Hell.

Cirencester, 15 miles west of Burford, is heady with Roman ruins. It was the Roman town of Corinium, set at the intersection of main roads, which makes it a lively market town even today. The Corinium Museum ♛ is a find for anyone captivated by Roman mosaics, artifacts, and reconstructions of a Roman kitchen and dining room. Between Cirencester and Cheltenham is Chedworth Roman Villa ♛ ♛, the remains of a luxurious, multiroom estate that included two types of baths, steam heat and sauna. The villa was found by chance when a ferret keeper dug up a rabbit burrow.

South of Cirencester, A433 leads to Tetbury, with an appealing 17th-century Market Hall ♛ ♛ in the town center. At the 18th-century St. Mary the Virgin Church, you'll see an altarpiece titled *The Holy Family,* painted by the American artist Benjamin West. Just outside the church are two unusual 15th-century, larger-than-life stone statues. Lately, Tetbury has become something of a tourist cynosure because the Prince and Princess of Wales bought an estate, Highgrove, at the edge of town. If you keep your eyes peeled as you round the bend on A433, heading for Westonbirt Arboretum, you'll see it.

Near the southern edge of the Cotswolds is Castle Combe ♛ ♛ ♛, an almost stereotypically scenic village. It prides itself on its sobriquet "prettiest village in England," and there's hardly a geranium out of place alongside the neat little stone cottages and walls. The village was the setting some years ago for the Rex Harrison movie *Dr. Dolittle.* During Castle Combe's heyday as a wool-and-weaving center, the first woolen blanket was supposedly woven here.

PERILS & PITFALLS

Weekends bring hordes of tourists to Castle Combe, creating traffic snarls along the narrow village lanes and in the numerous antique shops. If you can't make a weekday stop, we'd advise you to skip it. There are other equally pretty Cotswolds villages.

Cheltenham, on the western edge of the Cotswolds, is a sophisticated town of Regency buildings, crescents, wide streets, and what may be England's most handsome shopping street, the tree-shaded Promenade. There are music and literature festivals here, and you may still "take the waters" that made the town a popular 18th-century spa.

Six miles north of Cheltenham is Winchcombe, another joy. It was host to a Benedictine abbey from about A.D. 800 until it was razed by Henry VIII. The village's 15th-century church has an altarcloth by Catherine of Aragon. But Winchcombe is best known for 15th-century Royal Sudeley Castle ♛ ♛ ♛, the last home of Henry VIII's sixth wife, Catherine Parr. In addition to a dungeon tower, peacocks, and herb garden, the castle boasts art by Constable, Turner, Rubens, and Van Dyck, and features falconry exhibitions four days a week, May through August.

INSIDERS' TIPS

You can rent a wood-beamed Sudeley Castle farm cottage (three-night minimum). They hold from two to seven people and are comfortably modernized inside. Rent includes entrance to the castle, woods, and gardens. Information: Lady Ashcombe, Sudeley Castle, Winchcombe. Tel. (0242) 602-308.

The River Eye links the beautiful and still uncommercialized villages of Upper and Lower Slaughter and actually flows through the center of the lower town. Lower Slaughter's stone houses, cottages, and foot bridges, its brick corn mill, and its water wheel are visual delights. The 17th-century manor is now a hotel (Manor), and in the village square you may spy a lion-shaped water pump. Stow-on-the-Wold (where the Royalists and Roundheads fought their last battle) and Moreton-in-Marsh are also delightful little villages, two more of many in the area.

INSIDERS' TIPS

Two miles from Stow-on-the-Wold on A44, and just outside Bourton-on-the-Hill, is little-known (the owners like it that way) Sezincote ♛ ♛ ♛ ♛, a fantasy Mogul "palace" of graceful spires and onion dome, tucked into the Cotswold hills. The house is open *only* to special prearranged groups, but the romantic and extraordinarily beautiful gardens, "guarded" by large ceramic Brahma bulls, are open Thursdays, Fridays, and Bank Holiday Mondays 2–6 P.M.

Broadway is the Cotswolds' most famous and popular— and expensive—village. Just 15 miles southwest of Stratford, it is a favorite "base" for Americans sightseeing the area. Broadway's wide High Street is bordered for blocks by sturdy Cotswold stone buildings now given over to boutiques, gourmet delicacies, pubs, and inns, among which the standout is the 14th–17th-century landmark Lygon Arms. Here you may see the inglenook lounge that once was the kitchen, the room where Cromwell slept before the Battle of Worcester in 1651, and dine in the wood-paneled Great Hall, with its minstrel's gallery and Tudor fireplace.

INSIDERS' TIPS

For the traveler with extra time, the area west of the Cotswolds is studded with charming little towns. Special gems include Gloucester (with one of the great English cathedrals); the half-timbered towns of Ledbury and Ludlow; Tewkesbury (a marvelous 11th-century abbey); Shrewsbury (a splendid Tudor town with castle); and Worcester (noted for its cathedral and Royal Worcester Porcelain Works).

Three miles to the east is Chipping (in the 13th century the name meant "market") Campden, a village whose High Street includes the sprawling 1340 Woolstaplers Hall ♛ ♛, where miscellaneous exhibits feature one of Europe's largest collections of iron mantraps. The beauties of the town include the tree-shaded 14th- and 15th-century homes of wealthy wool merchants (stone buildings shoulder-to-shoulder along High Street) and an open-sided market hall, a 1627 structure now owned by the National Trust. The local church has some worthy brasses.

Hidcote Manor Garden ♛ ♛ ♛ ♛, 4 miles north of Chipping Campden, is famous among connoisseurs of gardens, for its 17th-century house and 11 acres of rare trees, shrubs, and plants and its long alleys of grass and holly tree hedges. Individual gardens in a single color or species are separated from one another by unusual hedges or walls, creating a series of delightful, eye-catching effects.

STRATFORD-UPON-AVON

Stratford-upon-Avon is virtually synonymous with Shakespeare. For generations this town 92 miles northwest of London has been a mecca for Shakespeare lovers and those seeking a glimpse of the thatch-and-timber town in which he was born. (Two McDonald's burger palaces are an index of the popularity that Stratford's easy accessibility—via train, coach, and cars—has brought.)

Stratford, established in 1196 by King John, still has its original plan—3 parallel streets crossed by 3 others at right angles—as its basic grid today. The major sights are easily walkable. Elizabethan and Jacobean half-timbered stucco façades with leaded windows are to be seen throughout the town—some genuinely ancient, some not.

Theater buffs gravitate to the Avon's banks, where the theater of the Royal Shakespeare Company is located. The building dates back only to 1932, when it replaced the company's original, fire-destroyed 1879 building.

During its Easter-through-August season, the RSC continually presents Shakespeare's plays, often in inventive, novel stagings. In addition, the Elizabethan-style Swan Theatre was opened in 1986 to present plays by Shakespeare's contemporaries. And a third theater, The Other Place, premieres new plays. The 3 feature some of Britain's finest actors (many familiar from Masterpiece Theatre and other BBC or ITV television programs).

INSIDERS' TIPS

A bonus for aficionados is Saturday sessions at The Other Place, which feature open rehearsals, demonstrations, workshops, and talks by RSC actors, directors, and designers. Tours backstage and through the RSC costume and stage history collection are also offered.

One of the oldest streets in town is High/Chapel/Church. Here you will see Harvard House ♛ ♛, a splendid example of a Tudor "town house." Rebuilt in 1596, it was the home of John Harvard's mother, Katherine Rogers, and it boasts authentic flagstone floors, ornately carved woodwork, and period furniture. (It was given by the Chicago millionaire Edward Morris to Harvard University in 1909, and is open to view.)

Across the street is the Town Hall, and on the same side is New Place, the site of the house (then the town's largest, demolished in 1759) to which Shakespeare retired in 1610 and where he died after extensive celebration with his friends, it is reported, on his fifty-second birthday in 1616. On the site today is a carefully tended Elizabethan garden, reached through the Nash House, home of the poet's granddaughter, Elizabeth Nash. Within its 16th-century rooms are some archaeological exhibits.

The block-long, 15th-century timbered guildhall and grammar school (which Shakespeare is believed to have attended) is a marvel. Peek inside the attached Gothic-style Guild Chapel ♛ ♛ on the corner of Chapel Lane and Church. Dating from 1269, the chapel's walls bear traces of the frescoes that once covered them, but were defaced in 1563. Over the chancel arch, traces of one, called "The Doom," still linger.

Across Clopton Bridge is Alveston Manor, parts of which antedate the Domesday Book of 1086. Tradition has it that *A Midsummer Night's Dream* was first performed under a cedar in the gardens.

The Tudor "Shakespeare's Birthplace" house is now the centerpiece of a slick, show-biz museum complex. The modern touches include video monitors, an exhibition (extra fee) of costumes used in the BBC series of the Bard's plays, and souvenir-laden sales counters before and after the old house.

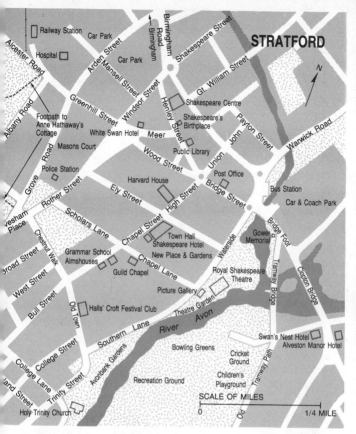

The two-story timbered house itself has only one of its original windows and is heavily restored. It is furnished with antiques of the period. Shakespeare's father, a glover, was the town's bailiff (mayor) and used part of the house for business. On display are the 16th-century keys he used for unlocking the town safe. Also to be seen is a 16th-century desk from the local grammar school where Will was a student.

PERILS & PITFALLS

The flood of tourists has encouraged a variety of activities and exhibits intended to attract them. Of course, butterfly farms, imitation brass-rubbing shops, "motor museums," and audiovisual presentations about "the world of Shakespeare" may be just what you're seeking in Stratford.

Though the "Birthplace" has acquired an aura of near-religious sanctity, one document on view states succinctly that "Shakespeare's birth on the premises cannot be proved by a birth certificate or other types of modern records which did not exist in his time." Nevertheless, we do know for sure that this is the house to which young Will brought his new teenage bride, Anne Hathaway.

William inherited the house when his father died, and rented it to his sister (at 12p per year), who in turn rented out the "commercial" part of it. After 1603, that became the Swan and Maidenhead Tavern. P. T. Barnum's attempt to buy the building for $210,000 to display it in the U.S. was thwarted by a public subscription (to which Dickens contributed £5) to keep the building in England.

You can take a footpath from Evesham Place to Anne Hathaway's 12-room "cottage" ♛ ♛ ♛ at Shottery, a mile from Stratford. Shakespeare may have walked this meadow route when he wooed the prosperous yeoman's daughter whom he later married when she was three months pregnant. The thatched timber-and-wattle construction with leaded windows is the epitome of an idealized Tudor farmhouse, surrounded by gardens and orchard. Furnishings and implements belonged to Hathaway descendants who occupied the cottage until 1892.

Three miles north of Stratford in the village of Wilmcote is the timbered, tile-roofed house where Shakespeare's mother, Mary Arden, lived as a child. It is another yeoman farmer's "cottage," with a farming museum in its barns.

To complete the visit, a Shakespeare pilgrim will walk to the peaceful Holy Trinity Church beside the Avon, where the poet is buried.

INSIDERS' TIPS

Around the corner on Old Town Street is Hall's Croft Festival Club, a building originally owned by Shakespeare's daughter Susanna. For a small weekly fee you can become a member, privileged to use the garden, reading rooms, or lounge, receive your mail, and hear lectures and poetry readings. Modest luncheons and snacks are available.

Through willows and water meadows the Avon wends its way to Charlecote Park ♛ ♛ ♛, the home today, as in Shakespeare's time, of the Lucy family. Sir Thomas Lucy reportedly fined Shakespeare for poaching his deer (scholars say there were none on the property in those years), and young Will, according to legend, left ribald graffiti on Charlecote's gatehouse wall, then fled to London. (The doddering Justice Shallow in *Henry IV* and *The Merry Wives of Windsor* is supposedly Shakespeare's portrait of Sir Thomas.)

Charlecote Park is a National Trust property, and its Victorian kitchen, brewhouse, coach house, formal gardens, and deer park (by Capability Brown) overlooking the Avon are all open to view.

WARWICK CASTLE

Eight miles north of Stratford is Warwick Castle ♛♛♛♛♛, the very model of a 14th-century fortress. Sir Walter Scott called it "the fairest monument of ancient and chivalrous splendour which yet remains uninjured by time." Its massive gray stone turrets dominate the area from a clifftop vantage point above the Avon.

As you enter the main gate, a sign lists the event menu of the day. On our last visit it read "Today's Special Attraction: The Red Knight, mounted and dressed as a 14th Century Knight." We saw him in the courtyard, his horse fully caparisoned in red with gold crosses to match the mail-clad knight's shield and robes, impersonating the 11th Earl of Warwick who fought at Poitiers in 1356 and with the Black Prince in Spain.

Inside there are other surprises, as you might expect on learning that Madame Tussaud's has installed an award-winning tableau of nobby life ("A Royal Weekend Party— 1898"), which is actually well presented, with mannequins in the appropriate clothes and postures.

Purists who want their castles un-hoked-up can take heart. In the many buildings of the fortress you will find choice collections of art (portraits by Cranach, Holbein, Rubens, Van Dyck), furniture, and a remarkable array of armor, plus the usual castle necessities: a dungeon, torture chamber, haunted tower, stables, and peacocks—in addition to the state, guest, and family rooms. The enormous Great Hall♛♛♛♛ fits everyone's image of a medieval castle.

The Castle is so dominant that it is easy to overlook the town, but Warwick Town has appealing features also. The

Lord Leycester Hospital, High Street, founded in 1571 by Robert Dudley, Earl of Leicester, has a half-timbered courtyard that is a delight. Above all, stop by the Collegiate Church of St. Mary♛ ♛ ♛, Church Street, a treasure trove of English Perpendicular Gothic architecture, with crypt—all that remains of the 1068 Norman church—14th-century chapter house, chancel, and Dean's Chapel with superb fan vaulting.

Don't miss the unique, elaborately ornamented Beauchamp Chapel, a Gothic masterpiece. Here are the tomb and life-size 15th-century portrait in gilded bronze of Richard Beauchamp, Earl of Warwick, a contemporary of Henry V (and equally powerful), and builder of the chapel. Hands apart and eyes wide, the earl's effigy gazes, awestruck, at Mary, Queen of Heaven, in the vaulted ceiling above. The once-glorious Flemish stained glass in the windows was smashed by the Roundheads in 1641, which accounts for the glass portrait of the Earl in armor wearing the patched-on head of his daughter.

Kenilworth Castle♛ ♛ lies in ruins 5 miles north of Warwick. Elizabeth I gave it to Robert Dudley in 1563 and visited it often with her court. Her celebrated 19-day court visit in 1575 (which cost her host £1,000 per day and absorbed 38,400 gallons of beer) is described in Scott's novel *Kenilworth*.

INSIDERS' TIPS

From April through September, many special events (some alfresco), take place at National Trust properties in this area. Examples: May Day dancing at Coughton Court, Baddesley Clinton, Berrington Hall; raft race, dressage, and concerts at Charlecote Park; "Midsummer Music at Chedworth" Roman villa; "Loves Labours Won" (extracts from Shakespeare) at Hanbury Hall; Dene River jazz concert in the open at Packwood House. Information: The National Trust, Severn Regional Office, 34 Church St., Tewkesbury, Gloucestershire GL20 5SN; tel. (0684) 297-747.

For a touch of American history, you may want to detour to Sulgrave Manor, 7½ miles east of Banbury on the Northampton road. This is the Early English home of

George Washington's ancestor Lawrence Washington, whose son left England in 1656 for Virginia. In the 14th-century church are the Washington family pew and memorials to Lawrence Washington and his wife and 11 children.

INSIDERS' INFORMATION FOR OXFORD, THE COTSWOLDS, AND STRATFORD

Aston Clinton (Buckinghamshire; Area Code Aylesbury 0296)

Hotel

Bell Inn 🏵 🏵 🏵
A41, London Rd. HP22 5HP. Tel. 630-252.
2 persons in twin, $90–120.
Family-run 16th-century coaching inn, handy to Heathrow and London. 21 rooms, cosy bar, French restaurant noted for game, outstanding wine list, croquet, garden, helipad. Tops in personal comfort, antique furnishings, all amenities.

PERILS & PITFALLS.

British addresses and telephone numbers. For small towns, we have often given just the postal code (zip code) for your use in writing for reservations. Telephone numbers in some small towns have only 3 digits; other small towns have been put on more modern systems and will have 7 digits. There are even a few in between, with 4, 5, and 6 digits. If everything were uniform, would Britain be Britain?

Aylesbury (Buckinghamshire; Area Code Aylesbury 0296)

Restaurant

Pebbles 🏵 🏵 🏵
Pebble Lane. Tel. 86622.
Average dinner: $22.
Anton Mosimann–trained, chef-owner David Cavalier specializes in *nouvelle* English/French cooking.

Bibury (Gloucestershire; Area Code Bibury 028-574)

Hotel

The Swan♛
GL7 5NW. Tel. 204.
2 persons in twin, $67.50–90.
Coaching inn on Coln River. 23 rooms, restaurant, garden, large rooms, open wood fires, old-fashioned comfort.

Bray-on-Thames (Berkshire; Area Code Maidenhead 0628)

Restaurant

Waterside Inn♛♛♛♛♛
Ferry Rd., Tel. 20691.
Average dinner: $55.
Indisputably one of England's best, most luxurious restaurants, near London and Heathrow. Elegant *haute cuisine* French dishes, mouth-watering desserts, splendid wine list, Thames setting, impeccable (if slightly forbidding) service, reflect Roux Brothers' proprietorship.

Broadway (Hereford and Wordester; Area Code: 0386)

Hotel

Lygon Arms♛♛♛♛
High St. WR12 7DU. Tel. 852-255.
2 persons in twin, $127.50–180.
300-year-old inn on main street of delightful Cotswold village. 64 rooms, 2 bars, much-improved cuisine (♛♛) in impressive Great Hall. Tennis, helipad, fresh flowers, wood fires, beamed ceilings, and antiques lend charm and character; Cromwell Room and inglenooks are especially atmospheric; service is friendly, expert.

Restaurants
Hunter's Lodge ♛
High St. Tel. 853-247.
Average dinner: $30.
Swiss-accented French menu in ivy-covered Cotswold stone house.
Small Talk Tea Shoppe ♛
32 High St. Tel. 853-676.
Light lunches, afternoon teas, delicious pastries. Also B&B, doubles $40.

Wine Bar
Goblets Wine Bar, High St. Old stone house, beamed ceilings, wood fires, moderate-priced snacks.

Shopping (among many shops along High Street)
Armstrongs. Men's clothing, accessories.
The Edinburgh Woollen Mill. Good buys in men's and women's woolen clothing.
Gavina Ewart. Antiques and art, silver, copper.
Richard Hagen Ltd. Quality antiques.
H. B. Heyworth. Quality men's shop.
H. W. Keil Ltd. Antiques.
J. J. Luckett & Son. Wide range of antiques.
Methuen Saddlery of Broadway. Everything you need in riding gear.
Picton House Gallery. Paintings and other art.
Stratford Trevers. 20,000 antique and out-of-print books.

Buckland (Gloucestershire; Area Code Broadway 0386)

Hotel

Buckland Manor ♛ ♛ ♛ ♛
Near Broadway WR12 7LY. Tel. 852626.
2 persons in twin, $105–150.
Country house on manicured grounds in Cotswolds. 11 rooms, bar, deservedly praised French restaurant(♛ ♛ ♛), swimming pool, tennis, riding, croquet, helipad. Anton Mosimann–trained chef, spacious rooms, luxurious decor and details.

Castle Combe (Wiltshire; Area Code Castle Combe 0249)

Hotels

Manor House ♛ ♛ ♛
Near Chippenham SN14 7HR. Tel. 782-206.
2 persons in twin, $90–120.
Sprawling country house on gorgeous grounds in quaint village. 33 rooms, lounge, restaurant, swimming pool, tennis, fishing. Welcoming touches: wood fires, fresh flowers, antiques throughout; friendly staff, spacious rooms, some with four-posters.

Castle Hotel ♛ ♛
Castle Combe SN14 7HN. Tel. 782-461.
2 persons in twin, $84–124.
Vintage inn in village center. 9 rooms, bar, restaurant. Cozy public rooms, oak beams, open fires, rustic charm.

Pub

White Hart
Tel. 782-295.
Perfect sightseeing stop for pub lunch or home-cooked snacks in cozy surroundings. Free house with good beer selection. Try Taunton cider, a specialty.

Cheltenham (Gloucestershire; Area Code Cheltenham 0242)

Hotels

The Greenway ♛ ♛ ♛ ♛
Shurdington GL51 5UG. Tel. 862352.
2 persons in twin, $90–120.
400-year-old manor house in peaceful setting outside Cheltenham. 11 rooms, bar, stylish restaurant, croquet. Great comfort in this family-owned-and-run place; friendly manner, handsome furnishings, many antiques.

Hotel de la Bere (and country club) ♛ ♛ ♛
Southam GL52 3NH. Tel. 37771.
2 persons in twin, $67.50–120.
Magnificent Tudor house (dating back to the War of the

Roses) 2 miles from Cheltenham. 34 rooms, bar, 2 restaurants, swimming pool, tennis, squash, gym, badminton, disco. Charming interior evokes the past, but facilities are 20th-century. Ornate wood paneling, exposed-beamed rooms, wood fires.

Queen's ♛ ♛
Promenade GL50 1NN. Tel. 514724.
2 persons in twin, average $88.50.
Convenient-to-shopping locale in town center. 77 rooms, bar, restaurant, garden. Large gracious guest rooms and public rooms, attractive decor.

Restaurants

La Ciboulette ♛ ♛
24–26 Suffolk Rd., Cheltenham GL50 9Q7. Tel. (0242) 573-449.
Average dinner: $30.
Much better than average French food in simple bistro setting. Attractive presentations, super sauces, fresh ingredients used.

Montpelier Wine Bar & Bistro ♛
Bayshill Lodge, Montpelier St., Tel. 27-774.
Average dinner: $12–15.
Lively, informal ambience, good wine selection by the glass, acceptable food for the price.

Number Twelve ♛
12 Suffolk Parade. Tel. 584-544.
Average dinner: $15–25.
Both decor and menu have French flair, done with insouciance. Good value for the money.

Chesterton (Oxfordshire; Area Code Bicester 0869)

Restaurant

Woods ♛ ♛
Bignell View. Chesterton OX6 8UJ. Tel. (0869) 241-444.
Average dinner: $18–30.
Fish, game, and meat deftly prepared with a French flair in this old prettified Cotswold barn. Try the pheasant with apricot & ginger. Fine service. Good value.

Chipping Campden (Gloucestershire; Area Code Evesham 0386)

Hotels

Kings Arms♛
Market Sq. GL55 6AW. Tel. 840256.
2 persons in twin, range $25.50–36.
16th-century inn on main street of delightful Cotswold village. 19 rooms, bar, restaurant, garden. Comfortable, simple surroundings, modest prices, good value for the area. Great bar snacks.

Noel Arms♛
The Square GL55 6AT. Tel. 840317.
2 persons in twin, $50.25–75.
Oldest inn in village, centrally located on main street. 19 rooms, 2 lounges, bar, well-thought-of restaurant. Guns, swords, and deer antlers, oak beams, paneling, all hallmarks of old-time inn. Both old and modern rooms available.

Rosary Cottage♛
Market Sq. GL55 6AW.
2 rooms. $14.25 per person.
A tiny, archetypal B&B Cotswold stone cottage, quaint interior. Village center.

Restaurants

The Badger Food & Wine Bar♛
High St.
Bistro setting, snacks, teas, light meals, reasonable prices.

Bagatelle♛
High St. Tel. 840-598.
Average dinner: $11–15.
Cozy stone house, beamed ceilings, terrace, French menu, fair prices.

Shopping

Bennetts & Willmotts
High St.
Large wine and spirits selection; shop shared with deli, featuring cheeses and Indian foods.

Campden Pottery
High St.
Hand-thrown pottery, dinnerware, cups produced here.

The Sheepskin Shop
High St.
Big selection of woolly goods.

Chipping Norton (Oxfordshire; Area Code Chipping Norton 0608)

Hotel
Crown and Cushion🐾
23 High St. OX7 5AD. Tel. 2533.
2 persons in twin, $30–67.50
16th-century Cotswold coaching inn in town center. 12 rooms, bar, restaurant, sauna, solarium. Handy, homelike, reasonably priced.

Restaurant
La Madonette🐾
7 Horsefair. Tel. 2320.
Average dinner: $25.
Small place, chef-owned; reliable French cooking, fairly priced.

Cirencester (Gloucestershire; Area Code Cirencester 0285)

Hotel
Fleece🐾
Market Sq. GL7 4NZ. Tel. 68507.
2 persons in twin, $67.50–90.
Tudor/Georgian gabled building in center of busy market town. 19 rooms, wine bar, restaurant. Agreeable ambience mixes modern convenience with vintage touches; modern English cooking a pleasant surprise.

Restaurant
Rajdoot Tandoori🐾
35 Castle St. Tel. 2651.
Average dinner: $15–18.
Well-spiced, predictable Indian cooking.

Clanfield (Oxfordshire; Area Code Clanfield 036-781)

Hotel

The Plough♛ ♛
Clanfield OX8 2RB. Tel. 222.
2 persons in twin, $67.50–90.
Well-preserved 1560 Tudor manor house, near Oxford. 5 rooms, bar, 2 restaurants, garden. Handsomely refurbished rooms, spacious public areas, excellent service, outstanding wine list.

Great Milton (Oxfordshire; Area Code Great Milton 084-46)

Hotel

Le Manoir aux Quat' Saisons♛ ♛ ♛ ♛
Church Rd. OX9 7RD. Tel. 8881.
2 persons in twin, $120–150.
Imposing gabled manor in secluded park and gardens near Oxford. 10 rooms, lounge bar, swimming pool, tennis, helipad, exquisite surroundings, flowers, antiques, personal accoutrements. One of Britain's *great* restaurants, *Le Manoir*(♛ ♛ ♛ ♛ ♛) with outstanding wine list. Average dinner: $65–70. Chef Raymond Blanc's fish, game, and pigeon dishes and desserts are ambrosial, with extraordinary original touches. Worth the price if food is important to your travel experience.

Gulworthy (Devon; Area Code Tavistock 0822)

Restaurant

Horn of Plenty♛
3 miles west of Tavistock, off A390. Tel. 832-528.
Average dinner: $21–35.
Notable French food; salmon in sorrel sauce is a long-time favorite. Scenic views of Tamar River. 6 rooms available too.

Maidenhead (Berkshire; Area Code Maidenhead 0628)

Hotel

Fredrick's♛ ♛
Shoppenhangers Rd. SL6 2PZ. Tel. 35934.
2 persons in twin, $90–120.
Solid, no-nonsense house just a short hop from London. 34 rooms, bar, notable *nouvelle* French restaurant (♛ ♛). Well-kept house and cheerful staff play second fiddle to inventive restaurant.

Marlow (Buckinghamshire; Area Code Marlow 06284)

Hotel

The Compleat Angler♛ ♛
Marlow Bridge SL7 1RG. Tel. 4444.
2 persons in twin, $120–150.
A well-situated country house on the Thames handy to London. 42 rooms; bar, *Valaisan* restaurant, terrace, tennis, fishing, croquet. An oldtime favorite, furnished with antiques, quiet charm and comfort, river views.

Moreton-in-Marsh (Gloucestershire; Area Code 0608)

Hotel

Manor House♛
High St. GL56 OLJ. Tel. 50501.
2 persons in twin, $72–90.
Golden stone 16th-century manor house in center of Cotswold village. 41 rooms, bar, restaurant, sauna, indoor swimming pool, riding. Fresh flowers, wood fires, four-poster beds, antiques.

Oxford (Oxfordshire; Area Code Oxford 0865)

Hotel

Randolph♛
Beaumont St. OX1 2LN. Tel. 247481.
2 persons in twin, $90–120.

Well-kept Victorian hotel in town center. 109 rooms, bar, restaurant, coffee shop. Turn-of-century rooms, modern facilities and service.

Restaurants
Elizabeth♛
84 St. Aldate's. Tel. 242-230.
Average dinner: $30.
Expert French cooking, fine wine list, attractive upstairs setting.
Le Petit Blanc♛♛♛
272 Banbury Rd., Summertown. Tel. 53540.
Average dinner: $23–35.
Attractive informal setting, expert service, indigenous ingredients, standout wine list all complement knowledgeable French cooking, super desserts. Related to Manoir aux Quat' Saisons, up the road.

Pubs
Turf Tavern♛♛
4 Bath Place, Holywell. Tel. 432-35.
A college favorite, hearty above-average (and cheap) pub grub, toasty rooms, congenial ambience, lively beer garden in rear, a few guest rooms.
The Bear♛
Alfred St.
13th-century, popular. College tie snips decorate walls.

Stratford-Upon-Avon (Warwickshire; Area Code Stratford 0789)

Hotels
Ettington Park♛♛♛♛
Alderminster CV37 8BS. Tel. 740-740.
2 persons in twin, $82.50–127.50.
Monumental Victorian Gothic estate 8 miles south of Stratford on A34. 49 rooms, bar, superlative restaurant(♛♛♛♛), indoor swimming pool, sauna, tennis, riding, croquet, fishing, helipad. Brand-new as a hotel, potentially one of England's grandest. Former Ritz chef Michael Quinn's skill makes restaurant outstanding.
Ragley Hall♛♛♛♛
Alcester, Warwickshire. Tel. 762-090.
2 persons in twin, $540 (includes 2 meals, champagne

reception, all drinks). Palatial home of Marquess of Hertford, 9 miles from Stratford. 3 rooms. Not a hotel, but a unique "experience" as paying guests of Lord and Lady Hertford in 115-room 1680 manor on 8,000 acres.

The Shakespeare♕♕♕

Chapel St. CV37 6ER. Tel. 294771.

2 persons in twin, $90–120.

Rambling, half-timbered 1637 hostelry in city center. 66 rooms, bar, 2 restaurants, garden, open fires, beamed ceilings, endearing eccentric walls, floors, leaded windows. Authentic antiquity compensates for smallish guest rooms. Rooms named after the Bard's plays.

The Falcon♕♕

Chapel St. CV37 6HA. Tel. 205777.

2 persons in twin, $87–108.

Big half-timbered building in handy central location; 73 rooms, bar, restaurant, garden; snug lounges, vast public areas, popular with tour groups.

Restaurants

Box Tree♕

Royal Shakespeare Theatre, Waterside. Tel. 293-226.

Average dinner: $18–30.

Handy in-theater place to dine when theatergoing.

Garrick Inn♕

High St. Tel. 292-186.

Colorful pub, with open fire, inexpensive pub grub and snacks.

Hussains♕

Chapel St. Tel. 67506.

Average dinner: $15–20.

Indian ambience and reliable spicy food.

Shopping

Antiques Centre

Ely St.

Wide selection of antiques.

Burman Antiques and Fine Arts

3 Chapel St.

Quality antiques.

Debenham

Wood St.

Branch of fashion-conscious department store.

The Edinburgh Woollen Shop
31 Bridge St.
Good scottish woolen buys in men's and women's clothing.
Laura Ashley
42 Henley St.
Fabrics and fashion.
Marks & Spencer
29–30 Bridge St.
Big variety of clothes for family, good prices.
Peter Dingley Gallery
8 Chapel St.
Excellent exhibits of ceramics, glass, and paintings.
Pitlochery of Scotland
9 Chapel St.
Scots goods with style.
Robert Vaughan
20 Chapel St.
Antiquarian books.
Ruskin Galleries Ltd.
11 Chapel St.
Attractive paintings.

Theaters

The Other Place
Southern Lane. Tel. 292-271.
Royal Shakespeare Company's "fringe" theater featuring experimental plays, also classics and some Shakespeare.
Royal Shakespeare Theatre
Waterside. Tel. 292-271.
Home to Royal Shakespeare Company. Always Shakespeare plays, plus others produced here.

Streatley-on-Thames (Berkshire; Area Code Goring-on-Thames 0491)

Hotel

Swan ♛ ♛
4 miles northwest of Pangbourne, Streatley RG8 9HR. Tel. 873-737.
2 persons in twin, $90–120.
Renovated 17th-century inn right on Thames river. 25 rooms, 2 bars, Oxford college barge available. Comfortable, well-tended rooms, but the real star is the ele-

gant French dining room, in the skilled hands of former Connaught chef(♛ ♛).

Pub

The Bull at Streatley
High St. Tel. 041-872-392
Convivial, bubbly, popular, with wood fire, good pub food.

Shopping

Wells Stores ♛ ♛ ♛ ♛
High St.
Remarkable cheese store, stocking 150 French and more than 50 unusual British cheeses. A "must" stop for gourmets.

Taplow (Berkshire; Area Code Burnham 06286)

Hotel

Cliveden ♛ ♛ ♛ ♛
Cliveden Estate, Taplow, Maidenhead SL6 0JF. Tel. 68561.
2 persons in twin, $225–300.
Former Astor country home (now National Trust) in 400 wooded acres of park and gardens. 23 rooms, 2 dining rooms(♛ ♛ ♛), sauna, exercise room, boating, tennis, squash, swimming pool, gardens. Regal surroundings, exquisitely decorated public rooms, enormous guest rooms and baths, numerous amenities.

Tetbury (Gloucestershire; Area Code Tetbury 0666)

Hotels

Calcot Manor ♛ ♛ ♛
GL8 8YJ. Tel. 89-227.
2 persons in twin, $90–165.
Stone farmhouse on A4135 outside Tetbury. 10 rooms, bar, restaurant, swimming pool, croquet, gardens. Impeccably converted to hotel (1984), pristine housekeeping, wood fires, spacious rooms, 2 with whirlpool baths. Total comfort in peaceful country setting.
The Close at Tetbury ♛ ♛
8 Long St. GL8 8AQ. Tel. 52272.

2 persons in twin, $111.

16th-century wool merchant's house-turned-hotel in town center faces lovely garden and close in rear. 12 rooms, lounge, popular, attractive restaurant(♛ ♛), croquet. Ample individualized rooms, antiques, some four-posters, friendly staff, cheerful, welcoming environment.

Snooty Fox♛ ♛

Market Place GL8 8DD. Tel. 52436.

2 persons in twin, range $94–126.

Former 16th-century coaching inn faces picture-pretty market square. 12 rooms, large lounge-bar, restaurant. Large, comfortably furnished public rooms combine with enormous guest rooms, nicely decorated, and friendly staff.

Restaurant

Gentle Gardener♛

Long St. Tel. 52884.

Average dinner: $18–22.

French-accented menu, innovative cooking, *intime* setting.

Upper Slaughter (Gloucestershire; Area Code; Cotswold 0451)

Hotel

Lords of the Manor♛ ♛

Near Bourton-on-the-Water, GL54 2JD. Tel. 20243.

2 persons in twin, $67.50–90.

Classic Cotswold manor house in wooded setting with lake nearby. 15 rooms, bar, restaurant, garden, croquet. Comfortable rooms, antiques, large public areas, good service.

Warwick (Warwickshire; Area Code Warwick 0926)

Restaurant

Randolph's♛

19-21 Coten End. Tel. 491-292.

Average dinner: $30–35. (Dinner only.)

Game's the specialty in this *intime*, exposed-beam eatery, well-prepared, stylishly presented.

Windsor (Berkshire)

Hotel

Oakley Court♔♔♔
Windsor Rd. SL4 5UR. Tel. (0628) 74141.
2 persons in twin, $90–120.
Victorian Gothic mansion facing the Thames. 91 rooms, bar, modern French restaurant(♔), croquet, billiards, fishing, helipad. Elegant antique furnishings and splendid rooms help you forget house's past role in horror films.

Woodstock (Oxfordshire; Area Code Woodstock 0993)

Hotels

Feathers♔♔
Market St. OX7 2SX. Tel. 812291.
2 persons in twin, $90–100.
17th-century building in central location. 15 rooms, bar, respected French restaurant(♔♔), garden. Understated rooms, full comfort with many amenities, congenial lounges convey low-key comfort and informality. Good afternoon teas.

Bear♔
Park St. OX7 1SZ. Tel. 811-511.
2 persons in twin, $94–134.
Classic coaching inn on lively main thoroughfare. 44 rooms, 2 bars, restaurant. Antique-laden, vintage inn, a short walk from Blenheim Palace. Village is "smart," so inn is a bit pricey.

Marlborough Arms♔
Oxford St. OX7 1TS. Tel. 811-227.
2 persons in twin, $57–78.
500-year-old inn on town's main highway. 14 rooms, bar, restaurant. Some four-posters. Ask for quiet rear rooms in this well-run inn cited in Sir Walter Scott's *Woodstock*.

Restaurant

Vickers Hotel♔
Park St. Tel. 811-212.
Average dinner: $15–34.
Homey and pub-like, genial landlord, good pub food, super homemade pies and other desserts. Some simply furnished rooms at $67.50.

BATH AND THE SOUTHWEST

For us, Bath ♛ ♛ ♛ ♛ ♛ heads the list of sights outside London. Not only is this sophisticated city a joy in itself, but its location 106 miles west of London (a little over an hour by train from Paddington Station) makes it an ideal steppingstone to nearby historic and artistically rich places as well as the pastoral landscapes of Devon, Dorset, and Cornwall.

Those nicked for time are occasionally advised to "do" Bath on a day trip from London, but to us this seems a sacrilege. We suggest at least one full day in Bath, a second day for the main sights of Wells and Salisbury, a third and fourth day for the back roads of Avon, Somerset, and Wiltshire. A week would be even better, there is so much to see. The area around Bath boasts more than 20 stately homes, celebrated gardens, and villages, so the city is a natural pivot for day trips.

Bath itself has almost everything a sightseer might wish: remarkable, harmonious architecture, a history enlivened with intriguing figures, a well-developed cultural life (art galleries, first-rate theater, an international music and art festival), sophisticated shopping, restaurants, and hotels, and all the vitality of a modern city 5 times its size.

Bath (population 85,000) has had 3 remarkable lives: Roman Bath; 18th–19th-century Georgian Bath; and new Bath, a revived 20th-century tourist magnet. There is promise of still a fourth incarnation: plans are afloat to restore and rebuild the spa facilities (which became contaminated) and turn Bath into an international thermal spa.

Bath was supposedly founded in 863 B.C. by Prince Bladud, father of Shakespeare's King Lear. It became a thriving community, called Aquae Sulis (waters of Sulis, Celtic goddess), shortly after the Romans discovered hot springs on the site in A.D. 54. For centuries thereafter, Roman soldiers and visitors exulted in the 23 walled acres surrounding the sulfurous pool and series of heating chambers that constituted the bath. But when Saxons demolished the city in 577, the remarkable Roman structures were buried for some 1,200 years.

The English discovered and were using the hot springs again in the 16th century when Queen Elizabeth I visited in 1574 and noted that in Bath "an unsavoury town could become a most sweet town"—if the baths were cleaned up, sewers covered, and the abbey restored. She gave funds to make this possible. In 1668 Samuel Pepys commented about the bathing that "it cannot be clean to go so many bodies together in the same water."

Queen Anne arrived in 1702, seeking a cure for gout. She didn't find it, but she made Bath *the* place to visit, and in 1706 a Pump Room was built so the ill and hypochondriacal could come and "take the waters." Later, Daniel Defoe said, "We may say it is the resort of the sound as well as the sick and a place that helps the indolent and the gay to commit that worst of murders—to kill time."

When, in 1755, some old church buildings were being demolished, several Saxon coffins were discovered. When the coffins were raised, hot springs gushed forth from Roman masonry and gave hints of the Roman baths that once were. It wasn't until 1878 that serious excavations began, and the Roman baths were uncovered and restored. By this time, Bath as a resort was so developed, with so many splendid 18th- and 19th-century buildings that a dilemma arose: How can you demolish a harmonious and architecturally perfect 18th-century city to dig up the Roman city you *know* sleeps below?

The answer was that you *don't*. But what *has* been excavated, namely the Roman baths themselves, adds depth (no pun intended) to any tourist visit to the city.

The best way, in fact the *only* way, to see central Bath is on foot, for heavy traffic, limited parking space, and several pedestrian malls dictate that you leave your car in a car park (parking lot) and walk.

A good starting place for any Bath walk is at Abbey Churchyard. Across the paved plaza, where jugglers and musicians in 18th-century costumes perform, is the Bath Information Centre, where you can pick up a map or sign

---

INSIDERS' TIPS

Informative (and free) daily walking tours are offered by the Mayor's Corps of Honorary Guides, and depart from the abbey churchyard. Inquire at the Information Centre for times.

---

on for one of a number of recommended walking tours.

Just a few yards from the Abbey, down 20 steps and 2,000 years below the Pump Room, are the Roman Baths and Museum♛♛♛♛♛. The Baths are the richest Roman cache in Britain. They are an astonishing and unique sight for the extent of their preservation and engineering feats, from the sauna room with its piles of terra-cotta tiles used for heating, to the Sacred Spring, from which archaeologists have removed 16,000 Roman coins. Imposing statues of Roman emperors (actually Victorian copies) give a sense of majesty to the giant (40 × 80 × 6 feet) Great Bath, which still has its original lead bottom. Some 250,000 gallons of water still surge up daily from the old Roman reservoir.

For years it was known that a temple in honor of the goddess of the waters, Sul Minerva, lay beneath the elegant Georgian Pump Room, but excavation seemed impossible without destroying the stately 18th-century building in the process. Modern technology finally was applied, and in 1979 the substructures of the Pump Room were reinforced and a series of excavations uncovered the temple beneath.

The great treasure of the excavations is the bronze head of Sul Minerva. It is now in the city museum, along with mosaics, temple pediments, and other Roman monuments.

INSIDERS' TIPS

Roman ruins can be found in many places in Bath. Two of note where you are welcome to look: the cellar of the Crystal Palace Pub and the Sally Lunn House, believed to be the oldest house in Bath.

Bath Abbey♛♛♛ was built in 1499 in English Gothic Perpendicular style, and is especially notable for the 1515 chantry of Prior Byrde, with its carved canopied niches and fan-vaulted roof. The Abbey has so many huge windows it is called "Lantern of the West." Note the ancient Norman arch, dating back to 1122, when the church was first *re*built.

Memorial tablets on the walls commemorate Bath's past luminaries, such as Beau Nash, the gloomy population forecaster Thomas Robert Malthus, American senator William Bingham, and a governor of colonial Massachusetts, Thomas Pownall. There is a charming small relief of the botanist Dr. John Sibthorp. David Garrick's epitaph for a fellow 18th-century actor begins "That tongue which set the table on a roar, and charm'd the public ear is heard no more."

The elegant Pump Room♛♛♛, with its Chippendale chairs, Bath, and sedan chairs, was the main social gathering place during the city's heyday as a health resort for jaded Londoners. Here they met to gossip, flirt, play whist, gamble, and attend balls and concerts. Today you can stop by for morning coffee, a Bath bun, and a concert by the Pump Room Trio. The window overlooks the King's Bath. You can also try the famous mineral water, which Dickens's Sam Weller said had the "wery strong flavor o' warm flatirons." One sip of the sulfurous liquid will perhaps convince you that anything that odious has to be good for you.

Notice the statue of Richard "Beau" Nash above the Thomas Tompion clock (mentioned in Dickens's *Pickwick Papers*) in the Pump Room. Nash, an adventurer, gambler, and entrepeneurial genius, turned the city into the fashion center of 18th-century England. In fact, he was so responsible for it that the town might have been dubbed "Nashville."

As arbiter of taste at the time, Nash set rules of proper behavior that were famous and accepted as gospel. They are posted in the Pump Room. We like these especially: "That no gentleman gives his tickets for the balls to any but gentlewomen—N.B. unless he has none of his acquaintance," and "That the elder ladies and children be contented with a second bench at the ball, as being past, or not come to perfection."

Stop at the Theatre Royal♛♛, one of England's oldest theaters—rebuilt in 1804 and recently refurbished. By all means attend a play (often there are pre-London previews

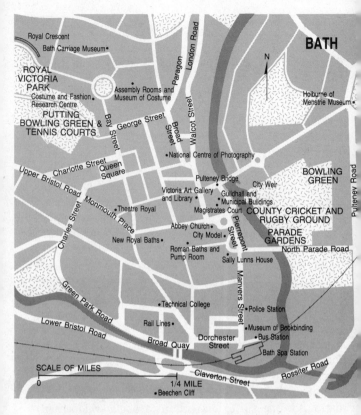

with star casts) and admire the plush-and-gilt interior. Be
alert for the celebrated in-house ghost, the elusive Gray
Lady, whose presence is detected by her jasmine scent.

Then stroll over to Pulteney Bridge ♛ ♛, designed by
Robert Adam in 1770. It is the only surviving shop-lined
bridge in Britain (*à la* Florence's Ponte Vecchio). It leads
across the Avon to the grand avenue, 100-foot-wide Great
Pulteney Street, and the Holburne of Menstrie Art
Museum ♛ ♛ ♛. This is another Adam edifice, well worth
a stop for its eclectic but fine collection of English (note
the remarkable Stubbs), Dutch, Flemish, and German
paintings, silver, and ceramics. The Craft Study Centre,
ensconced on the ground floor, features changing contemporary handicraft exhibits.

Jane Austen lived just across the street, at No. 4 Sydney
Place, in 1801. Back along Great Pulteney, you'll pass No.
36, where William Wilberforce, the slave trade abolitionist,
lived, and No. 27, the home of William Smith, "father of
English geology."

Have a look also at the Cleveland Bridge, built in 1827,

whose little Greek temples at each end were actually tollhouses.

As you head up Milsom Street, once and still the great shopping thoroughfare of Bath, look for the Royal Photographic Society's National Centre of Photography 👑 👑. It is installed in the well-restored Octagon, a historic 18th-century chapel just behind Milsom.

PERILS & PITFALLS

Entering the National Centre of Photography, you are forced to pass through a tacky entryway and shop, but don't let that deter you. The handsome eight-sided building, with its permanent History of Photography exhibit and special shows, lies just beyond.

Bath's two 18th-century architectural masterpieces were designed by a father and son, who transformed the city. With adroit planning and the backing of a local patron, Ralph Allen, what had been a sleepy provincial town was turned into a stunning resort center. The Circus 👑 👑 👑 👑, the creation of John Wood the elder in 1754, is a breathtaking circular stone structure surrounding a park. It consists of three crescents of attached three-story town houses, each with different decorations above the windows.

The Circus quickly became *the* address in town. William Pitt once lived at Numbers 7 and 8, the painter Thomas Gainsborough at No. 17, and Lord Clive of India at No. 14. You will find the home of Dr. David Livingstone (we presume) at No. 13.

John Wood the younger was responsible for the Royal Crescent 👑 👑 👑 👑 👑—30 attached houses designed as a semi-ellipse, with 114 Ionic columns that support a single, continuous, 600-foot-long cornice in the Palladian style. Many call it the most elegant crescent in Europe; it was built between 1767 and 1774.

To see how the best and the brightest of that time lived, you can visit No. 1 👑 👑 👑, which Wood built for his father-in-law. (Wood's own house was the bow-fronted No. 41 Gay Street.) The Bath Preservation Trust has furnished it with superb 18th-century antiques.

The younger Wood also designed the Assembly Rooms 👑 👑 👑, whose main hall is a magnificent 100-foot-long Palladian ballroom where Liszt and Johann Strauss, among many others, performed. The state rooms, considered by some the finest suite of rooms in all Europe, were fire-bombed in World War II. They have been restored to their 18th-century splendor by the decorator Oliver Messel, using the original sparkling chandeliers. In the rooms now is the Museum of Costume ♛♛♛, a wonderful sociological index to changing times, fashions, and classes in England, from 1580 right up to Yves St. Laurent. You'll find clothes worn by Lord Byron, and even President Franklin Roosevelt's 1933 inaugural morning suit.

The beautifully proportioned Queen Square ♛♛♛ was Wood the elder's work, his first major opus in Bath. Wood actually lived at No. 24 (his mistress's ghost, General Braddock's daughter, still haunts the place, locals say), and one of Jane Austen's several local residences was No. 13, where she reportedly wrote her Bath novel, *Northanger Abbey*.

A popular walking tour is "Jane Austen's Bath." The author of *Pride and Prejudice* and *Emma* hated the town, but she used it in her novels, as did Dickens, Henry Fielding (who modeled Squire Allworthy in *Tom Jones* on Ralph Allen), Tobias Smollett, and many other 18th- and 19th-century writers.

In its heyday, Bath played a major role in British social, literary, and political history.

Fielding's home at Widcombe Lodge is across from a peaceful little church, St. Thomas à Becket ♛, that dates back to 1498. If you have the time and interest, you can find the onetime homes of James McNeill Whistler (No. 1 St. James Square) and John Wesley (Broad Street). General Wolfe was in Bath when he received his marching orders to Canada. Lord Nelson recuperated in Bath at No. 2 Pierrepont Street. The playwright Richard Sheridan eloped from Bath, sending a sedan chair from his house at No. 7 Terrace Walk to fetch his bride at No. 11 Royal Crescent.

Sir Walter Scott lived at No. 6 South Parade. William Wordsworth lived at No. 9 North Parade; Edmund Burke and Oliver Goldsmith both lived, at different times, at No. 11. Josiah Wedgwood, the potter, called No. 30 Gay Street home. The Georgian house of the 18th-century astronomer William Herschel, from which he discovered the planet

Uranus, is at No. 19 New King Street and open to the public as a museum ♛.

See also the Bath Carriage Museum ♛ ♛ on Circus Mews, with more than 35 splendid carriages, as well as costumes and horse regalia from the coaching era. (Carriage rides are offered in temperate weather.) The Guildhall ♛ ♛ ♛, High Street, an Adams-designed 18th-century banqueting room, is a jewel, used for concerts and special events. If you are traveling with children, Burrows Toy Museum ♛ ♛, York Street, has two floors of enchanting toys, dollhouses, and children's books of the past 150 years.

EXCURSIONS FROM BATH

One mile to the southeast in Combe Down is Prior Park ♛ ♛ ♛, a Palladian masterpiece built in 1743 by the elder Wood for Ralph Allen, whose quarries supplied the golden stone used in most Bath buildings. The magnificent house is now a Catholic school, which can be visited at specified hours. Beckford's Tower ♛ ♛, to the north of town, was built by a wealthy eccentric, William Beckford, in 1825. On a clear day, from the top of the Tower, which looms high on Lansdown Hill, you can peer right into Wales.

Two and one half miles east of Bath is the American Museum ♛ ♛ ♛ ♛ in Claverton Manor, where Churchill delivered his first political speech, in 1897. Why visit an *American* museum in Britain? Because it offers a vast and surprising display of Americana with a distinctly English perspective ("to see ourselves as the English see us"). In addition to 18 period rooms, expertly furnished with American antiques and choice folk art that span two centuries, there are, among many delights, a replica of Washington's Mount Vernon garden, an 1830 Conestoga wagon, and an Indian tipi (a great favorite with English kids).

Just 3 miles south of Chippenham is Lacock Abbey ♛ ♛ ♛, at the edge of Lacock Village ♛ ♛ ♛. The 1232 Augustinian Abbey was saved from demolition in 1539, when Henry VIII shut down the religious orders, by being sold and converted to a private manor house. The graceful 15th-century cloister and chapter house were kept, a 16th-century brewery has been restored, and an octagonal tower and Great Hall have been added.

Just outside the Abbey walls is the William Henry Fox Talbot Photography Museum ♛ ♛, lodged in a 16th-century barn. Talbot made the first photographic negative in 1835. Lacock Village is a serene grouping of 15th- to 18th-century weavers' houses, an entire village saved and managed by the National Trust. On Church Street is the 15th-century gargoyle-edged St. Cyriac's Church (restored in 1861), where generations of Talbots rest in its Lady Chapel.

PERILS & PITFALLS

The splendid Talbot Museum is open only from 2 P.M. to 6 P.M. Why it can't be open mornings only God and the National Trust know. A major pitfall in traveling through England, as we continue to lament, is the lack of consistency of open-to-view hours.

Not more than 8 miles southwest of Lacock is Bradford-on-Avon ♛ ♛, one of England's best preserved Georgian towns. Its rarest gem is the small, severe, stone Saxon Church of St. Laurence ♛ ♛, that transports us back 13 centuries to its origin around A.D. 700. Few of Bradford's handsome buildings are open to the public, but the town is a joy to wander through.

Also nearby and worth a stop is Corsham Court ♛ ♛ ♛ ♛, an Elizabethan and later "Gothick" manor house in Chippenham. Its Georgian state rooms and picture gallery boast many first-rate works of art by Andrea del Sarto, Filippo Lippi, Correggio, Van Dyck, Gainsborough, Reynolds, and Romney. A portion of the house hosts the Bath Academy of Art, where many of England's contemporary artists (abstractionists like Bryan Wynter, Peter Lanyon, and Terry Frost) have studied. Gardens and park were designed by Capability Brown and Humphrey Repton.

Eight miles north of Bath is Dyrham Park ♛ ♛ ♛, a National Trust property that consists of a beautiful late-17th-century house, made of Bath stone, surrounded by a deer park, a 1680s garden, and grounds that would make any amateur gardener weep with envy. Cows nibble grass on a hillside next to the house, which was built for William Blathwayt, William III's secretary of state. Inside, you'll find Blathwayt's Dutch-influenced furniture, tooled leather walls, and Dutch paintings in many splendid rooms.

Some 13 miles northwest of Bath is Bristol, a lively port and commercial center with historic connections. John Cabot sailed to North America from Bristol in 1497. Thousands of emigrants followed, including Francis Cabot Lodge, who founded the American cotton textile industry in Massachusetts.

There are many sights of interest in Bristol, but you have to battle traffic to find them. Weave your way through Bristol's urban traffic and modern buildings (77 bombing raids from 1940 to 1942 erased many Bristol landmarks) to the Church of St. Mary Redcliffe ♛ ♛ ♛, praised by Elizabeth I as "fairest, goodliest and most famous parish church in the Kingdom." It is notable for its 1290 tower, fluted columns, and gilded roof bosses. Bristol Cathedral ♛ ♛ ♛ is esteemed for its Norman gatehouse and chapter house. Have a look at the City Museum and Art Gallery ♛ ♛ ♛, Queens Road, with paintings by Jan Steen, Cranach, Gainsborough, Constable, and a fine Hogarth altarpiece. The 17th-century Merchants' Almshouses on King's Street have been restored.

Also along King Street you will find the Theatre Royal ♛ ♛, one of Britain's oldest (1766). It is the home of the Bristol Old Vic Company. Look for Llandoger Trow ♛ ♛ ♛, an atmospheric half-timbered inn, a survivor from the 17th century, where pirates and seadogs gathered and Daniel Defoe was supposedly inspired by seamen's lore to write *Robinson Crusoe*. The inn also played a role in Robert Louis Stevenson's *Treasure Island,* and even has a resident ghost, a crippled boy water carrier.

If you are a wine lover, a "must" stop is Harvey's Wine Museum ♛ ♛ ♛, 12 Denmark Street, with guided tours, a tiny tavern, and an excellent collection of wine memorabilia, including glasses the Jacobites used clandestinely to toast their exiled king. Both the museum and Harvey's restaurant were designed by Conran's. The restaurant is located in the barrel-vaulted halls of what was once a 12th-century Augustinian monastery. It specializes in French cuisine, and has one of the world's great wine lists.

Longleat

Between Bath and Salisbury, 4 miles southwest of Warminster, is Longleat♛ ♛ ♛ ♛, one of Britain's most publicized stately homes and the first to be opened to the public full-time. The imposing Tudor palace belongs to the Marquess of Bath. He is descended from the palace's first owner, Sir John Thynne, who began life as kitchen clerk to Henry VIII, and ended it as High Steward to the regent of the child king Edward VI.

For lovers of antiques, there are Longleat's furnishings, including ornate Italian treasures from several periods. For connoisseurs of porcelain there are display cases of Meissen, English, and French china. For those fascinated by "Upstairs/Downstairs," the Victorian kitchen, complete with mannequins, is a delight. For gardeners, the gardens, created by the ubiquitous Capability Brown, may be the main event. They complement a maze, an orangery, and a two-mile-long Azalea Drive.

For children there is the Safari Park on the grounds♛ ♛ ♛, one of the first and best of these ride-around parks where, in effect, you are in the cage and the monkeys, lions, and giraffes roam free. Longleat also features a boat trip on the lake, with the chance to throw fish to sea lions leaping from the deep.

PERILS & PITFALLS

Many owners of stately homes, needing to increase the "gate" for property maintenance, have added all kinds of sometimes dubious attractions, such as amusement parks or butterfly exhibits, that have nothing to do with the property. These gimmicks are easy to avoid. Just buy a ticket for the main attraction. At Longleat, the Safari Park really *is* worth seeing, especially if there are youngsters with you, but be on guard against more commercial diversions elsewhere.

Northwest of Warminster a few miles is the market town of Frome (pronounced Froom). We recommend it for three reasons: its church has hideously wry gargoyles all around the exterior walls; ancient and steep Cheap Street has a stream running down its middle; and Margaret Vaughan. This vivacious lady, proprietor of a restaurant on

Cheap Street called The Settle♛♛, has been a one-woman task force in reviving English cooking.

Stourhead

South of Longleat near Mere is Stourhead♛♛♛♛♛, famous for its extraordinary 18th-century gardens (the creations of owner Henry Hoare). They blend art and nature in an idyllic Claude Lorrain-like setting, enhanced by rare trees, rhododendrons, and a great lake with islands, temples, bridges, and grotto. The 1721 Palladian house, the work of Colen Campbell, is beautifully furnished with Chippendale pieces and paintings. Both are well worth a visit, but if you are limited in time, go with the gardens. They are among England's finest.

Between Frome and Wells is one of those tiny discoveries that add spice to a trip. Nunney is a minuscule village with a moated 14th-century castle, now in ruins. It was modeled on the Bastille, with 4 corner towers, of which 3 survive. Though privately owned, the grounds are open for wandering. Across the stream from the castle is 14th–15th-century All Saints Church, with a Norman font, a 15th-century screen, and 30-pound Civil War cannonballs. The setting is a photographer's dream.

PERILS & PITFALLS

Americans driving on the left side of the road have an added peril in Somerset's narrow roads bordered flush to the road by stone buildings and walls. Be alert for oncoming cars or vans overlapping your side of the road.

Wells

Wells is 21 miles southwest of Bath, if you come directly along A39. The compact, bustling market town seems to flow outward from its Gothic Perpendicular cathedral, one of the most beautiful in England. In fact, Wells is a rare example of a town that was created to service its cathedral, instead of the other way around. In turn, the cathedral's presence makes this town of 8,600 officially a city, the smallest in England.

Wells Cathedral ♛ ♛ ♛ ♛ ♛ was completed in the 13th century and has much to admire. There are 400 life-size statues of saints "marching" across the 150-foot west façade. There are breathtaking double scissors arches under the central tower inside, and a 14th-century astronomical clock created for the cathedral by a monk of Glastonbury.

The cathedral's pride and the town joy is "Jack Blandifer," who sits high up in the triforium above the north transept and who, since 1392, has been kicking up his heels every hour. This propels two mounted knights to try to unseat each other with battle axes, striking the bells as they do so.

The richly ornamented 13th-century octagonal chapter house is a special treasure, with 51 canopied seats around a central shaft, surrounded by 18 columns and 30 ribs of vaulting highlighted with carved bosses.

From the cathedral, stroll the manicured grounds of the close. Past the moat and drawbridge is the 13th–15th-century fortified Bishop's Palace ♛ ♛ ♛ ♛, with its unique decorated chapel. At night, both cathedral and palace are bathed in amber lights, which make the statues in the west façade more visible.

PERILS & PITFALLS

Near Wells, tucked into the forested and slightly forbidding Mendip Hills, are Wookey Hole and the Cheddar Gorge. Like many natural sights that have been overdeveloped, Cheddar Gorge may once have been a thing of beauty. It is no joy now, though. Cars and tourist buses clog the narrow streets, lined with shops touting Cheddar cheese (which is made locally in only one shop, for demonstration purposes), tearooms, and commercial snares. This drive has our vote for England's number-one tourist trap.

Glastonbury

Glastonbury, 7 miles south of Wells, was famous throughout the Middle Ages for its Benedictine Abbey ♛ ♛ ♛ ♛. It was long believed that around A.D. 60, Joseph of Arimathea was sent to Britain to preach the Gospel, and built a modest church on what later became abbey grounds. Myth has it that the graves of King Arthur and Queen Guinevere were found here in the 12th century, then destroyed in the 16th.

Today, all you can see of the original 13th-century Abbey is a dramatic array of ruins. From the scope of the grounds, you get a picture of the wealth and power these Benedictines once had. When Abbot Whiting of Glastonbury remained faithful to his religion instead of to his king (Henry VIII), he was branded a traitor and hanged from the top of Glastonbury Tor.

After you have wandered through the evocative ruins, walk down High Street to the old 15th-century inn, George and Pilgrims, and climb up to the third-floor bedroom named for Henry VIII. From the windows you can see the Abbey, from the same spot where the king supposedly stood to watch the Abbey burn—at his command.

If you climb the 500-foot height of Glastonbury Tor, you'll see the tower of St. Michael, at whose foot St. Joseph is reputed to have buried the Holy Grail. Legends are a way of life hereabouts.

At Glastonbury there is also a handsomely organized Somerset Rural Life Museum ♛, lodged in Abbey Barn, a large, timber-roofed building that was once part of the Abbey grounds. The museum exhibits the tools, crafts, and aspects of farm life hereabouts for the past century.

Ten miles to the south, near Langport, is another abbey, Muchelney ♛, one of Somerset's oldest. Although the Abbey is little more than a decorative ruin, you can see the hinged steps where overnight visitors were locked into their rooms, to keep them isolated from the monks' quarters. The 14th-century Priest's House ♛, a pristine house with thatched roof, Gothic-style windows, and tidy gardens, and the church across the road (with slightly racy 17th-century ceiling paintings) are worth a stop.

You are now positioned to make a pastoral foray into the verdant woods and wilds of Quantock Hills, a terrain that Wordsworth and Coleridge made their own. It appeals to nature lovers and hikers just as much today. In Nether Stowey you may visit Coleridge's onetime cottage. South a few miles is Taunton, a peaceful market town today, but known in the past as the scene of bloody Civil War battles.

Taunton Castle ♛ is now a museum with motley but interesting exhibits, especially the decorative tiles and mosaics. It has the Somerset Military Museum upstairs, with military uniforms, weapons, and mementos (including an American ship's flag captured on Lake Champlain in 1813).

From here you can easily drive (if you have time) farther west to Cornwall and its cliffside resort villages Bude, Tintagel, St. Ives, and Penzance. This is a remote landscape, ideal for those who crave solitude, scenery, and communion with nature. On the westernmost edge of England is Land's End, appropriately named. The 19th-century artist J. M. W. Turner painted some of his wild, impressionistic seascapes here, reflecting the way the Atlantic misbehaves at this point.

Cornwall, Devon, and Dartmoor National Park in Devon deserve a separate trip in themselves. They are ideal for leisurely drives or walks. Again, see *The National Trust Book of Long Walks* and *Walker's Britain* for information on walking tours.

If you loop back eastward from Taunton, A30 brings you to Wiltshire and Wilton to see Wilton House ♛ ♛ ♛ ♛, home of the Earls of Pembroke for 400 years. Inigo Jones rebuilt the present house in 1650, and there is an 1850 addition by James Watt. The house rings with history. Shakespeare, they say, performed here. Churchill painted here. The D-Day invasion in World War II was planned here. Paintings by Rubens, Rembrandt, Van Dyck, Teniers, Reynolds, Lawrence, and others grace the walls of this superbly decorated house.

Then comes Salisbury, two and one-half miles to the east, a town immortalized in John Constable's 19th-century landscapes. Dominating all is Salisbury Cathedral ♛ ♛ ♛ ♛ ♛ in the quintessential Perpendicular style. On the green sward in front of the amazingly unified Cathedral is an imposing golden bronze sculpture ("the donut," an English friend calls it) by Henry Moore. Inside the cathedral is a marble effigy of a Norman knight resting on a wooden bier—a nephew of William the Conqueror—who died in 1072.

Ten miles north on the sweeping Salisbury Plain is Stonehenge ♛ ♛ ♛ ♛, possibly Britain's most famous prehistoric monument, believed to date back as far as 1850 B.C. The Norse word *stanhengist,* from which the name Stonehenge is derived, means "hanging stones," for the massive stones forming lintels over others planted firmly on the ground. It was long believed they were part of Druid worship, but the stones predate the Druids. The prevailing theory is that the two concentric circles of stone were part of an ancient cult of the dead, perhaps used as a temple of the sun.

PERILS & PITFALLS

The approach to Stonehenge is blocked off, and it is necessary to park and walk under the road and into the field. Hordes of trailers and campers nearby often diminish the impression of haunted, mystical isolation. The magic is gone.

From Stonehenge it is less than 40 miles back to Bath, or you can drive east on A303 and the M3 motorway for a fast 75 miles to central London.

INSIDERS' INFORMATION FOR BATH AND THE SOUTHWEST

Bath (Avon; Area Code Bath 0225)

Hotels

Hunstrete House ♛ ♛ ♛ ♛ ♛
Chelwood. Tel. (07618) 578.
2 persons in twin, $123–210.
Beautiful country setting for 18th-century manor 8 miles from Bath. 18 rooms, bar, superb restaurant (♛ ♛ ♛ ♛), swimming pool, tennis, deer park. Pampering and peaceful environment.

Ston Easton Park ♛ ♛ ♛ ♛ ♛
Ston Easton, near Bath BA3 4DF. Tel. (076-121) 631.
2 persons in twin, $97.50–172.50.
18th-century Georgian manor in dreamlike country setting 14 miles from Bath. 20 rooms, 60-member staff, superb restaurant (♛ ♛ ♛ ♛), impressive wine list. Perfection in every detail: Food, service (staff even washes your car), decor, elegant period furniture, ambience.

Homewood Park ♛ ♛ ♛ ♛
Hinton Charterhouse BA3 6BB. Tel. (022-122) 2642.
2 persons in twin, $60–120.

Handsome country home in 10 acres of woods, 5 miles from Bath. 15 rooms, bar, celebrated French-motif restaurant (♕ ♕ ♕), tennis, croquet. Casually elegant, like the home of a friend with superb taste.

Priory♕ ♕ ♕
Weston Rd. BA1 2XT. Tel. 331-922.
2 persons in twin, $120–150.
Georgian manor in pretty setting at edge of town. 21 rooms, 2 dining rooms (♕ ♕), swimming pool. Deluxe rooms exuberantly decorated, spacious and comfortable.

Royal Crescent♕ ♕ ♕
16 Royal Crescent BA1 2LS. Tel. 319090.
2 persons in twin, $120–150.
In center of historic Royal Crescent. 35 rooms, bar, conservatory-lounge, restaurant (♕ ♕), fine wine list, croquet, garden. Exquisite furnishings, architectural perfection; avoid tiny, pricey third-floor rooms.

The Hole in the Wall♕ ♕ ♕
16 George St. BA1 2EN. Tel. 25242.
2 persons in twin, $67.50–90.
Central location, long famous as restaurant, now has 8 rooms, handsomely furnished. Restaurant (♕ ♕ ♕) features fresh ingredients, imaginative renderings, *nouvelle* English/French. Average dinner: $37.50.

Restaurants

Clos du Roy♕ ♕ ♕
7 Edgar Buildings, George St. Tel. 64356.
Average dinner: $25.
Downtown location, imaginative *nouvelle* French menu and chef.

Popjoy's♕ ♕ ♕
Beau Nash's House, Sawclose. Tel. 60494.
Average dinner: $18.
Creative cooking in historic old house in town center, seasonal menu changes, fresh ingredients, unusual combinations, food now in an "up" phase.

The Canary♕
3 Queen St. Tel. 24-848.
Average lunch: $9.
Cheerful little tearoom and lunch place, English specialties, convenient to sights.

Chikako's ♛
Theatre Royal, Sawclose. Tel. 64125.
Average dinner: $11.50.
Westernized Japanese dishes, attractive setting.
Woods ♛
9–13 Alfred St. Tel. 314-812.
Average dinner: $12–18.
Informal bistro, menu old standards and *nouvelle* surprises, moderate prices.

Tearooms

La Silhouette Patisserie
7 Green St.
Homemade cakes.
Sally Lunn's House
4 North Parade Passage. Tel. 314-812.
Average lunch: $9
For lunch or tea and Sally Lunn cakes in oldest house in Bath, near Bath Abbey; then peek at old Roman "digs" in cellar.

Shopping

The Bartlett Street Antique Centre, 7–10 Bartlett St. Quality bargains in all kinds of antiques:china, glass, furniture.

The China Doll, 31 Walcot St. Repairs and reproduces antique dolls.

Coexistence, 10 Argyle St. Rugs, pottery, wallpapers, everything for the interior.

Collections, 4 Green St. 4 floors of great international clothes and objects.

The French Collections, 4 Monmouth St. Wondrous Victoriana, clothes.

Good Buy Bookshop, North Parade. Half-price book buys.

John Keil of Bath, 10 Quiet St. Superb antique furniture.

Kitchens, 4–5 Quiet St. 4 floors of kitchen supplies.

La Maison du France, 7 Broad St. English and French cheeses, deli, and wines. A good picnic stop.

MacHumble Antiques, 11 Queen St. Splendid array.

Rossiters of Bath, 38–41 Broad St. Kitchen and home accessories.

T. E. Robinson, 3–4 Bartlett St. Antique furniture of the past 3 centuries.

Market

Guinea Lane Market, Guinea Lane. Open Wednesday mornings; look for china and jewelry.

Theater

Theatre Royal, Sawclose. Tel. 65065. Tryouts of pre-London shows, also Royal Shakespeare Co. productions.

Beanacre (Wiltshire; Area Code Melksham 0225)

Hotel

Beechfield House ♛ ♛ ♛ ♛
A350 (between Lacock and Melksham), Beanacre SN12 7PU. Tel. 703-700.
2 persons in twin, $67.50–90.
Victorian mansion, handy to Bath. 16 rooms, first-rate restaurant(♛ ♛ ♛), swimming pool, tennis, croquet, garden, antiques, Victoriana, numerous luxurious touches add personality. Look for llamas on the grass.

Bristol (Avon; Area Code 0272)

Hotel

Ladbroke Dragonara ♛
Redcliff Way BS1 6NJ. Tel. 20044.
2 persons in twin, $90–120.
Modern hotel, handy downtown location. 201 rooms, bar, restaurant, coffee shop. Short on charm, long on convenience.

Restaurants

Harveys ♛ ♛ ♛
12a Denmark St. Tel. 277-665.
Average dinner: $25.
Medieval monastery vaults are the backdrop for elegant,

Conran-designed decor and a classical French menu, superb wines (one of Britain's best wine lists).
Bistro Twenty One ♛
21 Cotham Road South, Kingsdown. Tel. 421-744.
Average dinner: $16.50–22.50.
Cramped, crowded, informal, small menu but surprisingly informed kitchen; a fun place.
Rajdoot ♛
83 Park St. Tel. 28033.
Average dinner: $13.
India's Punjabi dishes are a specialty in this old-time, reliable, and reasonable place.

Markets

Clifton Antiques Market, 26–28 The Mall, Clifton. 60 stalls of antiques, open daily except Sunday and Monday.

Exchange Market, Corn St. For antiques and handicrafts; open daily.

Theaters

Theatre Royal, King St. Tel. 24388. Home of the renowned Bristol Old Vic company.

Hippodrome, St. Augustine's Parade. Tel. 299-444. Concerts and plays.

Chagford (Devon; Area Code Chagford 064-73)

Hotels

Gidleigh Park ♛ ♛ ♛ ♛
Chagford TQ13 8HH. Tel. 2367.
2 persons in twin, $90–120.
Secluded, Tudor-style timbered house in gardens and woods near Dartmoor. 12 rooms, bar, widely acclaimed restaurant (♛ ♛ ♛), exceptional wine list, swimming pool, tennis, fishing, riding, croquet. Average dinner: $28–55. Sophisticated menu, *nouvelle* French/English variations. Warm and welcoming retreat, American-owned and -run.

Teignworthy♛♛
Frenchbeer TQ13 8EX. Tel. 3355.
2 persons in twin, $48–67.50.
Low-key country house on 14 serene acres. 9 rooms, bar, restaurant, tennis, sauna, helipad. Genial hosts, gargantuan breakfasts, cozy ambience characterize this moorland retreat.

Dartmouth (Devon; Area Code Dartmouth 080-43)

Restaurant

Carved Angel♛♛♛♛
2 South Embankment. Tel. 2465.
Average dinner: $27–35.
A "must" detour for traveling gourmets. Classic French with exquisite original touches, seasonal menu using best local ingredients, good English cheese selection, well-chosen wine list. Scenic water views.

Frome (Somerset; Area Code Frome 0373)

Hotel

Selwood Manor♛
Frome BA11 3NL. Tel. 63605.
2 persons in twin, $90.
Country house in pastoral landscape, dotted with sheep, donkeys, farm animals. 6 rooms, dinners on request ($20.25 for 4 courses), family-run.

Restaurant

The Settle♛♛
Cheap St. Tel. 5975.
Average meal: $10–15.
Chef-owner Margaret Vaughan serves old English fare and her own creative innovations in a rustic setting; bakery attached. Try Margaret's specialty, Frome Bobbins. Super afternoon teas.

Glastonbury (Somerset; Area Code Glastonbury 0458)

Hotel

George and Pilgrims ♛
High St. Tel. 31146.
2 persons in twin, $45–80.
Historic inn (1475), used by abbey guests in medieval times. 15 rooms (6 with private baths), bar, okay restaurant. All rooms furnished differently, some with four-posters. Abbot Selwood room especially nice.

Restaurant

No. 3 ♛
Magdalene St. Tel. 32129.
Average dinner: $22.50–35.
English standards plus fresh seafood (including lobster from Cornwall), roast beef, and Yorkshire pudding, all carefully prepared.

Helford (Cornwall; Area Code Manaccan 032-623)

Restaurant

Riverside ♛ ♛
Helford, near Helston. Tel. 443.
Average dinner: $35.
Well-prepared food, menu changes daily, French overtones. Charming setting. 12 cottage guest rooms.

Lacock (Wiltshire; Area Code Lacock 024973)

Hotel

Sign of the Angel Inn ♛
6 Church Street, near Chippenham SN15 2LB. Tel. 230.
2 persons in twin, range $67.50–90.
Tiny half-timbered house on quiet street of National Trust–preserved village. 6 rooms, pub, restaurant, fishing. A 15th-century wool merchant's house, full of quaint charm, antiques.

Penzance (Cornwall; Area Code 0736)

Hotels

The Abbey♛
Abbey St. TR18 4AR. Tel. 66906.
2 persons in twin, range $45–67.50.
Homelike tiny hotel in convenient location, 6 rooms, restaurant. Attractively decorated, well-kept rooms, friendly hosts.

Smugglers♛
14 Fore St., Newlyn TR18 5JN. Tel. 4207.
2 persons in twin, range $36–42.
250-year-old inn overlooking harbor. 14 rooms, 8 with baths, restaurant. Nautical motif throughout, a favorite with artists.

Salisbury (Wiltshire; Area Code Salisbury 0722)

Hotels

Rose & Crown♛
Harnham Rd. SP2 8JQ. Tel. 27908.
2 persons in twin, range $67.50–90.
Half-timbered building with modern addition on Avon River banks, across from town. 28 rooms, bar, restaurant. For greater character, antiques, four-posters, ask for room in old building.

White Hart♛
1 St. John Street SP1 2SD. Tel. 27476.
2 persons in twin, range $67.50–90.
Georgian hotel in handy in-town location. 68 rooms, 56 with bath, bar, restaurant. Slightly formal air pervades this traditional town hotel, softened somewhat by welcoming fires, comfortable lounge.

Restaurant

Crane's♛
90–92 Crane St. Tel. 333-471.
Average dinner: $22–27.
French classics with original touches in casual, friendly ambience.

Taunton (Somerset; Area Code Taunton 0823)

Hotel

Castle ♛ ♛ ♛
Castle Green TA1 1NF. Tel. 72671.
2 persons in twin, $90–150.
Family-run converted castle in center of bustling market
town. 44 rooms, bar, restaurant (♛ ♛ ♛). Individually
decorated rooms exude comfort and stylishness. Notable
service and fastidious maintenance. Fine afternoon teas.

Thornbury (Avon; Area Code Thornbury 0454)

Hotel

Thornbury Castle ♛ ♛ ♛
Near Bristol BS12 1HH. Tel. 418–511.
2 persons in twin, $90–120.
Authentic Henry VIII–owned castle in the country 11
miles north of Bristol. 12 rooms, bar, widely acclaimed
restaurant (♛ ♛ ♛), vineyard. Restored with theatrical
Gothic flair, the dining room is a dramatic backdrop for
expertly prepared *nouvelle* French food; guest rooms sumptuous and antiques-laden.

Torquay (Devon; Area Code Torquay 0803)

Hotel

Imperial ♛ ♛ ♛
Belgrave Rd. TO2 5HF. Tel. 23219.
2 persons in twin, $150.
Modern high-rise resort hotel. 164 rooms, bars, restaurant, indoor and outdoor swimming pools, sauna, tennis,
squash, disco, billiards, croquet, shop, health and beauty
center. Handsomely decorated, with abundant amenities.

Warminster (Wiltshire; Area Code Warminster 0985)

Hotel

Bishopstrow House ♛ ♛ ♛
Warminster BA12 9HH. Tel. 212312.
2 persons in twin, $102–172.50.
Georgian mansion on spacious grounds at town's edge. 25 rooms (some with Jacuzzis), bar, excellent French restaurant (♛ ♛ ♛), conservatory, sauna, indoor and outdoor swimming pools, tennis, fishing, solarium, helipad. Exuberant elegance and sybaritic comfort highlight every spacious corner here.

Restaurants

Agra ♛
32 East St. Tel. 212-713.
Average dinner: $18–22.
Tandoori and other Indian dishes make this an agreeable addition to Wiltshire dining.
Cooper's
28 High St. Tel. 216-911.
18th-century house, good food, reasonable prices.

Wells (Somerset; Area Code Wells 0749)

Hotel

Crown ♛
Market Pl. BA5 2RP. Tel. 73457.
2 persons in twin, $50–75.
15th-century coaching inn in cathedral's shadow. 18 rooms, lounge, restaurant. Mullioned windows, exposed beams, open hearths, much the same as when William Penn spoke to crowds from inn window in 1695.

Market

Croscombe, 3 miles west of Wells; Tuesday 10 A.M.; handicrafts, home-grown, home-cooked foods; tiny indoor space.

Winchester (Hampshire; Area Code Winchester 0962)

Hotels

Lainston House ♔ ♔ ♔
Sparsholt SO21 2LT. Tel. 63588.
2 persons in twin, $120–150.
An imposing William-and-Mary house on 63 wooded acres, 3 miles from town. 32 rooms, bar, restaurant (♔ ♔), tennis, croquet. Predominantly Swiss menu, well-chosen antiques, fine architectural detailing, sizable rooms give unique flavor.

Wessex ♔ ♔
Paternoster Row SO23 9LQ. Tel. 61611.
2 persons in twin, $90–120.
Modern redbrick building with head-on cathedral views. 94 rooms, bar, restaurant, coffee shop. What it lacks in character it makes up in sightseeing convenience and ample rooms. Good afternoon teas.

Restaurant

Old Chesil Rectory ♔
1 Chesil St. Tel. 53177.
Average dinner: $21. Dinner only.
3-course *prix fixe* French-style menus. Good value.

Pub

Eclipse Inn
The Square.
Tudor pub, ancient beams, low windows for easy chats with passersby.

CANTERBURY AND THE SOUTHEAST

Canterbury, center stage so often in English history, is just 56 miles southeast of London, a 1-hour-18-minute train ride, making it an easy one-day or, if necessary (but please God, no!), half-day excursion from the capital.

With 2 days by car you can drive through Kent, from Canterbury on to Dover, Rye, and Hastings. Add 2 days along the coast to Brighton, Arundel, and Chichester, then back to London. This lopsided loop will catapult you back 10 centuries, show you the battleground of the Norman Conquest as well as stately homes and magnificent gardens, offer samples of Britain's "garden district" fare, and nourish your psyche.

Kent, you will find, is a well-nurtured countryside, with cherry and apple orchards and generous crops. You will see curious cone-shaped brick buildings called oast houses. These are for drying hops, the plant used in making beer. They are unique to Kent, and many have been converted into bed-and-breakfast guest houses, boutiques, restaurants, and even a theater. (That's gentrification, Kent-style. The yuppies are here.)

Kent is also Dickens country, and a fan will find many associations with the 19th-century novelist. A quick first stop might be the busy industrial city and port of Rochester, 30 miles east of London, to see the Charles Dickens Centre♛♛ on High Street. It has memorabilia and exhibits about the author, and can pinpoint many places mentioned in the early *Pickwick Papers*, *Great Expectations*, and *Edwin Drood*. At Gad's Hill, just outside town in Higham on A226, Dickens spent the last years of his life. The big redbrick house ♛♛ (not open) across the highway from the Falstaff Inn is now part of a school.

Rochester has other features of interest. Its primarily Norman cathedral♛♛♛ (don't miss the crypt, one of England's largest and most appealing) is well worth a visit, and Rochester Castle ♛ ♛ (walls only) is impressive, as are the 17th-century Guildhall ♛ and Tudor-era Restoration House ♛ ♛ on Maidstone Road.

Just before you reach Rochester on the A2 is Cobham, a delightful village immortalized by mention of its timbered Leather Bottle Inn ♛ in *The Pickwick Papers.* Just opposite the cozy tavern (which serves a good pub lunch even today) is St. Mary Magdalene Church ♛ ♛, notable for its Gothic arches, stained-glass windows, ornate 16th-century Tudor tomb, and especially for its 16 13th–16th-century tomb brasses, one of Britain's largest collections. At the rear of the church is the New College of Cobham ♛ ♛ which incorporates the 14th-century almshouses.

INSIDERS' TIPS

Aficionados can make rubbings of the brasses for a small fee at specified times.

Maidstone, a few miles south of Rochester, is the site of Leeds Castle ♛ ♛ ♛ ♛, one of the most beautiful castles in the world. This former Norman stronghold, "gentrified" by Henry VIII into a royal palace, straddles two islands in the middle of a swan-and-duck-dappled lake amidst a rolling emerald landscape. The Castle itself is rich in medieval tapestries and furniture and—surprisingly—Impressionist paintings.

Just gawking at the crenellated towers and flag-hung parapets is spirit-lifting. But there are many organized activities on the vast, well-kept grounds, ranging from 9-hole golf and open-air concerts to English wine festivals and country craft "fayres." You will find parklands, gardens, a duckery, an aviary, greenhouses, and an ancient vineyard to wander through. There is even a Dog Collar Museum—a bizarre thought, but oddly fascinating in its assortment of antique silver, brass, and velvet collars belonging to pampered pets of the past.

A pleasant route to Canterbury from Maidstone is through Chilham ♛ ♛ ♛, one of Kent's prettiest villages. The road winds up to a hilltop castle and a charming small square, faced on three sides by redbrick and black-and-white timbered Tudor houses. Some are now attractive antique shops and village pubs. On the fourth side is the gate to Chilham Castle ♛, on the grounds of a onetime hunting lodge of Henry VIII.

At the castle, jousting tournaments are held each Sunday, medieval banquets are served in the Norman keep, and a Raptor Centre holds frequent flying demonstrations of its trained eagles, falcons, hawks, and owls. The castle gardens, park (designed by Capability Brown), and Norman keep are open daily.

PERILS & PITFALLS

Leeds Castle is marketed as a full day's outing in itself. The all-inclusive admission price is reasonable for a leisurely visit but steep for a quick look-see.

CANTERBURY

You arrive at last, like medieval pilgrims, in Canterbury, one of Britain's major treasure towns. There are considerably more local residents now (36,000) than when Geoffrey Chaucer wrote his *Canterbury Tales* in the 14th century. Yet even today, all streets lead to the Cathedral, the town's focal point.

The main approach to the Cathedral grounds is from Buttermarket Square. (This was once known as Bullstake, because it was the place for bull-baiting.) You enter the grounds through the 1520 Christ Church Gate♛♛♛, built to commemorate the marriage of Henry VII's son Arthur, Prince of Wales, to Catherine of Aragon.

Canterbury Cathedral♛♛♛♛♛ is an architectural jewel, a treasure house of sculpture, and a historic monument. There was a church on the site as early as 597, after St. Augustine appeared on the scene. Destruction by Danes and a later fire led to a whole new edifice, begun in Norman style in the late 11th century, and finished in Perpendicular Gothic in 1503.

Beautiful as the Cathedral is, it is hardly an exaggeration to say that it was murder that put it on the map—and atonement for that murder that kept it there.

The murder, immortalized in Tennyson's poem "Becket" and T. S. Eliot's play *Murder in the Cathedral,* occurred December 29, 1170. Four knights, "henchmen" of Henry II, believing it was the king's will, killed the independent-

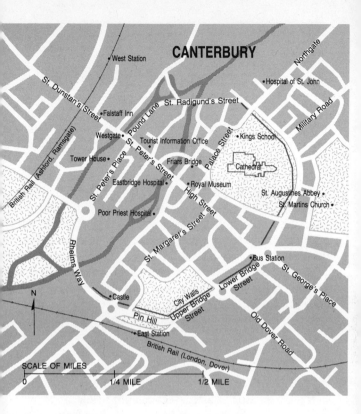

CANTERBURY

West Station

Hospital of St. John

St. Dunstan's Street

Northgate

Military Road

Falstaff Inn

St. Radigund's Street

Pound Lane

Westgate

Tourist Information Office

Palace Street

Kings School

Tower House

St. Peter's Place

St. Peter's Street

Friars Bridge

Cathedral

British Rail (Ashford, Ramsgate)

Eastbridge Hospital

Royal Museum

High Street

St. Augustines Abbey

St. Martins Church

Poor Priest Hospital

Rheims Way

St. Margaret's Street

Bus Station

St. George's Place

Lower Bridge Street

Castle

City Walls

Upper Bridge Street

Pin Hill

Old Dover Road

East Station

British Rail (London, Dover)

N

SCALE OF MILES

0   1/4 MILE   1/2 MILE

spirited Archbishop of Canterbury, Thomas à Becket, attacking him in the Cathedral.

In doing so, they created a martyr (later canonized a saint), sent the king on a humiliating public pilgrimage of penitence (forced on him by the Pope), and turned Canterbury into a premier pilgrimage center. For 350 years, hordes of religious pilgrims came to Canterbury to pray and pay their respects at the tomb of the martyred St. Thomas à Becket.

In 1538, Henry VIII had Becket's tomb destroyed and pocketed its jewels and treasures (it took eight men to lift the container). The Cathedral became the center of the Protestant Church of England, with the Archbishop of Canterbury its primate.

Today there is a dramatic triple cross over a new altar that marks the spot where Becket was slain. On the floor is a plaque reading, "In this place hallowed by the martyrdom of St. Thomas à Becket, Pope John Paul II and Robert Runcie, Archbishop of Canterbury, knelt together in prayer May 29, 1982."

There are scores of treasures worthy of your attention inside the Cathedral and on its walled grounds. We would like to suggest a few.

You will, of course, be duly impressed with the beauty of the 11th-century nave, the Norman Trinity Chapel and Choir (1200), the Dean's Chapel, and the chapel of St. Edward the Confessor.

The 12th- and 13th-century stained-glass windows tend to catch one's eye first. Mercifully, they were spared the destruction that Luftwaffe bombing raids wrought on the town. The early 13th-century series of glass, called "Poor Man's Bible," depicts scenes from both Old and New Testaments.

In the ambulatory of the Trinity Chapel, which was built to enclose Becket's shrine, are other 13th-century windows, called the Miracle Windows because they illustrate miracles performed at Becket's shrine or through the saint's help.

Look for the magnificent golden-burnished brass figure ♕ ♕ ♕ ♕ ♕ of Edward, son of King Edward III, dubbed the Black Prince. His life-size effigy is clad in battle armor, atop an alabaster tomb. His helmet and tunic are displayed above. Idol of the nation for his victories at Crécy and Poitiers, he died at age 46.

The placid tomb figures of Henry IV (the only English king entombed in Canterbury) and his second queen, Joan of Navarre, are masterfully done. (She was widely suspected of hastening his demise by witchcraft in 1413.)

Many of the tombs of past archbishops are also works of sculptural art to admire. That of Henry Chichele, showing him in magnificent church attire (above) and as an emaciated cadaver (below), is a striking reminder of transitory glory.

The tombs illustrate the interweaving of church and politics in early England. Hubert Walter, who was archbishop from 1193 to 1205, accompanied Richard the Lionhearted on his Crusade and negotiated "three yers, three weeks and three days" with Saladin for Richard's release. The tomb of John Mauthier, bishop of Bray, is here. He persuaded Edward IV's widow to place her sons, the young princes, in Richard III's care—and we know what befell them.

Look for the elaborate 16th-century tomb of Nicholas

Wotton, dean of Canterbury, who helped arrange the misleading Holbein portrait of Anne of Cleves, on the basis of which Henry VIII chose her as his wife. Wotton subsequently had the delicate task of informing her brother that the lady did not measure up to the King's standards of beauty. Henry rewarded him in his will.

Don't overlook the Crypt, the oldest part of the Cathedral. The low roof and rounded arches are in pure 11th-century Norman style, and the capitals of the pillars carry amusingly carved grotesqueries. Our Lady Undercroft, a 14th-century chapel in which the Black Prince wanted to be entombed, is also a gem. In the eastern crypt on a pillar is the shadowy painting of a man, known locally as "Becket's ghost."

A walk around the Cathedral grounds brings you to the Great Cloister, a 14th-century masterpiece; the Chapter House; the Water Tower (sometimes called the Baptistry) where the monks washed up en route to Cathedral services; and the Norman Staircase (now part of King's School on the grounds), a remarkable wooden-roofed structure considered one of the best remaining examples of Norman domestic architecture.

INSIDERS' TIPS

Note the tablet nearby, marking the spot where the ashes of Somerset Maugham, once a King's School student, are buried, an Old Boy come home to rest. (Joseph Conrad is also buried in Canterbury, in the Roman Catholic section of Canterbury Cemetery.)

From the Cathedral grounds you can walk easily to all the other local sights, saving time at the end for a shopping browse or lunch or tea along High Street—perhaps at Queen Elizabeth's Guest Chamber, a pilgrims' inn (you'll recognize it by the finely pargetted façade) where the queen turned down the Duke of Alençon's marriage offer.

Canterbury, or *Cantwarabyrig* as the Saxons called it, goes back to the Stone Age. The Romans used the town as their regional center for Kentish tribes. World War II bombing knocked out one-third of Canterbury's center, revealing old Roman underpinnings. Some of the tessellated pavement of a Roman townhouse is open to view under new postwar shops built on Butchery Lane.

INSIDERS' TIPS

The Canterbury Tourist Information Office, High Street, offers a walking tour of the town that begins at 2:15 P.M. daily, May through September.

Pilgrims walked through West Gate ♛ ♛ (the last of the city gates still standing) and High Street on their way to the Cathedral. Among them were William the Conqueror and Richard the Lionhearted. One French king on pilgrimage promised the monks of Christchurch an annual 200 hogsheads of wine. Deliveries stopped centuries ago; Canterburians refrain from mentioning this to French visitors.

Farther along, where High Street crosses the Stour River, are the beautiful houses of "the weavers" ♛ ♛ with their gables, bow windows, and window boxes of flowers hanging over the water. Here lived and worked some of the Flemish and Huguenot refugees of the 16th century who at times outnumbered the natives.

Across the street is St. Thomas's (or Eastbridge) Hospital ♛ ♛, a 12th-century hostel for poor pilgrims, today housing the elderly. Pop in to see the 13th-century chapel, Norman crypt, and mural of Christ in the hall.

Outside West Gate, the road is named St. Dunstan's Street and passes the old Falstaff Inn on its way to the 13th-century St. Dunstan's Church. Here the vault contains the head of St. Thomas More, returned to his daughter, Margaret Roper, after being displayed for 14 days on London Bridge. It was at St. Dunstan's that Henry II in 1174 dismounted and changed from kingly garb to penitent's robes to walk barefoot to the Cathedral as an ordinary pilgrim, as part of the penance imposed on him by the Pope for Becket's murder.

You may wish to visit the remains of St. Augustine's Abbey ♛ ♛, begun by the saint in 602 and extended over centuries until the Dissolution in 1538. Considered among the most important monastic ruins north of the Alps, the buildings were, until rescued in 1848 and subsequently restored, used for a brewery, beer garden, and cockpit. They are quieter today.

Nearby on Longport Road is England's oldest church in current use, St. Martin's ♛. The chancel predates St. Augustine, going back to Queen Bertha's time, before 597.

DOVER

From Canterbury, it is just 16 miles to the white cliffs of Dover on the English Channel—a fact to tuck away in case you want to see Canterbury before hopping the ferry to France. Dover was one of the original Cinque Ports, along with Hastings, Hythe, New Romney, and Sandwich. They were formed into a federation by Edward the Confessor to protect England's coast from Continental marauders in the 11th century.

Dover's chalk-white cliffs played a role in World War II as the white ribbon of security that Allied pilots looked for when returning from bombing raids across the Channel. Dover today is the closest port to the Continent, with all the facilities of a modern seaside resort as well. Dover Castle ♛, with its crenellated towers, well-preserved keep, and Norman memories, has portions that date from the 12th century and earlier. The Roman lighthouse was built about A.D. 50. The town hall is in the 13th–14th-century Maison Dieu Hall ♛ in Biggin Street, adjoined by the Maison Dieu House ♛ (1665), which is a library.

From Dover, skim westward along the coast to Hythe, New Romney, and Winchelsea, all ancient towns long associated with the Cinque Ports, smuggling, and fishing.

Winchelsea ♛ ♛ today is no longer on the coast but is still a delightful old town of narrow streets. Near the 1283 Church of St. Thomas the Martyr is Wesley's Tree, where John Wesley preached in 1790. Nearby is the Manna Plat Coffee House (*manna* = bread, *plat* = portion of land), which has beneath it a 13th-century wine cellar that you may visit, one of 3 left of 40 that once existed in town— legacies, perhaps, of the early smuggling days.

RYE

And so on to Rye ♛ ♛ ♛ ♛, once a port, now 5 miles inland. In the 14th century, Rye acquired all the privileges of the Cinque Ports. One of our very favorite English towns, Rye is a real "must" on any south-of-London itinerary.

In Rye it isn't the sights that are important, but the ambience. Narrow, cobbled streets weave up and down

---

PERILS & PITFALLS

Others think Rye is great, too, and on sunny weekends the town's narrow, hilly streets are jammed with English day-trippers. If possible, schedule your visit on a weekday.

---

hills, edged by half-timbered houses that predate Shakespeare. "Picturesque" is a much-abused word, but it is difficult to describe Rye's charms without resorting to it. No wonder writers and artists have been attracted to the little town. Admirers of E. F. Benson's series of books about Mapp and Lucia (televised on the American Public Broadcasting System) will recognize the town of Tilling as Rye.

The American novelist Henry James also succumbed to Rye's charms. For 16 years (1898–1914) he lived at Lamb House ♥ ♥, a stolid brick mansion, which he called "ravishing," adding that "all the good that I hoped of the place has, in fine, properly bloomed and flourished here." The house was built in 1722 by James Lamb, a Rye mayor. During James's ownership, Edith Wharton, Rudyard Kipling, G. K. Chesterton, H. G. Wells, Joseph Conrad, and other writers visited him here. After James's death, E. F. Benson lived in the house (until 1940), and later so did the novelist Rumer Godden.

Lamb House today is a National Trust property, and when you visit, you will see James's morning room with the French windows and the Dutch tiles he installed in the fireplace. What you *won't* see is the little Georgian pavilion in the rear garden that James called his "temple of the muse." It was savaged by firebombs in World War II. James once said he would "offer the whole bristling state of Connecticut in exchange for one brick from the wall" of his Rye garden.

Rye is a delight for wandering and shopping, with many art galleries and pottery studios, handsome shops, old

---

PERILS & PITFALLS

Lamb House is leased, so only the hall and three rooms are open to the public. James's fans may be disappointed by the paucity of James memorabilia; others will admire the handsomeness of the house.

---

inns, and tearooms. One of the most charming tearooms is Fletcher's House, a former vicarage where the Elizabethan poet and playwright John Fletcher was born in 1579. The old timbered house with leaded windows is on Lion Street, down the hill from St. Mary the Virgin Church♛, where Fletcher's father was vicar. The fine old stone parish church has wood-beamed ceilings, a clock with moving figures, and stained-glass windows. Rye Museum, inside Ypres Tower in Gungarden, across from the church, displays a collection of Cinque Port mementos, toys, and local history.

Smuggling (of wool and spirits, to avoid taxes) played such a role in Rye history that in 1773, when Wesley preached in the town, he said of the locals, "They will not part from the accursed thing." In 1781 Lord Pembroke asked rhetorically, "Will Washington take America or the smugglers England first?"

On cobbled Mermaid Street is the vintage Mermaid Inn, once infamous as a hangout for the Hawkhurst smuggling gang, but now a delightful overnight or mealtime stop. Have a look at the priest's hole halfway up the chimney. The prettiest guest room is named after a notorious character, Dr. Syn, and has a secret staircase (connecting to the bar) and room behind the bookcase.

From Rye there are compelling side trips inland. North of Rye, just outside Tenterden, is Smallhythe Place, a 16th-century timbered house with leaded windows, which the actress Ellen Terry made into her country home, edged by tidy gardens and hedges. Now the Ellen Terry Museum♛, run by the National Trust, it is a petite treasure, displaying Terry's theatrical memorabilia. Down the quiet country road is the 1509 brick Church of St. John the Baptist, where Terry was buried in 1928.

Tenterden is also home to the Kent & East Sussex Railway♛, "Britain's first light railway," with a museum and old-fashioned steam trains you can ride a short distance ("4 miles in 50 minutes").

Nearby is Sissinghurst Castle♛♛♛♛, magnificent gardens created by the late Vita Sackville-West and her husband, Sir Harold Nicholson, who bought the ruined Elizabethan mansion (not really a castle) in 1930. The gardens and the way they creatively use the castle tower and other parts as backdrop are a tour de force, a must-see for serious gardeners. Nicholson said the gardens combined "the element of expectation with the element of surprise." Indeed they do. Some gardens are planted with all-white flowers, and all were created to provide some color in all seasons.

Ten miles west of Sissinghurst is Tunbridge Wells, famed in the 17th and 18th centuries as a royal spa and fashionable watering place. Today it is simply a thriving market town and shopping center for Kent. One reason for a stop is to see the Pantiles♛, an unusual tiled promenade lined with lime trees, by a spring.

PERILS & PITFALLS

Possibly the last chance to see the Pantiles. On our recent visit the area looked forlorn and neglected, and the tiles themselves seemed to be deteriorating.

Follow B2176 west to Penshurst Place♛♛♛, an imposing medieval manor in the Gothic style, whose Great Hall dates from 1340. The poet Sir Philip Sydney was born here in 1554, and the house has been in the family of the Sydneys and their descendants, the De L'Isles, since the 16th century. The furniture, portraits and tapestries are notable.

Knole, Chartwell, and Hever Castle are all in the vicinity. You will find them described in the section on Excursions from London, pages 122–135.

South of Tunbridge Wells 20 miles or so, look for Burwash, another pristine Kent village with houses of redbrick or faced with scalloped red tiles. Burwash's claim to fame is Rudyard Kipling's home, Bateman's♛♛♛, which he bought in 1902 and lived in until his death in 1936. The 17th-century ironmaster's stone house, sprouting chimneys, is located down a steep hill from the village. The furnishings are mostly Kipling's own, including Tiffany lamps, many 17th-century antiques, splendid Indian carpets, a dining room whose walls are covered with leather in a *chinois* pattern, and oriental artifacts, such as a Tibetan brass jug. The entire house, and especially the study, with his oak bed, volumes of Indian source books, and the author's favorite novels, really evoke the man. Kipling's Rolls-Royce is preserved in an outbuilding, with notations indicating that although he didn't drive, he was a madman in the car. A mill and gardens laid out by the Kiplings are part of the treat.

INSIDERS' TIPS

The redbrick oast house on the grounds is now a National Trust shop with excellent buys in woolens.

Between Burwash and Rye is Bodium Castle♛, a romantic moat-surrounded fortress (built 1385–89) that looks the way a castle should.

On A259 again, heading west to Brighton, is Hastings, scene of the best-known battle in English history. Remains—walls and gatehouse—of Britain's first Norman castle still exist. In the Town Hall is the Hastings Embroidery♛♛, a commemorative handwork on 27 panels that highlights 81 scenes from English history.

As you head west toward Brighton, you might stop at the adjoining villages of Westham and Pevensey to see the very first church the Normans built after their 1066 landing nearby. Behind St. Mary the Virgin's♛♛ stout gray stone walls is a fine 15th-century wooden Gothic rood. It is a short walk from the church to the ruins of Pevensey Castle♛, which was a Roman fortress, for some splendid views. A few miles farther, just off the main road, is Alfriston♛♛, a dream village on Cuckmere River, with a beauty of an old market cross, half-timbered houses, and an old smugglers' inn.

Passing through Lewes, you might pause to inspect the town's American Revolution connections: Tom Paine lived

---

INSIDERS' TIPS

Charleston Farm, Vanessa Bell's country retreat for the "Bloomsbury Group" that included her sister Virginia Woolf, Duncan Grant, Lytton Strachey, and John Maynard Keynes, among others, is now open to visitors on a limited basis. Here the Omega Workshop decorative arts movement leaders applied their Post-Impressionist whims and fancies to every paintable surface, nook, cranny, and garden corner. Open by prearrangement. Contact Charleston Farmhouse, Firle near Lewes; tel. (032) 183-265. It is about 3 miles south of Glyndebourne and 4 miles east of Lewes in the East Sussex Downs.

in the house that is now a restaurant (Bull House), and met with fellow radicals at the White Horse Inn, both on High Street. Lewes is also known for its Cluniac Priory ruins ♛, Norman Keep ♛, and Anne of Cleves House ♛, the last being Henry VIII's divorce settlement to Anne. She never lived here. The house is now a folk museum, with Victorian dress, costumes, furniture, pottery, and toys.

BRIGHTON

And so westward to Brighton, Britain's premier seaside resort, a favorite with royalty and observers of royalty for more than 200 years. But Brighton isn't merely a nostalgia trip. True, the monumental old Victorian "wedding cake" hotels, Regency terraces, and old-fashioned pier evoke summers past, but Brighton *still* attracts day-trippers, weekenders, and vacationers with its lively shopping, antique markets, art shows, and theater (pre-London tryouts).

In Brighton the major magnet is the Royal Pavilion ♛ ♛ ♛ ♛, an architectural fantasy created in 1815 by architect John Nash for the Prince of Wales, later King George IV. With its massive Indian gate and fairy-tale turrets, this dream dwelling evokes the spirit of Empire. Inside, India gives way to China, with hall after grandiose hall a fantasy of elongated oriental lanterns, scroll paintings, lacquerware, and huge Chinese vases. George IV reportedly cried for joy when the pavilion was first unveiled in all its oriental splendor.

The Banqueting Room ♛ ♛ ♛ ♛ ♛ is extraordinary. A huge, lotus-shaped crystal chandelier is "held" by an enormous gilded winged dragon suspended from a 45-foot-high domed ceiling on which is painted a plantain tree with three-dimensional copper leaves. An elongated table (seating 40 or so) is set with Royal Derby porcelain and sparkling crystal. Around the room are ornate rosewood sideboards, ornamented with decorative gilded dragons, displaying elaborate silver candelabras, trays, and bowls. Calling it regal is an understatement. Regal no, Imperial yes.

A self-conducted tour leads you to the enormous, beautifully restored kitchen (one of 14 in the pavilion), lined with gleaming copper pots. Replicas of whole lambs, skinned and dressed, are hung by the copper-hooded fireplace. On tables, replicas of hares, pheasants, and quail are being readied, along with rolls, vegetables, and other foodstuffs, as if for a kingly feast that very night. The realism of the display extends even to a "rat" on the floor.

A block from the Royal Pavilion is the Brighton Art Gallery and Museum ♛ ♛, housed in a cluster of buildings designed as stables and a riding house for the Prince Regent in 1808. Numerous unrelated exhibits give a motley first impression. But in fact, each exhibit is extremely well displayed, with an informed presentation that piques your interest. A 20th-century design collection contains first-rate examples of Art Nouveau and Art Deco.

The ethnology collection is small but has choice examples from Africa, Ceylon, Burma, New Guinea, and Northwest and Southwest American Indians. There is an exhibit of old and rare musical instruments, furniture, and paintings (including works by William Blake, Edward Lear, Max Ernst, and Salvador Dali).

The exhibits range all over the lot, from one on the history of tea, to fashion ("Why Do We Wear Clothes?") and "The China Trade 1600–1860." Their only link is highly intelligent presentation.

Other Brighton lures include the Preston Manor Museum ♛ ♛, Preston Park, which has an exemplary English furniture and silver collection, and the Booth Museum of Natural History ♛ ♛, opposite Dyke Park Road, with a remarkable collection of British birds mounted in their natural habitats. Shoppers will save time for The Lanes, narrow pedestrian streets studded with trendy boutiques and antiques shops in what were once fishermen's cottages.

WEST SUSSEX

From Brighton it is only 55 miles north to London (one hour by train). An alternative, if you have time available, is to continue your coastal drive west on A27 some 30 miles to pretty little Arundel, to see Arundel Castle ♛, whose keep predates the Norman Conquest. Though ancient, the castle (seat of the Duke of Norfolk) was razed by

Roundheads in the Civil War in 1643, rebuilt in the 18th century, and added to in 1890. Inside, you will find 16th-century furnishings and paintings by Van Dyck, Reynolds, and others. Arundel's Saturday-morning antiques market is a big draw for Londoners.

West of Arundel 20 miles is Chichester, which still has its original Roman street plan, augmented now by some splendid 18th-century Georgian buildings. The Norman Cathedral♛♛♛ is rich in treasures: Romanesque stone carvings; works by modern artists Sutherland, Skelton, and others; a modern tapestry; and fine windows and nave. The Chichester Festival (May–September) attracts international visitors.

This part of West Sussex has many surprises. In Hardham, a village a mile south of Pulborough on A29 (the old Roman road to London), is a tiny, ancient Saxon church called St. Botolph♛. It has a rough-hewn wood-beamed ceiling, and walls covered with russet-and-mustard-colored frescoes. These paintings date from 1100 and are believed to be the earliest in England. Most startling, and very different from the others, are two Picasso-like depictions of Adam and Eve, after the Fall, with extended tummies that look a bit racy in church. Could someone have perpetrated a hoax? No one knows.

At Bignor Roman Villa♛♛, outside Pulborough, another surprise awaits: In the middle of nowhere are groups of vividly covered, perfectly preserved Roman mosaics and house fragments. A dolphin-like Ganymede and an eagle, as well as a shrouded female head depicting "Winter"—are part of the decorative flooring to be seen here. The mosaics were first uncovered by a farmer in 1811. Other mosaics still lie hidden under the Sussex fields, archeologists believe.

Petworth, 14 miles northwest of Pulborough, is another charming West Sussex town, with a beautiful old square, many half-timbered buildings, and Petworth House ♛♛♛♛. This magnificent, rebuilt (1688–96) manor is blessed with an enormous and important collection of furniture, sculpture, and paintings. Its pictures include works by Titian, Blake, Van Dyck, Reynolds, and a stunning room full of paintings by Turner (14 of them), who often painted while a houseguest here. The house overlooks a park landscaped by Capability Brown and also painted by Turner.

As we were saying, Britain is full of surprises.

INSIDERS' INFORMATION FOR CANTERBURY AND THE SOUTHEAST

Alfriston (East Sussex; Area Code Alfriston 0323)

Hotel

The Star ♛
High St. Tel. 870-248.
2 persons in twin, $75.
13th-century pilgrims' hospice, handy center-of-town location. 34 rooms, pub, restaurant. Classic old English hostelry of considerable charm.

Shopping

Valley Wine Cellars, The English Wine Centre, Drusillas Corner BN26 5QS. Tel. 870-532. Daytime and evening tours and tastings.

Arundel (West Sussex; Area Code Arundel 0903)

Hotel

Norfolk Arms ♛
22 High St. BN18 9AD. Tel. 882-101.
2 persons in twin, $48–67.50.
Coaching inn from 1787, central location. 35 rooms (32 private baths), 2 bars, dining room. Handy for sightseeing in this historic town.

Ashford (Kent; Area Code Ashford 0233)

Hotel

Eastwell Manor ♛ ♛ ♛ ♛
Eastwell Park, Boughton Aluph TN25 4HR. Tel. 35751.
2 persons in twin, $90–120.
Enormous manor house with character, surrounded by 62

acres of sheep-grazed greenery. 24 rooms, lounge, excellent *nouvelle* French restaurant (♛ ♛ ♛), tennis, croquet. Spacious public and private rooms, hospitable staff, welcoming atmosphere.

Restaurant

Terazza ♛
45 Church Rd. Tel. 44887.
Average dinner: $30.
Italian specialties, notable desserts.

Pub

Flying Horse, Boughton Aluph, near Eastwell Manor. Tel. 20914. Courage House, friendly, good hot lunch and dinner snacks. 4 guest rooms.

Bagshot (Surrey; Area Code Bagshot 0276)

Hotel

Pennyhill Park ♛ ♛ ♛ ♛
College Ride GU19 5ET. Tel. 71774.
2 persons in twin, $105–150.
Edwardian country house in parklike grounds. 50 rooms, bar, conservatory, restaurant, sauna, swimming pool, 9-hole golf course, riding, tennis, fishing, helipad. Luxurious setting, antiques, spacious rooms.

Battle (East Sussex; Area Code Battle 042-46)

Hotel

Netherfield Place ♛ ♛ ♛
Netherfield TN33 9PP. Tel. 4455.
2 persons in twin, $67.50–90.
Georgian manor house in parklike setting on 30 acres. 12 large, airy rooms, each decorated differently; comfortable. Restaurant, garden.

Shopping

Battle Antiques Market Halfway between Battle Abbey and the Norman Church. Tel. 3364. Open Monday through Saturday, 10 A.M.–5 P.M.

Brighton (East Sussex; Area Code 0273)

Hotel

Brighton Metropole ♛
King's Road BN1 2FU. Tel. 775432.
2 persons in twin, $90–120.
A large, well-kept seafront hotel, handily located. 333 rooms, bar, pub, restaurant, nightclub, sauna, beauty shop. Convenient up-to-date facility with only a hint of Victorian past.

Restaurants

Le Francais ♛
1 Paston Place, Kemp Town. Tel. 680-716.
Average dinner: $38.
Knowledgeably prepared, French-accented dishes, somewhat pricey.

Muang Thai
77 St. James's St. Tel. 605-223.
Average dinner: $9–15.
Nice try. Attractive oriental setting. More Thai spicing needed.

Shopping

Churchill Square, Branches of Marks & Spencer and other London stores.

The Lanes, Full of antiques shops, jewelers, boutiques.

Regent Arcade, Jewelry stores and fashion boutiques.

Market

Upper Gardner Street, Saturday-morning flea market.

Theaters

Dome, 29 New Rd. Tel. 682-127. Concerts (rock, jazz, other).

Theatre Royal, New Rd. Tel. 28488. Professional repertory productions.

Burwash (Kent; Area Code 0435)

Pub

Bell Inn, High St. TN19 7EH. Tel. 882-304. Cosy oak-beamed pub, serving real ale, simple meals. 4 guest rooms.

Byworth (West Sussex; Area Code Petworth 0798)

Pub

Black Horse♛ Near Petworth. Tel. 42424. Charming vintage pub, known for good English food and real ale. Upstairs dining room, beamed ceilings, garden overlooking stream.

Canterbury (Kent; Area Code Canterbury 0227)

Hotels

County♛ ♛
High St. CT1 2RX. Tel. 66266.
2 persons in twin, $73–90.
Atmospheric town-center hotel, 5 minutes from cathedral. 74 rooms, Tudor bar, lounge, restaurant, coffee shop. Refurbished rooms well equipped, some four-posters, quiet charm.

Chaucer♛
Ivy Lane CT1 1TT. Tel. 464427.
2 persons in twin, $67.50–120.
Large, comfortable, Regency-style hotel on busy street. 45 rooms, bar/lounge, restaurant. Spacious public areas, handy for sightseeing.

Restaurants

Restaurant Seventy Four♛ ♛ ♛
74 Wincheap. Tel. 67411.
Average dinner: $25.
The place where Kent gourmets head for special-occasion dining; *nouvelle cuisine.* Lodged in a 16th-century wine merchant's house at the town's edge.

Queen Elizabeth's Guest Chamber♛
44 High St. Tel. 64080.
Good choice for moderately priced, wholesome English lunches, afternoon teas. Upstairs in half-timbered building. Historic spot where Elizabeth I turned down the Duke of Alençon's proposal.

Tuo e Mio♛
16 The Borough. Tel. 61471.
Average dinner: $15–25.

Handsome decor, central location, homemade pasta, reliable Italian dishes.

Waterfields♛

5a Best Lane. Tel. 450276.

Average dinner: $15.

Scenic city-center locale on River Stour; emphasis on sophisticated English fare, decent prices.

Pub

Olive Branch, Buttermarket. Good pub lunches, across from cathedral gate.

Chilham (Kent; Area Code Chilham 022-776)

Hotel

Woolpack Inn♛

High St. CT4 8DL. Tel. 730-208.

2 persons in twin, $51–66.

Village inn over 400 years old. 13 rooms, 11 with private baths, bar, restaurant. Oak beams, huge inglenook fireplace, atmospheric locale in picture-pretty village.

Pub

White Horse♛, The Square. Tel. 355. Good lunch or snack choice, homemade dishes, including ice cream. Tiny rooms with fire, beer garden in rear.

East Grinstead (West Sussex; Area Code Sharpthorne 0342)

Hotel

Gravetye Manor♛ ♛ ♛ ♛ ♛

West Hoathly RH19 4LJ. Tel. 810-567.

2 persons in twin, $80–100.

Ivy-covered country house in pastoral wood-and-garden setting. 14 rooms, bar, lounges, elegant restaurant (♛ ♛ ♛ ♛), croquet, fishing, gorgeous gardens. Each room different, graced with antiques, some with Tudor fireplaces, handsome public rooms, superb service, every amenity.

Eastbourne (East Sussex; Area Code Eastbourne 0323)

Hotel

Grand ♕ ♕ ♕
King Edward's Parade BN21 4EQ. Tel. 22611.
2 persons in twin, $90–150.
Massive seafront hotel along waterfront. 178 rooms, bars, restaurant, indoor and outdoor swimming pools, sauna, solarium, gym, beauty shop, game rooms. Traditional all-in-one vacation hotel, with modern touches and comforts.

Edenbridge (Kent; Area Code Edenbridge 0732)

Pub

King Henry VIII Inn, Hever. Tel. 862-457. Unpretentious pub across from Hever Castle, a handy lunch spot. Wood fire, Tudor lounge, few guest rooms ($50 for 2), clean and neat, cheerful staff.

Egham (Surrey; Area Code Egham 0784)

Hotel

Great Fosters ♕ ♕
Stroude Rd. TW20 9UR. Tel. 33822.
2 persons in twin, $67.50–120.
Magnificent moated Tudor building (former royal hunting lodge) in "stage set" formal gardens. 44 rooms, bar, restaurant, swimming pool, tennis, sauna. Antiques, mullioned windows, tapestries create a special sense of grandeur.

Haslemere (Surrey; Area Code Haslemere 0428)

Hotel

Lythe Hill ♕ ♕
Petworth Road GU27 3BQ. Tel. 51251.
2 persons in twin, $67.50–120.
Rambling, timbered farmhouse in 14 acres of Surrey hills woodland. 38 rooms, bar, restaurant, tennis, sauna, cro-

quiet, helipad. Exposed beams, leaded windows, antiques give character to this fine old house.

Restaurant

Morels ♛ ♛
25 Lower St. Tel. 51462.
Average dinner: $18.
French style, unusual dishes, in pretty French country setting.

Mersham (Kent; Area Code Aldington 023372)

Hotel

Stone Green Hall ♛ ♛
Near Ashford TN25 7HE. Tel. 418.
2 persons in twin, $48–67.50.
Victorian redbrick house tucked into Kent countryside. 3 rooms, lounge, first-rate restaurant (♛ ♛), patio, tennis. Best known for well-prepared, eclectically international menu (don't miss the local lamb). Reasonable.

New Milton (Hampshire; Area Code Highcliffe 04252)

Hotel

Chewton Glen ♛ ♛ ♛ ♛ ♛
New Milton BH25 6QS. Tel. 5341.
2 persons in twin, $120–150.
Georgian manor house nestled into 30 parklike acres in New Forest, about 8 miles east of Bournemouth. 44 rooms, bar, *Marryat Room* restaurant (♛ ♛ ♛), outstanding wine list, swimming pool, tennis, croquet, library, helipad. Exquisite furnishings throughout, fresh flowers, flawless service, friendly staff. French restaurant lives up to the same luxurious standards as the hotel.

Richmond (Surrey; Area Code 01)

Restaurants

Lichfield's ♛ ♛ ♛
13 Lichfield Terr., Sheen Rd. Tel. 940-4343.
Average dinner: $25–44.

Market-fresh ingredients, a knowing way with fish, unusual combinations, super sauces, and luscious desserts give this stylish restaurant a special pizzazz.

The Original Maids of Honour ♛
288–90 Kew Road, Kew Gardens. Tel. 940-2752.
Delightful for afternoon teas.

Rye (East Sussex; Area Code Rye 0797)

Hotels

Mermaid Inn ♛ ♛ ♛
Mermaid St. TN31 7EY. Tel. 223065.
2 persons in twin, $67.50–90.
Historic timbered Tudor inn, *rebuilt* in 1420, on cobbled side street. 30 rooms, 21 with bath; bar, restaurant. Ghosts, smugglers, beamed ceilings, linenfold paneled dining room, priest's hiding hole, secret staircase, all give unique character to this, one of our favorite inns.

Hope Anchor Inn ♛
Watchbell St. Tel. 2216.
2 persons in twin, $60–75.
15 rooms, bar, restaurant. Cozy rooms, folksy ambience, honest English cooking, little-known "sleeper."

Restaurant

Simmons ♛
68 The Mint. Tel. 222-026.
Average dinner: $19–28.
Handsome 500-year-old house sets the stage for capable renderings of modish English and French dishes, using finest local ingredients.

Tea Shops

Fletcher's House, Lion St. Timbered 15th-century house where playwright John Fletcher was born, now serves delicious teas and light lunches.

Simon the Pieman, Lion St. 16th-century house, excellent for afternoon teas.

Shopping

Iden Pottery, Conduit St. Hand-thrown bowls, dinnerware.

Kurrein Gallery, 7 Lion St. Original handicrafts, fine pottery, and contemporary jewelry.

Monastery Pottery, Conduit St. Workshop for quality hand-made pottery.

Rye Pottery, Ferry Road. Workshop and shop. Interesting ceramics.

Storrington (West Sussex; Area Code Storrington 090-66)

Hotel
Little Thakeham♛ ♛
Merrywood Lane RH20 3HE. Tel. 4416.
2 persons in twin, $90–150.
Country house designed by Sir Edwin Lutyens, set amidst vivid gardens. 10 rooms, bar, esteemed restaurant, swimming pool, tennis. Splendid public rooms, antiques, and ample guest rooms contribute to sumptuous air.

Restaurant
Manleys♛ ♛ ♛
Manleys Hill. Tel. 2331.
Average dinner: $33–39.
Chef/owner Karl Loderer's standards are high, evidenced in a versatile Austrian-accented menu, pristine accoutrements, and punctilious service.

Tunbridge Wells (Kent; Area Code Tunbridge Wells 0892)

Hotel
Spa♛ ♛
Mount Ephraim TN4 8XJ. Tel. 20331.
2 persons in twin, range $67.50–120.
Large, imposing country mansion at town's edge. 69 rooms, bar, restaurant, gym, sauna, swimming pool, solarium, health and beauty salon, tennis, croquet. Comfortable, all-purpose resort hotel, large rooms, many services.

Restaurant
Thackeray's House♛
85 London Road TN1 1EA. Tel. 37558.

Average dinner: $22–30.
Chic setting with creative French food to match.

Pub

George & Dragon ♛, Speldhurst. Tel. (089-286) 3125. Charming 13th-century oak furnishings, tasty pub grub and choice of real ale, also a restaurant. Good family choice.

Uckfield (East Sussex; Area Code 0825)

Hotel

Horsted Place (too new to be reviewed)
Little Horsted TN22 5TS. Tel. 75581.
2 persons in twin, $187.50–338.
Magnificent Victorian-Tudor mansion renovated (1986) as Kent country-house hotel. 18 suites, king-size beds, bar, restaurant, tennis, indoor swimming pool, gardens. Former home of Lord Nevill, Prince Philip's treasurer. Promise of elegance.

Woodbridge (Suffolk; Area Code Woodbridge 039-43)

Hotel

Seckford Hall ♛
Off A12, Woodbridge IP13 6NU. Tel. 5678.
2 persons in twin, $78–84.
Imposing Tudor brick house in serene lake and park setting. 24 rooms, bar, restaurant, fishing. Garish decorating and some small rooms don't impair the beauty of Sir Thomas Seckford's 16th-century manor. Modern amenities.

Wye (Kent; Area Code Wye 0233)

Restaurant

Wife of Bath ♛
4 Upper Bridge St. Tel. 812-540.
Average dinner: $20–25.
Competent French country cooking in no-frills setting.

CAMBRIDGE, THE EAST, AND LINCOLN

Among the least tourist-visited of any region in England is East Anglia. Yet this area northeast of London has an abundance of treats—in museums, stately homes, churches, unspoiled villages and pastoral landscapes.

Our suggestion, if you have just one day, is to spend it at Cambridge. The university town has far more than a day's worth of treasures. With a week to spare, the visitor with a car can circle east of Cambridge into East Anglia, visiting Ipswich, then north to Norwich, west to King's Lynn, Peterborough, and Stamford. A side trip north to Lincoln can be added if there is time.

From London, head north 37 miles on the M11. Turn off at exit 9 to Saffron Walden, a remarkable medieval village of 15th–16th-century timbered houses and unusual parget-ted (relief wall designs) buildings, on a prehistoric site settled in turn by Britons, Saxons, and Normans. Until 1790, saffron crocuses were big business here, used for dye, medicine, and food coloring, hence the town's name. Note the 200-foot-long Church of St. Mary the Virgin ♛ (Cromwell's forces used it as a club room), which has the tomb of Henry VIII's chancellor, Lord Audley.

Just west of town one mile on A11 is Audley End House ♛ ♛, a monumental 1616 manor house. James I reportedly called it too large for a king, but said "it might just do" for a Lord Treasurer. That's who built it—Sir Thomas Howard. Sir John Vanbrugh, no slouch at building monuments, recommended eliminating two-thirds of it. Half was demolished in the 18th century, and the current mansion features a Jacobean Great Hall, along with rooms decorated by Robert Adam.

Back on the M11, it is 23 miles north to Cambridge ♛ ♛ ♛ ♛ ♛, the small city (100,700) on the River Cam with one of Britain's (and Europe's) most extraordinary concentrations of superb architecture and the arts.

Beautiful, compact, and nonindustrial, Cambridge, in short, is the classic ivory-towered college town. The 31 colleges that constitute the famed university form the major attractions for visitors.

INSIDERS' TIPS

Two-hour tours with licensed guides for £1.75 ($2.63) meet at the Tourist Information Office on Wheeler Street, across from the Guildhall.

If time is tight, these are the colleges essential to see: King's, Queens', Trinity, Magdalene, St. John's, Jesus. All are within an easy walk of one another.

INSIDERS' TIPS

For an unforgettable one-hour feast for eye and spirit, rent a punt—a flat-bottomed boat that you pole—at the quayside by the Magdalene Street bridge, and glide on the shallow Cam along the campus area, with St. John's, Trinity, Clare, King's, and St. Catherine's colleges in succession on one side and the lawns, gardens, willow-shaded fields, and "Backs" (parkland) on the other. Learn *how* to punt before you shove off, however!

The Fitzwilliam Museum ♛ ♛ ♛ ♛, one of Britain's finest, is on Trumpington Street, a good starting place for a walking tour. It was founded in 1816 by the seventh Viscount of Merion, a 1764 Cambridge graduate, with his art collection of 144 paintings, Rembrandt etchings, medieval illuminated manuscripts, and a bequest of £100,000. That was just the beginning. The collection has expanded greatly since.

On show in the Lower Galleries are examples of Assyrian and Egyptian, Greek and Roman sculptures and reliefs, Oriental ceramics, European armor, porcelains and glassware, and medieval manuscripts and letters. The painting collection in the Upper Galleries includes Titian's famed *Tarquin and Lucretia*, Veronese's *Hermes, Herse, and Aglauros*, Italian paintings from the 13th century onward, and works by Corot, Dufy, Monet, Renoir, Lorrain, Seurat (a study for *La Grande Jatte*), Vuillard, Matisse, Rouault, Modigliani, and Picasso. There are British works by Hogarth ("Before" and "After" a seduction), Augustus

John, Lord Leighton, Constable, Turner, the sculptor Jacob Epstein, and others.

PERILS & PITFALLS

Most of the Upper Galleries section is open only in the afternoon, the Lower Galleries in the mornings. Plan accordingly.

North on Trumpington, you come first to Peterhouse ♛ ♛ ♛, Cambridge's oldest college. Though founded in 1284 by the Bishop of Ely, most of the buildings are from much later. The chapel ♛ ♛ ♛ dates from 1632 and was designed by Christopher Wren's uncle, Matthew. Devotees of Pre-Raphaelite art will find in the 15th-century hall ♛ ♛ fireplace tiles by William Morris and stained glass by Burne-Jones and Madox Brown.

A few yards farther along on Trumpington is Pembroke College ♛ ♛ ♛, founded in 1347. Its 1666 chapel ♛ ♛ ♛ is believed (by Cantabrigians) to be Christopher Wren's first architectural work (Oxonians insist their Sheldonian Theatre was first). See also the fine 1690 plaster ceiling in the Old Library (the original old chapel). Pembroke's gardens are especially beautiful.

At the next street intersection is St. Benet's Church ♛, whose Anglo-Saxon tower is perhaps Cambridge's oldest structure.

Next on Trumpington is Corpus Christi College ♛ ♛, whose old courtyard (oldest college quad in England) dates from 1352, but has weathered badly. The medieval hall displays paintings by Romney, Poussin, Reynolds, and Kneller. Christopher Marlowe studied at Corpus Christi. That may be his portrait in the hall, but nobody is certain.

Cross Trumpington to Silver Street and Queens' College ♛ ♛ ♛, one of the most delightful. Founded in 1448 by Margaret of Anjou, wife of Henry VI, and in 1465 by Elizabeth Woodville, wife of Edward IV, it has fine brick quadrangles and a timbered 16th-century President's Gallery ♛ ♛ ♛.

In Queens' Old Court, look for an extraordinary pre-1642 "sundial" that not only tells time by sun or moonlight, but gives the date, time of sunrise and sunset, and zodiacal sign. Erasmus lived at Queens' in 1511, and his opinion of the local beer was such that he imported his own wine. You won't find such criticism today.

From Queens' Lane to King's Lane you reach King's Parade (really Trumpington with a name change) and one of the peerless jewels of English architecture—King's College Chapel♛♛♛♛♛ in King's College. It bears comparison with the Sainte Chapelle in Paris, which inspired it.

The Chapel, whose foundation was laid in 1446 by Henry VI, was completed by Henry VIII in 1515. The carved wooden roodscreen separating nave and choir bears the arms and initials of Henry VIII and Anne Boleyn, thereby dating the work almost precisely. The altarpiece♛♛♛ is a glowing, almost fiery Rubens, *The Adoration of the Magi.* Also outstanding is the Gothic fan vaulting. Exquisite stained-glass windows♛♛♛♛ are, along with York Minster's, the only medieval ones in Britain to survive intact.

INSIDERS' TIPS

A Sunday concert in the Chapel is a memorable experience. Even more so is Christmas Eve, when the traditional "Nine Lessons and Carols" are sung. But this event is so popular you have to line up for admission nearly 24 hours ahead of time.

The 1722 Senate House♛♛♛, designed by James Gibbs (who designed London's St. Martin-in-the-Fields), is on the corner of King's Parade. This is where University degrees are conferred.

Across the street is the parish church, Great St. Mary's♛♛♛, built in the 15th century in Gothic Perpendicular style.

Behind the Senate House is Clare College♛♛, founded by the widowed Elizabeth de Clare in 1338. The original buildings are long gone, and the quadrangle you see dates from 1638 to 1715. The bridge behind it is Cambridge's oldest (and is an excellent vantage point for a view of the Backs), but the art at Clare is among the University's newest. Note the early Henry Moore *Unknown Warrior* in the grounds of Clare's new buildings.

Continue to Trinity College♛♛♛, Cambridge's largest. It was formed in 1546 when Henry VIII consolidated

the King's Hall (founded by Edward II in 1317) and
Michaelhouse (a religious foundation of 1323) into a single
institution. Fittingly, Henry's statue and arms decorate
the impressive Great Gate. In Trinity's library ♛ ♛, a
sober, classical Christopher Wren design, are carvings by
Grinling Gibbons, a statue of former student Lord Byron
writing *Childe Harold* (Westminster Abbey rejected the
statue a century ago because of the poet's scandalous life),
and the glorious 1280 *Trinity Apocalypse* illuminated
manuscript. Sir Isaac Newton and, more recently, Prince
Charles, studied here.

St. John's College ♛ ♛ ♛ adjoins Trinity and was
founded in 1511 by Henry VIII's grandmother, Lady Margaret Beaufort. Notice above the magnificent ornamental
gateway ♛ ♛ ♛ a statue of St. John and two yales
(fabulous horned beasts) holding the Beaufort arms. The
College has three redbrick courtyards and a splendid 17th-
century library, but most visitors remember best its lovely
gardens and graceful bridge across the Cam, modeled after
its Venetian forerunner, the Bridge of Sighs. The bridge
connects St. John's older part with New Court and is seen
at its best from the Wren bridge nearby.

Just north of the Cam is Magdalene (pronounced *maudlin*) College ♛ ♛ ♛, started in 1542 on the site of a 15th-
century Benedictine hostel. Magdalene was the alma
mater of Samuel Pepys, who bestowed on it his famous
diaries and 3,000 books in a library he designed for them.
(It's in the second court.)

Cambridge has many unusual museums. Across the
street from Magadalene is the Folk Museum ♛ at Northampton and Castle streets, which houses a good visual
presentation of Cantabrigian life through the ages.

INSIDERS' TIPS

Key Cambridge events: May Week activities the last of May
and first week in June, with plays, pranks, punting, and the
annual Footlights Revue (which launched many of today's
international stars) at the Art Theatre; City Festival (the last
two weeks in July), with concerts, organ recitals, theater
and dance in college buildings, singing on the river, and
more.

Across Northampton is Kettle's Yard, which may sound like a pub, but is actually an intriguing contemporary art museum, collected and displayed by J. S. Ede in 4 slum buildings he renovated in the 1950s for the purpose. Here you will find works by the British artists Ben Nicholson, Christopher Wood, Alfred Wallis, and David Jones.

Both Magdalene and Northampton streets are graced by some of the oldest and handsomest two- and three-story half-timbered houses in Cambridge.

Jesus College♛♛, on Jesus Lane, was founded in 1496. Note especially its cloister court, the chapel with ceiling decorations by William Morris, and the windows by Morris, Madox Brown, and Burne-Jones.

Emmanuel College♛♛♛ on St. Andrews Street may hold special interest for Americans. The college was founded in 1584 on the remains of a Dominican abbey. It became a center of radical Protestantism and educated many Puritans, some of whom settled in the Massachusetts Bay Colony. John Harvard, founder of the school in that *other* Cambridge, was educated here. Look for Christopher Wren's chapel♛♛ of 1677.

OUTSIDE THE COLLEGES

Pub life in Cambridge is lively. Note especially the Eagle Hotel, Benet Street. Besides being the last coaching inn in town, it has unique graffiti on the ceiling, mementos of World War II days, when American, British, and Canadian airmen based nearby wrote their names with candle smoke. The proprietor vowed he would never repaint. He hasn't yet.

A delightful walk, bicycle ride, short drive, or punt south of Cambridge brings you to Grantchester, a tiny village of cottages with timber-and-stucco walls and ornately thatched roofs that hark back to medieval times. On the road as you come into the village is the Old Vicarage, behind a brick wall. The poet Rupert Brooke, who died in World War I, boarded here during his Cambridge days. The novelist Jeffrey Archer lives in the house today.

Cambridge-area airfields played an important role in both World Wars, especially in the Battle of Britain. The

American 8th Air Force was stationed here in World War II. Military aviation buffs can visit the Imperial War Museum at Duxford, just 9 miles southwest of Cambridge on A505. On tranquil Sunday afternoons, the historic airplanes are exercised in the sky.

Also nearby at Madingly, 4 miles northwest of Cambridge on A1303, is the American Military Cemetery where 3,800 World War II veterans are buried. The chapel carries a large mural of the war zone.

ELY

Ely, one of Europe's most majestic cathedrals 👑 👑 👑 👑, is 12 miles north of Cambridge. Ely, an ancient, eel-rich island, is now high, dry, and eel-less. Its Norman cathedral, begun about 1090, has an unusual octagonal tower that beckons for miles across the surrounding countryside. The tower, a 14th-century structure made with 4 stout 63-foot oak columns, replaced one that had collapsed.

Inside the cathedral, note the carved 16th-century chantry chapels and 14th-century choir stalls and tombs. In the north triforium there is a stained-glass museum (much of it Victorian), with some panels by Burne-Jones, and a splendid view of the nave.

The vicarage (1636–47) of St. Mary's Church (where Cromwell and his family lived for a time) is behind the 15th-century Bishop's Palace.

Eight miles southwest of Cambridge on the A603 is Wimpole Hall and Park 👑 👑 👑 👑, which the National Trust calls "the most spectacular mansion in Cambridgeshire." The 350-acre park, dotted with a Chinese bridge, folly, and lake, shows off 17th–18th-century Wimpole Hall to perfection. The house was designed by the cream of Britain's architects (James Gibbs, Henry Flit-

PERILS & PITFALLS

Like many of Britain's churches, Ely Cathedral is strapped for money for upkeep, an understandable plight. Its solution is to rent interior space to trade shows, a disconcerting practice, for tacky booths set up in aisles detract from the cathedral's sweeping architectural grandeur. There must be another way.

croft, and Sir John Soane) and landscape architects (Humphrey Repton, Capability Brown, and Charles Bridgeman), and its interior features palatial staterooms. Wimpole Home Farm nearby consists of thatched 18th-century buildings and a great barn (150 feet long) housing a museum of farm implements.

BURY ST. EDMUNDS

Push on from Cambridge, then, into East Anglia. It's 26 miles east on A45 to Bury St. Edmunds, where King Edmund was brutally slain and beheaded by Danish raiders in 820. Miracles attributed to the dead king caused his canonization and reburial at the abbey. A plaque at the abbey ruins reminds us that in 1214, 25 of King John's barons swore on St. Edmund's high altar (the excavated spot is marked in the abbey ruins) to force the infamous king to sign the Magna Carta. All 25 names are listed. Ironically, most of their titles are now extinct.

Little remains of the medieval abbey today (part of the nave and transept of the abbey church have been incorporated into the town park), but it was once one of England's richest monasteries. Its monks in the 12th century produced exquisite illuminated manuscripts that are treasured today in major museums.

On Chequer Square you'll see a remarkably pure Norman 12th-century gateway tower ♛ ♛ ♛ that was once the abbey entrance, but is now the belfry of the Cathedral of St. James.

Note also the powerful Great Gatehouse of 1380 ♛ ♛ on Angel Hill. In the Borough Museum, lodged in two Norman houses (1140–90) called Moyses Hall that face Butter Market, the prize is a large Bronze Age hoard found in 1959. In the 15th-century Church of St. Mary ♛ ♛, which has a unique nave roof festooned with angels, Mary, Henry VIII's sister, is buried.

Bury has Dickens associations. At the Victorian Angel Hotel, you can see his room (No. 15). The columned house next door to the hotel is where France's Louis Philippe lived during his Bury stay. Note also the small Theatre Royal, the last existing Regency theater outside London (1819).

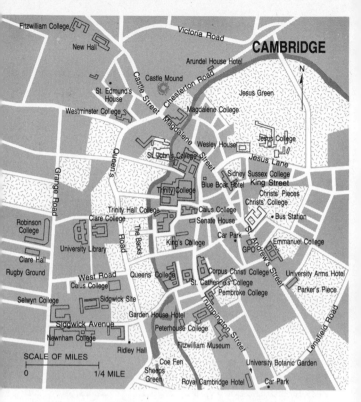

Ipswich, the major city of Suffolk, is 26 miles farther southeast on the A45, past flat, agricultural country like the Netherlands, reclaimed from the waters with dikes and water controls. (In fact, Dutch engineers supervised the work in the 17th century.)

If you take the A604 from Cambridge to Ipswich, you'll pass through several of East Anglia's prettiest villages. In Clare ♛ ♛, on the River Stour, are many pargetted houses, including a 15th-century priest's house and the Nethergate. In Cavendish ♛ ♛, notice the multicolored houses near the church.

East Anglia is a major wine-producing area of Britain. If you want to visit a winery, Cavendish Manor Vineyards, near Cavendish, are open all year at a small admission fee.

Long Melford ♛ ♛ ♛ (the ford by the mill) is a once-wealthy wool town whose wide High Street is built over the old Roman road. Its most imposing building is Melford Hall ♛ ♛ ♛, a turreted high-Tudor brick mansion where Queen Elizabeth was entertained in 1578. There are rich Regency interiors and priceless Chinese porcelain jardinieres and ivories—booty of a Spanish galleon captured by the house's owner, Captain Sir Hyde Parker, in 1762.

The Elizabethan Kentwell Hall ♛ ♛, at the other end of the village, has a grand lime tree avenue leading up to its moat and symmetrical redbrick building. Another Long Melford treasure is the Perpendicular Holy Trinity Church ♛ ♛, considered Suffolk's finest.

Gainsborough's birthplace in next-door Sudbury can be visited—it is filled with his works. Flatford Mill, where Constable's father was the miller, is a mile from the village on the River Stour. The Constable house is long gone, but you can see Willie Lott's Cottage, much as it was when Constable painted it.

LAVENHAM

Take a slight detour to our favorite East Anglian village, Lavenham ♛ ♛ ♛, pure Tudor in its tiny alleys and richly carved timbered and pargetted cottages. On the Market Place is the Guildhall ♛ ♛ ♛, one of England's finest. (Note the likeness of Lord de Vere, the Guild's founder, carved into the cornerpost.) Built in the 1520s, the Guildhall served subsequently as prison, workhouse, and storehouse, and is now a museum of weaving and the wool industry. The Old Swan Hotel incorporates the old Wool Hall; and on Shilling Street is the house where Jane Taylor looked up and wrote "Twinkle, twinkle, little star." (Store it away for trivia games.)

Lavenham's Church of St. Peter and St. Paul ♛ ♛ (1480–1530), is outstanding Perpendicular, with fine chantries, carved misericords, a 14th-century roodscreen, and a 140-foot tower (for superb views of the countryside).

IPSWICH

Ipswich is Suffolk's major city. Its major attraction is Christchurch Manor ♛ ♛ ♛, the town's free museum of art and local history, set in a pleasant park. Among the Manor's many treasures are superb 16th-century carved-oak Tudor rooms and furniture, a brick-walled kitchen and servants' hall, seven splendid Constable and two Gainsborough paintings, fine china, and decorative arts. Australian visitors will be surprised to see a portrait of 17-year-old Margaret Catchpole, who ended up in an Aussie penal colony for stealing her employer's horse.

Walk over to Buttermarket Street to see the Ancient House♛♛♛, whose extraordinarily sumptuous pargetting features Atlas and allegorical scenes. Hatchard's bookshop is installed inside.

Little Woodbridge, 4 miles east of Ipswich, has attractive Tudor and Georgian houses from the 15th to 18th centuries, but its outstanding monument is the 1575 Dutch-style Shire Hall♛ by Thomas Seckford. (Trivia Department: It was the sale here of gaudy souvenirs on St. Audry's Day that brought the word *tawdry* into the language.)

Walk along New and Cumberland streets and the Thoroughfare for best views, peek in at the Post Office's Jacobean ceilings, fireplaces, and staircase, and stop in the Bell Inn to see the old lever weighing machine, one of the few remaining in England. On the shore of the River Deben, where Viking invaders once landed, is the 18th-century Tide Mill and yacht harbor. Within sight of the Mill across the river is Sutton Hoo, where in 1939 an Anglo-Saxon burial ship was excavated. (Its treasures are in the British Museum.)

Northeast of Ipswich 15 miles is Framlingham, a village whose moated castle (now a ruin) dates from 1190. It was from here, where she lived in 1553, that Mary Queen of Scots pressed her claim to the English throne. You will enjoy the pargetting on Framlingham's 17th-century Ancient House and the almshouses of 1654 and 1703, but your main objective should be the Church of St. Michael♛♛♛. It was rebuilt in the 15th century. The roof of its nave and the 16th-century tombs of the Dukes of Richmond and Norfolk are especially beautiful.

As you drive north through Norfolk, you'll notice that thatched cottages, broad vistas, and open fields laced with lazy streams typify the area. Rich and fertile today, Norfolk was characterized in 1776 by the Earl of Leicester (who had a 40,000-acre estate there) as a place where "two rabbits might often be seen fighting for one blade of grass."

NORWICH

Norfolk's leading city, Norwich, is a scant 30 miles north of Ipswich on the A140. The city has many attractions, but art lovers will make a special trip for one reason above all: the Sainsbury Centre for Visual Arts ♛ ♛ ♛ ♛ at the University of East Anglia.

Don't be deterred by the exterior, a gleaming stainless-steel 1978 building that has all the appeal of an airport hangar. Inside is a world-class gallery whose outstanding exhibition techniques and spaciousness set off excellent special shows and a superb permanent collection.

What makes the permanent collection such a joy is the way in which primitive sculptures are juxtaposed with modern paintings. An elongated Modigliani portrait shares space with an African mask, causing comparisons. Among hundreds of high-quality sculptures are works from Melanesia, Polynesia, Asia, Africa, the Cyclades, Cambodia, Egypt, Europe, and the Americas. What the museum calls "tribal art" is always extraordinary, especially from Africa, the Pacific, and the Americas. Giacometti and Henry Moore rate special galleries, and there are continuing additions to the 20th-century collection, which already has fine examples by Bacon, Arp, Degas, Epstein, Modigliani, and Picasso, among many, many others.

Up a circular staircase, a mezzanine gallery displays Tiffany and other Art Nouveau objects and Lalique jewelry. All in all, this is a rare collection, imaginatively displayed.

Norwich's largely Norman Holy Trinity Cathedral ♛ ♛ ♛ dates from 1096 and is reminiscent of Salisbury Cathedral in form. It suffered extensive destruction from the Puritans, and was repaired in 1660. The vault bosses tell the story of the Crucifixion (bring your binoculars). Also notable are a Norman painted vaulting near the screen in the south aisle, misericord carvings, an 1100 stone effigy of Bishop Losinga, and England's only double-decker cloisters with fine carved stonework.

Much of old Norwich is clustered near the Cathedral, within the old city walls. Elm Hill ♛ is a restored, cobbled medieval street, illuminated at night by lanternlight. The city is rich in medieval churches (36 of them), of which the choicest might be St. Peter Mancroft (1430), the Church of

St. Julian, St. Gregory's Pottergate, and St. Peter Permountergate.

Northwest from Norwich, near the village of Fakenham, is a remarkable 18th-century English palace, the Palladian Houghton Hall ♛ ♛ ♛. It was designed by James Gibbs for Robert Walpole, First Lord of the Treasury to both King George I and II.

Practically untouched for 250 years, Houghton gives—inside and out—a marvelous view of coordinated design and furnishings in the finest taste and sensibility of that era. (Walpole was an art lover who assembled in 20 years the masterpieces that were sold by his impecunious grandson to Catherine the Great, and formed the core of the Hermitage's great collection.)

About 20 miles west on A148 is King's Lynn, a busy market town, where in 1215 King John feasted and was lavishly entertained. He died soon after "from a surfeit of lampreys," and, to top it off, the baggage train carrying his treasure was lost. Lampreys are still served in King's Lynn, and visitors today find the place attractive and eminently survivable. Two monumental squares, the Tuesday Market Place and the Saturday Market Place, are city focal points.

Eight miles north of King's Lynn on A149 is Sandringham ♛ ♛, a Jacobean-style house bought by Queen Victoria (and extensively rebuilt) for the Prince of Wales (who reportedly used it for some of his romantic interludes). As the Royal Family's country home since 1861, Sandringham is open from Easter through September when they are not in residence. (For information, call the Estate Office, Sandringham, at King's Lynn 772-675.) Expect lengthy waits in line.

There's a major flower show in midsummer, and the gardens and grounds are a treat at all times. The house is less so, unless you are a royalty fan eager to pore over photos, portraits, and souvenirs of, and gifts to, the royal family.

LINCOLN

It's 62 miles northwest of King's Lynn through Tennyson country for a side trip north to Lincoln, one of England's prettiest market towns. In A.D. 48 the Romans set up a military garrison on the hilltop at the intersection of their main north-south and east-west highways. (The south face of Newport Arch is original Roman stone.) In 1068 the Normans built a castle♛, and in 1072 Lincoln Cathedral♛♛♛♛, one of Europe's finest and the main reason for a visit, was begun. Fire and earthquake damage necessitated rebuilding in the 13th century. The central tower was completed in 1311.

The rhythm of the exterior beats with a rare Gothic purity. But inside, complex arches over the choir have been called "the crazy vaults of Lincoln." Of special note are the carved panels above the west entrance, the "Judgment Porch" on the west side, the choir stalls, misericords, and roodscreen, the chantry chapels, the Angel Choir with its stone angels, the chapter house and cloister. Other delights are the vast "Dean's Eye" and "Bishop's Eye," delicate tracery windows. And the Treasury contains an original copy of the Magna Carta. As this suggests, there is much to savor.

At Steep Hill and Christ's Hospital Terrace is the 12th-century House of Aaron the Jew♛♛, said to be England's oldest inhabited dwelling. Farther down cobbled, well-named Steep Hill (a pedestrian throughfare lined with antiques shops and tearooms) is the better-known, richer, stone Jew's House♛♛. Aaron, a Jew of the 12th century, was a moneylender operating in 25 counties (Christians were forbidden to lend money at interest).

Notice also on Steep Street a timbered building housing the Halifax Building Society. This was once an inn called the Cardinal's Hat, so named to flatter Cardinal Wolsey, who was Bishop of Lincoln in 1514–15. A tearoom called the Mayor's Chair (1732) was given that name because a onetime mayor put a chair there for passersby to rest while climbing the incredibly steep street. On the High Bridge♛♛ are several beautiful old timbered medieval houses facing "Glory Hole"—so designated in the days when people were pushed from the bridge "to their glory."

Stamford, the gray stone redoubt of the Burghleys, is 42 miles south of Lincoln via the A607 and A1. It was an old town when the Normans arrived and marked it down in the Domesday Book. Some consider it one of Europe's outstanding medieval towns because of its 13th-century Bastion, Browne's (1480) Hospital, and Burghley Hospital and Almshouses (dating originally from the 11th century).

Most of Stamford's most interesting existing buildings, especially those in St. George's Square, St. Mary's Hill, and High Street, have façades from the 17th century. St. Martin's Church♛ ♛ (1480), where Sir William Cecil, the first Lord Burghley, was buried in 1598, was a favorite of Sir Walter Scott and J. M. W. Turner. St. John the Baptist Church♛ ♛ (1450) has superb angel and cherub figureheads and stone gargoyles, and parts of All Saints Church♛ date back to 1220.

The George Hotel, a famous coaching house from the 16th century (Sir Walter Scott was a frequent guest), was an inn for pilgrims even in Norman times. A crypt and subterranean passage remain. It's a pleasant place for afternoon tea.

Stamford's real showpiece is Burghley House ♛ ♛ ♛ ♛, 1½ miles southeast of town in a spacious park. Built (1546–87) by Queen Elizabeth's Lord High Treasurer, William Cecil, to demonstrate his wealth, it is highlighted by an extraordinary double-hammerbeam Great Hall, baroque chapel, and cavernous arched kitchen with a gargantuan assemblage of copper pots. Equally arresting are the fittings and decorations. Carvings by Grinling Gibbons and Demontreuil; paintings by Van Dyck, Van Eyck, Rembrandt, Cranach, Breughel, Kneller, Gainsborough, Veronese, and Holbein; spectacular cloudlike murals by Verrio in the "Heaven Room"; and tapestries and fine furniture all make this a 240-room museum (18 open to view) to remember. Expect crowds.

Peterborough is 10 miles southeast of Stamford and offers its own rewards. Its cathedral♛ ♛ ♛, one of England's finest Norman-Romanesque buildings, was built from 1118 to 1143, though the rhythmic Gothic west front was added later. The painted wooden roof of 1220 (England's earliest that still survives) is extraordinary (bring those binoculars). Mary Queen of Scots and Catherine of Aragon are buried in the yard, and the gravedigger who buried them is immortalized in a painting on the west wall.

And so back to London via the M1.

INSIDERS' INFORMATION FOR CAMBRIDGE, THE EAST, AND LINCOLN

Bury St. Edmunds (Suffolk; Area Code Bury St. Edmunds 0284)

Hotel

Angel♛
Angel Hill IP33 1LT. Tel. 3926.
2 persons in twin, $67.50–90.
Ivy-covered, venerable (1452) town hotel, faces abbey ruins. 38 rooms, Pickwick Bar, 2 restaurants, afternoon tea. Dickens stayed in No. 15. Victorian ambience, 1980s comfort, tidy housekeeping.

Restaurants

Bradleys♛
St. Andrews St. South. Tel. 703825.
Average dinner: $30.
Chef-run; continental-style food, simple and attractive setting. Save room for luscious desserts.

Mortimer's♛
31 Churchgate St. Tel. 60623.
Average dinner: $25.
Steamed and grilled seafood the specialty; good desserts, excellent wine list.

Cambridge (Cambridgeshire; Area Code Cambridge 0223)

Hotels

Cambridgeshire Moat House♛♛
Bar Hill CB3 8BU. Tel. (Crafts Hill-0954) 80555.
2 persons in twin, $65–85.
Modern hotel just outside town on A604. 100 rooms, indoor swimming pool, sauna, tennis, squash, golf, gardens. Popular as a conference center. Rooms compact.

Garden House♛♛
Granta Place, Mill Lane CB2 1RT. Tel. 63421.
2 persons in twin, $90–120.
Modern brick building on the Cam River in town center. 117 rooms, bar, restaurant, punting. Balconies of snug

little rooms overlook river, help compensate for lack of character. All amenities, handy locale.

The Blue Boar♛
Trinity St. CB2 1TB. Tel. 63121.
Two persons in twin, average $67.50.
Ancient inn in town center; cozy rooms revive the past. 48 rooms, 11 private baths, atmospheric pub, restaurant.

Restaurant

Charlie Chan
14 Regent St. Tel. 61763.
Average dinner: $22.50.
Convenient location, minimal decor, acceptable if unremarkable Chinese food.

Pubs

Bath Hotel, Benet St. 16th-century inn, cozy rooms with fires.

Eagle Hotel, Benet St. Popular student hangout, World War II flyers' favorite. Lively outdoor area.

Shopping

Fitzbillies, Regent St. and Trumpington Rd. Bakery with delicious pastries.

Theaters

ADC Theatre, Park St. Tel. 59547. College and amateur productions.

Arts Theatre, Peas Hill. Tel. 352-000. Professional plays, operas, ballets, often with big-name stars.

Dedham (Essex; Area Code Colchester 0206)

Hotels

Dedham Vale♛♛
Stratford Rd., near Colchester CO7 6HW. Tel. 322-273.
2 persons in twin, $90–112.50.
Vine-covered Victorian house in wooded landscape, near A12. 6 rooms, bar, first-rate *Terrace* restaurant (♛♛♛). Spacious suites, attractive decor, admirable service.

Maison Talbooth♛♛♛
Gun Hill, near Colchester CO7 6HN. Tel. 322-367.
2 persons in twin, $112.50–158.
Austere Victorian house in a lush country setting with magnificent views. 10 rooms, lounge, breakfast served in

rooms. All rooms are huge suites, theatrically decorated, king-size beds. Meals served at Le Talbooth, nearby.

Restaurant
Le Talbooth ♛ ♛ ♛
Gun Hill, near Colchester. Tel. 323-150.
Average dinner: $40.
River Stour setting, stylish dining on seafood, meat, and game, expertly prepared and served. Elegance all the way.

Ipswich (Suffolk; Area Code 0473)

Hotel
Hintlesham Hall ♛ ♛ ♛ ♛
Hintlesham IP8 3NS. Tel. 87-268.
2 persons in twin, $90–142.50.
Classic Georgian house-turned-country-hotel 5 miles west of Ipswich. 10 rooms, bar, 2 stylish dining rooms with fireplaces. Each room different. Excellent *nouvelle* cooking(♛ ♛ ♛ ♛), subtle, with flair.

Lavenham (Suffolk; Area Code Lavenham 0787)

Hotel
Swan ♛ ♛
High St. CO10 9QA. Tel. 247477.
2 persons in twin, $67.50–120.
Timbered 15th-century hostelry in ancient wool town. 48 rooms, 2 bars, restaurant. Cozy lounges, wood fires, beamed ceilings highlight this classic old inn.

Lincoln (Lincolnshire; Area Code Lincoln 0522)

Hotel
White Hart ♛ ♛
Bailgate LN1 3AR. Tel.26222.
2 persons in twin, $90–120.
Famous vintage hotel handy to cathedral and castle. 52 rooms, 2 bars, restaurant, patio. Quiet elegance, generous rooms and lounges, slightly impersonal air characterize this ancient hotel that is often host to royalty.

Restaurant
White's ♕ ♕ ♕
Jews House, 15 The Strait. Tel. 24851.
Average dinner: $35.
One of Europe's oldest houses is the backdrop for imaginative Continental dishes prepared with great flair.

Long Melford (Suffolk; Area Code Sudbury 0787)

Hotel
The Bull ♕
Hall St. CO10 9JG. Tel. 78494.
2 persons in twin, $67.50–120.
Timbered Tudor wool merchant's house in town center. 27 rooms, 2 bars, restaurant. An inn since 1580, with wide hearths, rooms of varying shapes and sizes, considerable charm.

Stamford (Lincolnshire; Area Code Stamford 0780)

Hotel
George of Stamford ♕ ♕
St. Martin's High St. PE9 2LB. Tel. 55171.
2 persons in twin, $67.50–90.
16th-century coaching inn in the bustling town center. 44 rooms, 2 bars, restaurant, croquet. Period look, original architecture, comfortable, personal service, which may be why it appealed to Charles I and other royals.

Wymondham (Norfolk; Area Code Wymondham 0953)

Restaurant
Adlard's ♕
16 Damgate St. Tel. 603-533.
Average dinner: $25. Dinner only.
Finely tuned English cooking in informal, homey 17th-century cottage; easy side trip from Norwich, best food in area.

THE NORTH: CHESTER, YORK, AND THE LAKE DISTRICT

Visitors to Britain who fly into Manchester have interesting options available. It is possible (and quick) to land in England's Midlands and immediately zip 30 miles west to the great city of Chester, which is also a convenient gateway to Wales. It is also possible to scoot 60 miles east to York, the capital of Yorkshire, or to the Lake District. All are easily accessible from London, too. Here is a look at what these options offer.

CHESTER

Chester is easily reached by train from London in 3 hours or by car via the M56 motorway.

Twice daily, dressed in knee breeches, buckled shoes, and long coat, and wearing a stovepipe topper, the town crier appears at Chester's City Cross, clangs his handbell, and shouts the news of the day (with suitably topical commercials). In Chester, surrounded as he is by medieval timbered buildings built on ruins of the Roman 20th Legion's fortress, the crier and his 18th-century garb do not seem especially anachronistic.

In fact, this is a city (62,000 population) where anachronism is a way of life. Ninety-five percent of its striking black and white timber-and-wattle buildings are Victorian, not Elizabethan. The leading department store, Brown's, promotes its 13th-century crypt, which incidentally houses a restaurant, and other stores invite shoppers to admire Roman columns and a hypocaust among the modern sale merchandise in their basement display areas.

Chester's history is complex. The 20th Roman Legion built and occupied Deva, as it was then called, for 200 years to keep in line both the Welsh Ordovices and the English Brigantes peoples.

William the Conqueror laid waste the entire area in 1069–70, wiping out Chester's stubborn resistance to the Norman Conquest. By 1086 Chester had rebounded from the slaughter of its males and the total destruction of more than 400 buildings. And it soon became a bustling international port.

The city sided with Charles I in the Civil War and was pounded and starved into surrender by Cromwell's army. During the Napoleonic wars, 3 shipyards built British warships in Chester.

Today, Chester is a major tourism center. This is unusual, because it has no beaches, medicinal springs, or spa, no cult of poet or preacher, no Disneyland, casinos, or amusement parks. Its closest approach to such allures is its Roodee (not rowdy) racecourse below the city walls, along a loop in the River Dee.

But the tourists come anyway, to walk 2 miles of ramparts ♛ ♛ ♛, built directly on the Roman walls, that completely encircle old Chester. They photograph the unique 1897 Victoria Jubilee clock ♛ ♛ ♛ and revel in the unexcelled vistas of Eastgate (the Roman Via Principalis) and Foregate streets. They visit the Cathedral ♛ ♛ ♛ (which began in 958 as the church of St. Werbrugh, a Mercian princess), enjoy the 12th-century baptistry, 13th-century cloisters, and 14th-century carved choir stalls, have tea in its rebuilt refectory, and walk about Abbey Square ♛ ♛, its Georgian close.

From King Charles I's Tower ♛ ♛, above Kaleyards Gate, they can survey the city. It's a vantage point from which the King saw the defeat of his army, in September 1645, by the Parliamentarians at Rowton Moor.

They can use Kaleyards Gate to pass through the old city wall. The monks petitioned Edward I for permission to make a gate here so they could shortcut the route to their fields. He agreed, but ordered it shut nightly at 9 P.M., a curfew aimed at Welshmen and outlanders. To this day Kaleyards Gate is closed at 9.

At the top of any visitor's list are "The Rows" ♛ ♛ ♛ ♛, Chester's unique, galleried Tudor-style buildings that house modern shops along Eastgate and Northgate Streets. These timbered three- and four-story gabled buildings feature handsome carved and ornamented open loggias on their ground and first floors. They make it possible to stroll and window-shop while protected from the elements at all times. And Chester does have some of the finest upscale shops and shopping to be found in England.

Most visitors start at the Tourist Information Centre on Town Hall Square. City tours 💐 💐 💐 led by qualified "Blue Badge" volunteer guides begin here. Other tours (such as the "Roman Legionnaire"), begin at the Chester Visitor Centre 💐 💐, located outside the walls, past the partially excavated Roman amphitheater (built to seat 7,000) on Vicar's Lane.

INSIDERS' TIPS

A program in which overseas visitors are invited to local homes lets you see how a Chester family lives. Inquire at the Tourist Information Centre or Chester Visitor Centre if you'd like the experience.

Chester owes much to the Grosvenors, who own much of the city and inspired its 19th-century enthusiasm for Tudor architecture. They are direct descendants of Hugh Lupus, who was given Chester and its surroundings by his uncle, William the Conqueror. The Grosvenors' 10,000-acre ancestral home is at Eaton Park nearby. Their impact is readily evident on every side: Grosvenor Bridge, Grosvenor Park, Chester Grosvenor Hotel, Grosvenor Road—you get the idea.

You can see portraits of prominent members of the Grosvenor clan in the Town Hall's Assembly Room and stained-glass windows. (The present earl, whose cash flow was once estimated at $16,000 per hour, is Duke of Westminster, his 17th-century ancestor having married Mary Davies, who just happened to inherit what are now London's Belgravia and Mayfair sections.)

Some 30 miles southeast of Manchester is the village of Rowsley, in the Peak District National Park. And near it, overlooking the Derwent River, is one of Britain's greatest stately homes, Chatsworth 💐 💐 💐 💐 💐. Begun in 1687 by architects William Talman and Thomas Archer for the first Duke of Devonshire, its most recent changes were in the 1820s under Jeffry Wyatville and Joseph Paxton, who designed the Crystal Palace for the Great Exhibition of 1851 in London.

For this Palladian palace, Paxton designed the baroque interiors, the spectacular "Grand Cascade" terraced waterworks, the "Emperor Fountain" with its 267-foot jet, and the French and Italian gardens, all of which make the trip worthwhile. But the Cavendishes (the Duke's family name) have more, much more, to show in fine furniture, furnishings, and art.

The single most opulent room is the State Bedroom where George II was laid out in state. The art collection is so large that only a portion can be shown at any one time, and the prints can be seen only by scholars applying to the librarian. Among the outstanding paintings usually on view are works by Rembrandt, Hals, Poussin, Van Dyck, Gainsborough, and Venetian masters, and, among contemporaries, family portraits by Lucian Freud. The 6th Duke's love of sculpture (especially by Canova) is apparent in a spacious and unique gallery of 19th-century works.

YORK

From London, York is a 190-mile drive or a 2-hour express train ride.

As is the case with so many cities in Britain, York's riches, history, and monuments require more than a hasty stop. But if you are on a tight schedule, set aside at least a day, with additional days for the rest of Yorkshire. A week would give you time to add the Lake District, and possibly Durham and Hadrian's Wall. There are abbeys, stately homes, gardens, and Brontë sites to be visited throughout the area.

Of all places one might visit in Yorkshire, York itself should certainly be number one. Its very name reflects the city's variegated history. It comes from the Roman *Eborecum*, or "Place of the Boar." The Vikings translated this as *yorbic*, which led eventually to York.

Well-preserved walls and gates make York one of the most medieval-looking cities in England, but it actually began life as a Roman garrison town in A.D. 71–74. Hadrian used Eborecum as a base for his northern campaigns. When the Emperor Constantius Chlorus died in York in 306, his son, Constantine the Great, was proclaimed Emperor, the only time such a Roman proclamation emanated from Britain. The Saxons arrived in the 7th century and ensconced themselves inside the old Roman fortress walls. They were dislodged in 867 by marauding Vikings, who turned the town into an important port.

When the Normans conquered England in 1066, York was mercilessly suppressed by William the Conqueror. In the 13th century, massive stone walls were built around the city, a great abbey was erected, followed by more than 40 churches, and York became one of the great religious centers of England. That didn't mean York was free of strife.

Shakespeare's historic plays seethe with the animus and battles between Yorkists and Lancastrians (the Wars of the Roses) that raged for 30 years in the 15th century. When the last York king, Richard III, died at the Battle of Bosworth Field in 1485, Henry VII took the throne and began the reign of the House of Tudor. York records summed up the event this way:

"This day was our good King Richard III piteously slain and murdered; to the great heaviness of the city."

Was Richard a murderer or maligned hero? Chauvinistic Yorkshiremen will tell you that the victorious Tudors rewrote history and that Richard III was not the villain incarnate that Shakespeare, who wrote for a Tudor audience, and others portrayed.

Whether this centuries-old controversy sends your adrenaline racing or not, you will find many memories of York's last king still echoing through the city. There is a stained-glass window depicting a white boar (Richard III's emblem) in St. Martin's Church, Micklegate. The King's Arms, a local pub, was named for Richard and bears his coat of arms.

Following Richard's trail further, you might visit Middleham Castle, 43 miles northwest of York at Leyburn, where he spent his youth; it has one of the largest great keeps in England. Only 10 miles north at Sheriff Hutton is a ruined castle once owned by Richard. You can see his son's alabaster tomb effigy in the village church.

York's powerful stone walls had their last test in the

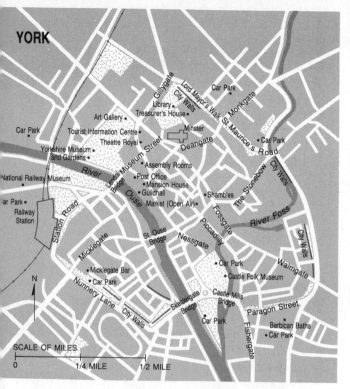

YORK

Gillygate
Lord Mayor's Walk
St. Monkgate
St. Maurice's Road
Car Park
Library
Treasurer's House
City Walls
Art Gallery
Tourist Information Centre
Minster
Car Park
Theatre Royal
Deangate
Car Park
Yorkshire Museum and Gardens
River
Leendal Museum Street
Assembly Rooms
Post Office
Mansion House
The Stonebow
National Railway Museum
Ouse
Guildhall
Shambles
City Walls
ar Park
Railway Station
Station Road
Market (Open Air)
Fossgate
River Foss
Piccadilly
St. Ouse Bridge
Nessgate
City Walls
Micklegate
Walmgate
Micklegate Bar
Car Park
Car Park
Castle Folk Museum
Nunnery Lane
City Walls
Skeldergate Bridge
Castle Mills Bridge
Paragon Street
Fishergate
N
Car Park
Barbican Baths
Car Park

SCALE OF MILES
0   1/4 MILE   1/2 MILE

battle of 1644, when Charles I's forces surrendered to Oliver Cromwell's.

The old city is so self-contained within the 3 miles of 13th-century walls that it is ready-made for walking. All major sights are within easy reach of one another, and there is the promise of fascinating discoveries along the way.

PERILS & PITFALLS

Parking is a terrible problem inside York's old walls. We strongly recommend "ditching" your car outside the walls, and taking to your heels for sightseeing.

Delightful free walking tours are led by well-informed volunteer guides. Many are retired residents, versed in local anecdotes. The 1½-hour tours begin at 10:15 A.M. and 2:15 P.M. at the Tourist Information Centre (which sponsors the tours), DeGrey House, Exhibition Square.

It is easy to find your way on your own. Just pick up a city map at the Tourist Information Centre and take off. A good companion on your walk is *A Walk Around the Snickel-*

ways of York, a paperback book by Mark W. Jones, about $3 in any of York's numerous bookshops. Jones defines a "snickleway" as "a narrow passageway or alley between walls, fences or buildings," and describes many historic ones.

PERILS & PITFALLS
Wear comfortable walking shoes, as many of York's streets are cobbled.

Near Exhibition Square is York's oldest section, with a cluster of touristic sights. Next to the Tourist Information Centre is the Theatre Royal (1740). Across St. Leonard's Place is the City Art Gallery ♛ ♛, which has some important Italian Renaissance paintings plus British and European paintings from the 14th to the 20th century, including works by Watteau, Van Dyck, Lely, Gainsborough, and the Barbizon School.

King's Manor ♛, now part of the University of York, has a long history, dating from its early days as the home of St. Mary's Abbot. The initials *C.R.* in the Royal Arms over the doorways denote the time, before and during the Civil War, when Charles I was in residence. *J.R.* in the arms recalls James I's visit, when he stopped here on his way from Scotland to be crowned in Westminster.

Yorkshire Museum ♛ ♛, on Museum Street, has a fine head of Constantine the Great, among other rare Roman, Bronze Age, and Iron Age implements found in York. Nearby is the Hospitium ♛, a 16th-century guest house of the abbey, now a geology and natural history museum.

The Museum Botanical Gardens ♛ ♛ were laid out in the 19th century among the ruins of the Benedictine monastery called St. Mary's Abbey ♛. Peacocks strut among the vivid flower beds by the Tower (*rebuilt* by the Romans in A.D. 300) and the ruins of arched windows. This land was granted to the monks by William Rufus, son of William the Conqueror.

Every 3 years these historic grounds are an open-air stage for the York Cycle of Mystery Plays. No whodunnits, these are famous medieval dramatizations of the Bible, which were first performed here in 1340. Fireworks, choirs, brass bands, special effects, balloons, and performances by professional actors highlight this unique event.

Proceed through Bootham Bar, York's oldest gate, from which you can walk the walls for a full 3 miles if you choose. (The wall walk from here to Monk Bar is the most interesting stretch, offering marvelous overviews of York Minster.) Bootham Bar is a misnomer, since its portcullis is no longer functional. The word *bar*, incidentally, means "gate," and York street names ending in *gate*, such as Skeltergate, Micklegate, and Petergate derive from the Danish word *gade* for "street."

From Bootham Bar, turn on to High Petergate, which leads to York's pivotal attraction, York Minster♛♛♛♛♛, a Gothic cathedral that is Britain's largest and one of its most magnificent. Its claim to fame is the beauty of its stained-glass windows, the most abundant and beautiful in Britain. The Great East Window, with a profusion of glass, is the size of a tennis court. The Minster's 130 windows contain glass ranging in age from the 12th to the 20th century. Don't miss the 13th-century geometric Five Sisters Window, a favorite of Charles Dickens. Look also at the roodscreen, with its life-size statues of every king from William the Conquerer to Henry VI.

If you attend a *son et lumière* performance inside the Minster (with narration by Sir John Gielgud, Eric Porter, and Judi Dench), you'll learn that this Minster is the fourth church built on the same site. The first was a wooden chapel built by King Edwin, Anglo-Saxon ruler of Northumbria, for his baptism in 627. This Gothic cathedral, which took 250 years to build, was finished in 1480.

In 1984 lightning zapped the Minster's south transept, starting a fire that collapsed the ceiling and splintered the building's 13th-century oak beams. York thrives on mystery, and local residents make much of the fact that there were lightning rods wired into the roof, and 6 new smoke detectors in the Minster's ceiling, yet no alarm sounded.

To many in York, the fire was a warning from "above." The reason? Just 3 days before the fire a controversial clergyman was consecrated in York Minster as Bishop of Durham. He had aroused ire in traditional Church of England circles for statements questioning the Resurrection and the Virgin Birth.

That wasn't the only theory. Others suggested that the fire was caused by a Yorkshire farmer's prayer for rain, divine punishment, a UFO, or St. Elmo's fire. The extensive damage left 90 percent of the building intact, but cracks were discovered in many of the 73 panels of glass in the great 16th-century Rose Window. This depicts the momentous 1486 marriage between Henry VII of Lancaster to Elizabeth of York, ending the Wars of the Roses. Though restoration continues, the Minster is eminently visitable regardless.

Look in at the Crypt with its Norman-carved Doomstone, and the Undercroft Museum, whose exhibits explain the Minster's history in detail. There you'll also see remains of Roman buildings. The Chapter House ♛ ♛ ♛ is a 13–14th-century architectural feat, a Gothic octagon without a central support pillar. There are amusing and grotesque gargoyles carved on the pillared stalls.

Across from the Minster is the Treasurer's House ♛ ♛, whose foundations are Roman, though much of the present house dates from the 17th century, with a splendid collection of 17th- and 18th-century furniture and paintings.

INSIDERS' TIPS

Christmas in York is special. The Minster is at its most traditional and impressive when brilliantly robed prelates and choirboys proceed up the main aisle and sing the "Nine Lessons and Carols." This series of ancient carols and Bible readings evokes medieval times. An old-fashioned tree is lit in St. Helen's Square, and there are usually carols by the Kirkgate Singers and costumed readings of Dickens stories in the heavily beamed 14th-century Merchant Adventurers' Hall. Many hotels offer special activities and rates. All told, York at this season is a delightful nostalgic journey.

Near the Minster, note Young's Hotel, the house where Guy Fawkes was born in 1570. This revolutionary who tried to blow up Parliament was baptized at St. Michael-le-Belfrey Church ♛ ♛, a fine 1536 example of Tudor architecture. Stonegate Street was the original Roman road leading from the River Ouse to the Roman barracks. Along it were carted the stones that built the Minster. Today it is a lively shopping street. York is a terrific place for shopping buys in woolens, books, and antiques.

Back on Petergate, your walk leads to the Shambles ♛ ♛, a street so narrow that you can stand in one shop and almost touch the shop across the way. The name Shambles comes from medieval times when this was a passageway between butcher shops, lined with butchers' benches or *fleshammel*. Only two butcher shops are left, but the meathooks and meat counters can still be seen along other shopfronts. At No. 35 is the house of Margaret Clitherow, a butcher's wife who was executed in 1586 by being crushed beneath a door weighted down with rocks for having harbored Jesuits. She was canonized St. Margaret of York in 1970.

At the end of the Shambles you'll come to an open area known as the Pavement, infamous for its stocks and gibbets. Charles Percy, Earl of Northumberland, was beheaded here in 1572, and a Cromwell effigy was burned here in 1660. Across the street, notice the white and black timbered house with double peaked roof that was once the home of Sir Thomas Herbert, physician to Charles I and the last person to see him alive.

Tucked behind the Shambles is York Market, full of stalls selling flowers, produce, and other assorted goods. Farther along, at Fossgate, you'll see the splendid half-timbered 14th-century Merchant Adventurers' Hall ♛ ♛ ♛, one of the finest surviving medieval guildhalls.

Near Fishergate Postern Tower is the Castle Museum ♛ ♛ ♛ ♛, the largest folk museum in Britain and a major York sight. It is housed in two 18th-century buildings with identical façades, believed to have been built by Sir John Vanbrugh. Though they look like Georgian mansions, one was a women's prison, the other a debtors' prison.

Inside is a revelation: a series of authentically furnished rooms of various periods, including a 1690s Jacobean Hall with dark oak paneling, a 1790 Georgian dining room, a moorland cottage of 1850, a Victorian parlor, weavers' cottages, and shops from Tudor to Edwardian times. You will see here an Edwardian street, the King William IV Hotel, a Victorian photographer's studio, a British officers' mess circa 1890, and a reconstruction of the Scarborough seafront in the 1870s. Other treasures to pore over include a costume collection, military uniforms, weapons, and a delightful section on folkways and superstitions.

A block away is Clifford's Tower♛, an unusual mid-13th-century quatrefoil shape. It replaced a wooden tower, part of William the Conqueror's castle, that was destroyed by fire in 1190 during a massacre of Jews. A plaque commemorating the 150 Jews who died in the pogrom was unveiled in 1978 at the foot of the tower.

At Goodramgate is Our Lady's Row, the oldest surviving group of York houses (from 1316). Opposite is tiny Holy Trinity Church♛♛, which dates from 1250, has 18th-century box pews like cattle stalls, and holds services only once a year.

There are 18 pre-Reformation churches distributed about York's center. St. Mary's, a 15th-century church at Castlegate, is now a Heritage Centre that replays York history extremely well. Other notable churches are All Saints♛, on North Street, a Norman church with 14th–15th-century stained-glass windows; St. Michael♛♛, Spurriergate, with 12th-century arcades, 18th-century reredos, rare 15th-century chalice brass, medieval glass, and a lovely interior; and the city's oldest, St. Cuthburt♛♛ (687), at Peasholme Green, built with Roman stones. General Wolfe's parents worshiped here when they lived opposite in the timbered house that is now the Black Swan Inn♛♛. Pop inside to see the Delft-tiled fireplace and carved wood paneling.

Another pub worth a visit is the Roman Bath, at St. Sampson's Square, where a Roman steambath was discovered. York is said to have hundreds of pubs, and Yorkshire ale is famous. Try Stone's Best Bitter and Samuel Smith (made 12 miles from town).

As you explore the snickleways, notice the many black iron streetlights with gilded crests that date back to the 1820s. Although gaslights have been replaced by electricity, the bulbs are the shape of the original gas mantles, and cast a similar soft light.

Residents proudly claim that York has many ghosts. In fact, some of England's most fascinating shades hover here. After all, what other city can top the sighting of the entire Roman Legion marching past in the cellars of the Treasurer's House behind the Minster? The legionnaires were most recently seen by Harry Martindale, a York policeman.

On a local tour, "Haunted and Historic York," you will

learn about Brother Jochundus, an inebriated monk who haunts the Theatre Royal because its cellar incorporates parts of vaulted cloisters from the medieval St. Leonard's Hospice. The theater also has a ghostly nun who was walled up under the present dressing room, and a mysterious, floating Gray Lady.

York's newest historic sight is Jorvik Viking Centre, a Disney-like recreation of the Viking period in York. You ride a dozen minutes in "time cars" through a darkened interior that simulates the living/sleeping/cooking huts of a Viking settlement of A.D. 948. Dimly seen figures speak in "Old Norse." Beyond, in display cases, are various artifacts—primitive bone combs, horsehide "skates," pins and shards—excavated from a recent dig at Coppergate.

PERILS & PITFALLS

Crowds wait in line sometimes over an hour to spend minutes riding through this simulated Viking village. In our minority view, Jorvik Viking Centre is commercial and not worth the time or money.

The major city attraction outside the old walls is the National Railway Museum ♥ ♥ ♥, on Leeman Road. You don't even need to be a railroad buff to enjoy Queen Victoria's favorite 1869 saloon car. It is outfitted with silk-covered chairs and couches, and its exterior gleams as though ready for her instant departure. Queen Adelaide's "bed carriage" (1842), with gold-plated handles and elaborate furniture, is another treasure. There are 25 locomotives and engines in the Great Hall, arranged around two turntables, with carloads of other railway lore for the dedicated railway buff.

OUTSIDE YORK

Nature lovers who want to wander the dales and moors for which Yorkshire is famous will find opportunities galore in the Yorkshire Dales National Park ♥ ♥ ♥ and North Yorkshire Moors National Park ♥ ♥ ♥, both easy day drives northwest and north, respectively, from York.

But Yorkshire has many other fascinations besides scenery.

It is 21 miles from York to Harrogate, a once-magnificent, still-lively spa center, where Victorian gentry "took the waters" and Queen Victoria held cabinet meetings. Harrogate, as Agatha Christie fans will recall, is where the author turned up after being mysteriously missing for some days.

Harrogate still enjoys the regal Royal Bath Assembly Rooms, and it is worth a visit for its stylish shops, voluminous flower beds, and attractive tearooms (where you can sample such Yorkshire delicacies as parkin, Leeds rhubarb pie, Yorkshire curd tarts, Brontë fruitcake, and brandy snaps).

Nine miles north of Harrogate is Ripon, known especially for its eclectic 17th-century cathedral♛♛ with Saxon crypt, and the 13th-century Wakeman's House♛♛.

Just outside town is one of England's most romantic ruins, Fountains Abbey♛♛♛♛♛. You can wander through cloisters, roofless rooms, a chapel of 22 bays, and vaulted dormitories of the 12th-century Cistercian monastery. There is a two-mile round-trip walk—a pastoral delight—past a lake, a canal, "Anne Boleyn's Seat," "Moon Pond," and a folly called "The Temple of Fame."

Some 25 miles southeast of Harrogate is Haworth (*HOW-worth*), a 19th-century village of grim-looking stone houses with slate roofs, hugging a hillside bordering the moors. Haworth, the home of the literary Brontës, leaves little doubt in our minds why Emily wrote *Wuthering Heights* and Charlotte wrote *Jane Eyre.*

The bleak parsonage♛♛♛ where Patrick Brontë and his family lived lies behind St. Michael's Church, where all the Brontës (except Anne) are buried in a chapel to the right of the altar. The Brontë siblings died of tuberculosis within months of one another: Bramwell was 31, Anne 29, Emily 30, Charlotte 39. Their mother had died at 36. Only their father, Patrick, lived on into his eighties.

The Brontë parsonage, a small house with a slate roof like most other houses in Haworth, overlooks the church cemetery. Small wonder that Charlotte once described the house as "a tomb with windows." Most of the furnishings in the house today belonged to the family, including the somber horsehair sofa on which Emily died of consumption. Several upstairs rooms are filled with glass cases full of Brontë mementos: Charlotte's black silk shoes, cords made of Emily's and Anne's hair, a copy of Bramwell's portrait of his three sisters (the original is in London's National Portrait Gallery).

Down the street from the parsonage is the Black Bull Hotel, in whose pub Bramwell drank himself to death, not the cheeriest thought on which to sample a pint.

Following the Brontë trail further, either by walking over well-defined footpaths or by taking a pony and trap ride, leads over Haworth Moor to the Brontë Waterfall (a mere trickle), and a huge stone nearby called the Brontë Chair, because the sisters rested there on their walks. Two miles farther on is Top Withens, supposedly the inspiration for *Wuthering Heights*, its hilltop made gloomier by the ruins of an old house.

Your walk will also take you along the Pennine Way (Britain's longest footpath, extending 250 miles), to Ponden Hall, an 18th-century farmhouse believed to be the inspiration for Thrushcross Grange in *Wuthering Heights*. This is a handy place to stop for lunch or tea and a browse through the hand-weaving shop installed in the house.

Two of Britain's most splendid stately homes are in Yorkshire: Harewood House and Castle Howard.

Harewood ♛ ♛ ♛ ♛, 5 miles south of Harrogate, is the home of the Earl and Countess of Harewood. It is a placid 18th-century manor house designed by Robert Adam and John Carr of York. It has a Capability Brown park with waterfall, lake, and rose garden, and the house furniture was made to order by Chippendale. There is a noted collection of Italian paintings (Titian, Tintoretto, Veronese), as well as Sevres and Chinese porcelains.

Perhaps Yorkshire's most famous house is Castle Howard ♛ ♛ ♛ ♛ ♛, 15 miles northeast of York, near Malton. When is a house not a home? When it is a palace, which this creation of Sir John Vanbrugh (his first major work) and Nicholas Hawksmoor surely is. Castle Howard is a major showpiece, commanding 10,000 acres. The property is so big, in fact, that you travel by "train" from car park to house.

Castle Howard inevitably evokes scenes from *Brideshead Revisited*, the television adaptation of Evelyn Waugh's book, which was shot here. The drive, the Great Hall (whose dome soars 80 feet), or the fountain will surely bring the story to mind. The interiors are opulent with tapestries, oriental rugs, collections of Roman, Egyptian, and Greek sculpture, porcelains, and furniture, plus paintings by Van Dyck, Holbein, Gainsborough, and Rubens.

Another collection of stirring ruins is Riveaulx Abbey♛ ♛ ♛ on the edge of the North Yorkshire Moors National Park. From Riveaulx Terrace♛ ♛ ♛ ♛, a magnificently landscaped half-mile height with a Greek temple and a folly, you can look down upon the Gothic ruins that were once the first Cistercian abbey in Britain. Riveaulx is a half-day outing from York or a stop en route from York to Scotland.

Traveling to Riveaulx, you will pass through Thirsk, a noisy market town in James Herriot country. The author of *All Creatures Great and Small* guards his privacy and address carefully.

Laurence Sterne, who wrote *Tristram Shandy* and *A Sentimental Journey*, lived in Shandy Hall, a 15th-century medieval hall to which Sterne added a Georgian façade, in the tidy little village of Coxwold, as cheerful as Haworth is depressing. Across from Shandy Hall is a 15th-century church where, as vicar, Sterne preached. Coxwold is just 6 miles south of Riveaulx.

On the coast is Scarborough, a great Victorian seaside resort that appealed to T. S. Eliot in his later years. Here you can see Woods End, the Sitwell family's summer home, where Dame Edith was born in 1887.

Another 19 miles up the coast is Whitby, a cheerful seaside town on a long harbor. On a hilltop are the ruins of 13th-century Whitby Abbey♛, and on Grape Lane Captain Cook lived and supervised the building of his ships. Wilkie Collins set his eerie novel *The Moonstone* in Whitby, but it is difficult to see how the town may have caused Bram Stoker to create *Dracula* here. Naturally, hotels in town now offer Dracula weekends.

DURHAM

Perhaps 60 miles north of York is Durham, whose mighty cathedral and castle grow out of the solid rock peninsula all but surrounded by the Wear River. The cathedral ♛ ♛ ♛ ♛ ♛ is built upon a Saxon church site and was well under way by 1096. It is one of Britain's greatest Romanesque churches, as the powerful pillars and rhythmic arches plainly state. There is a 12th-century Lady Chapel in which the Venerable Bede's 16th-century tomb is placed. Note the fine altar screen of the 14th-century, and superb 17th-century woodwork (removed by the Victorians and later restored). There are 12th- and 13th-century wall paintings in the north aisle and east wall.

The cloisters, chapter house (12th century), monk's dormitory (14th century), and old library are in excellent condition. In the new chapter library, the former dormitory, is the 7th-century wooden coffin of St. Cuthbert in which the saint's body traveled far and wide. Also on view are religious artifacts.

Across the green is the Castle of the Bishops ♛ ♛ ♛, which began as the fortress of William the Conqueror in 1072. A visit takes you through the kitchen, the 13th-century Great Hall, the 16th-century gallery and chapel. You climb to the Norman gallery and take the spiral staircase down to the Norman chapel, which was part of the original construction. Durham University occupies the Castle buildings, and students and academics are seen about the area.

Another University building worth seeking out is the Oriental Museum/Gulbenkian Museum ♛ ♛ ♛ on Elvet Hill. Here are displayed Indian, Burmese, Chinese, and other oriental sculptures, pottery, jade, and archeological finds.

Some 70 miles north of York is Hadrian's Wall ♛ ♛ ♛, a magnet for Romaniacs. This 2d-century fortification across the narrow neck of Britain once ran 73 miles, uninterrupted except by the turrets and forts that were spaced along it. Over the years, much of it was dismantled; General Wade, for example, used it as a quarry to build fortifications after the Jacobite uprising of 1715. A Roman road ran along parallel to it, and you will drive on that road today.

To see it best, stop at Housesteads, where an excavated fort and an excellent small museum explain how the Romans manned the Wall and used it. At Walltown is a fair stretch of the Wall and a signal turret.

THE LAKE DISTRICT

Carlisle, at the southern end of the Wall, is on the northern border of England's lovely Lake District ♛ ♛ ♛ ♛. This is a 32-square-mile national park, noted as much for its three mountain peaks (each topping 3,000 feet), as for the dozen and a half meres (lakes) that snuggle into mist-hung valleys between the mountain heights. The undisputed star of the Lake District is the scenery, at its most spectacular around Ullswater, but enjoyable from almost any vantage point. One view to conjure with is from the castle ruins at Kendal ♛ ♛, where Catherine Parr, Henry VIII's sixth wife, was born.

Literary mavens may want to look in on Dove Cottage ♛ ♛ in Grasmere, where the Romantic poet William Wordsworth lived and worked from 1799 to 1808. The Wordsworth Museum next door has manuscripts and first editions of his works. Actually, the Lake District was home turf to Wordsworth. He was born in 1770 in Cockermouth, 25 miles away. His birthplace, the 1745 Wordsworth House ♛ ♛, is open to view.

Another literary shrine is Hill Top ♛ ♛, Beatrix Potter's farmhouse in Near Sawrey. The author of *The Tale of Peter Rabbit* and other animal stories bought this undistinguished 1906 cottage on a 200-acre working farm and raised flocks of pedigreed Hardwick sheep here until her death in 1943. The house displays her original drawings and paintings.

> ### PERILS & PITFALLS
> One sight you may profitably spare yourself: The so-called Laurel and Hardy Museum in Ullswater, where Stan Laurel was born in 1890, contains little more than a brass bed, pens, and a collection of photocopies of newspaper clippings about the comedians.

The real pleasure of the Lake District is that it invites a kind of lazy wandering. (See the section on Oxford, the Cotswolds, and Stratford on page 165 for recommended books about walking tours.) If you don't want to wander by foot or car, there are delightful boat rides. You can cruise Lake Coniston, for one, via a restored steam-propelled yacht, *Gondola,* which was launched in 1859. Boats cruise all the major lakes, and you can rent boats also.

INSIDERS' INFORMATION FOR
THE NORTH OF ENGLAND

Abberley (Hereford and Worcester; Area Code Great Witley 029-921)

Hotel

Elms♛ ♛ ♛
Abberley, Route A443 near Worcester WR6 6AT. Tel. 666.
2 persons in twin, $90–120.
1710 Queen Anne house in country setting. 27 rooms, fine *nouvelle cuisine* restaurant, bar, tennis, croquet, putting green, garden, helipad. Regency decor, antiques, some four-poster beds.

Ambleside (Cumbria; Area Code Ambleside 0966)

Hotels

Rothay Manor♛ ♛ ♛
Rothay Bridge LA22 0EH. Tel. 33605.
2 persons in twin, $75–120.
Imposing Regency house with lake views. 16 rooms, bar, 2 dining rooms, croquet, garden. Family-run, fine English cooking, cheerful atmosphere, handy for Lake District outings.

Kirkstone Foot♛ ♛
Kirkstone Pass Rd. LA22 9EH. Tel. 32232.
2 persons in twin, $48–67.50.
Attractive 17th-century house on well-kept grounds, near town. 14 rooms, restaurant features English food, croquet, garden. Modified American Plan (2 meals included in room charge). Comfortable and unpretentious.

Bakewell (Derbyshire; Area Code Great Longstone 062-987)

Hotel

Hassop Hall♛ ♛ ♛ ♛
Hassop DE4 1NS. Tel. 488.
2 persons in twin, $67.50–120.

Magnificent 500-year-old estate in wooded setting. 12 rooms, bar, restaurant, tennis, croquet, garden. Luxurious and spacious rooms, deluxe extras (robes, linen sheets), great comfort and quiet.

Restaurant
Fischer's ♕ ♕ ♕
Bath St., Woodhouse. Tel. 2687.
Average dinner: $30.
Cozy cottage setting for fine dining; chef-owner specializes in *nouvelle* English, emphasis on game, fish, market-fresh ingredients.

Birmingham (West Midlands; Area Code 021)

Hotels
Metropole & Warwick ♕ ♕ ♕
National Exhibition Centre B40 1PP. Tel. 780-4242.
2 persons in twin, $67.50–120.
Modern facility in handy location. 700 rooms, 3 bars, restaurants, sauna, squash, in-house movies, hairdresser, solarium. Huge, well-run, packed with amenities, handy for business travelers.
The Plough & Harrow ♕ ♕ ♕
135 Hagley Rd., Edgebaston B16 8LS. Tel. 454-4111.
2 persons in twin, $120–150.
Large redbrick hotel just a mile from Birmingham center. 44 rooms, bar, high-quality French restaurant(♕ ♕ ♕), sauna, garden. Large rooms, attractive furnishings, great comfort and service, elegant restaurant with imaginative menu.

Restaurants
Sloans ♕ ♕
27–29 Chad Square, Hawthorne Rd., Edgbaston B15 3TQ. Tel. 455-6697.
Average dinner: $30.
Fresh seafood dishes with a French accent.
Rajdoot ♕
12 Albert St. BA4 7UD. Tel. 643-8805.
Average dinner: $12.
Large, popular North Indian restaurant features tandoori, excellent *nan*, also vegetarian dishes.

Chester (Cheshire; Area Code Chester 0244)

Hotel
Chester Grosvenor ♛ ♛ ♛ ♛
Eastgate St. CH1 1LT. Tel. 24024.
2 persons in twin, $97.50–165.
Handy city-center location. 98 rooms, 2 bars, fine French
restaurant ♛ ♛. Historic timbered façade contrasts with
sophisticated, up-to-date rooms and suites, lavish with
extras and upscale touches. A joy.

Durham (Durham; Area Code Durham 0385)

Hotel
Seven Stars Inn ♛
Shincliffe Village DH1 2NU. Tel. 48454.
2 persons in twin, $32.25–48.
Small coaching inn in a charming village one mile from
Durham. 8 rooms, bar, restaurant. Open fireplaces and
exposed beams add character to this traditional inn.

Ely (Cambridgeshire; Area Code Ely 0353)

Restaurant
Old Fire Engine House ♛ ♛
25 St. Mary's St. Tel. 2582.
Average dinner: $20.
Robust, well-prepared meals in a restored firehouse. Emphasis is on wholesome, hearty dishes—beef, game, hare,
good soups. Generous portions, good value.

Grasmere (Cumbria; Area Code Grasmere 096-65)

Hotels
Michael's Nook ♛ ♛
Grasmere, near Ambleside LA22 9RP. Tel. 496.
2 persons in twin, $67.50–90.
Secluded Victorian country house in the Lake District.

11 rooms, bar, much-praised restaurant(♛♛), croquet. Eclectic assemblage of antiques forms backdrop for a clever blend of classic and original cuisine.

Wordsworth ♛♛
Near Ambleside LA22 9SW. Tel. 592.
2 persons in twin, $90–120.
Gabled Victorian house in tree-shaded setting. 35 rooms, bar, attractive restaurant, indoor swimming pool, sauna, solarium, fishing. Cheery mix of Victorian and modern decor in large rooms.

White Moss House ♛
Rydal Water LA22 9SE. Tel. 295.
2 persons in twin, $67.50–90.
Comfortable stone house overlooking Rydal Water. 6 rooms, Modified American Plan (2 meals included with room charge). Fishing, respected restaurant(♛♛) featuring English classics, offers good value.

Hambleton (Leicestershire; Area Code Oakham 0572)

Hotel
Hambleton Hall ♛♛♛♛
Oakham LL15 8TH. Tel. 56991.
2 persons in twin, $123 up.
Imposing Victorian manor with hilltop view of Rutland Water. 15 rooms, bar, deservedly esteemed restaurant (♛♛♛), outstanding wine list. Tennis. Handsomely decorated lounges, spacious guest rooms and baths, personal service, all make this family-run country hotel special.

Harrogate (North Yorkshire; Area Code Harrogate 0423)

Hotels
Harrogate International ♛♛♛
Kings Rd. HG1 1XX. Tel. 500-000.
2 persons in twin, $102.
Handsome gleaming glass high-rise just outside town. 214 rooms, bars, 2 restaurants, conference facilities. Good service, conveniences, all modern.

Majestic 👑 👑
Ripon Rd. HG1 2HV. Tel. 68972.
2 persons in twin, $90–150.
Enormous *fin de siècle* hotel in center of this spa town.
160 rooms, bar, restaurant, indoor swimming pool, tennis,
squash, helipad. Though large and impersonal, many
facilities, good service, and ample rooms compensate.

Hexham (Northumberland; Area Code Hexham 0434)

Restaurant
Diwan-e-am Tandoori 👑
23 Priest Popple. Tel. 606-175
Average dinner: $15–18
Delicious Indian food.

Ilkley (West Yorkshire; Area Code Ilkley 0943)

Restaurants
Box Tree 👑 👑 👑 👑
29 Church St. Tel. 608-484.
Average dinner: $45.
Long among Britain's best, well worth a detour for dinner
(no lunch). From this small, old-fashioned stone house in
town center come original re-creations of French classics
and remarkable desserts. Service is as friendly and caring
as the food.
Olive Tree 👑 👑
31 Church St. Tel. 601-481.
Average dinner: $21.
Greek specialties exceptionally well done, including some
vegetarian dishes. Dinner only.

Kendal (Cumbria; Area Code 0539)

Hotel
Woolpack 👑 👑
Stricklandgate LA9 4ND. Tel. 23852.
2 persons in twin, $67.50–90.
Historic 18th-century coaching inn, centrally located.
58 rooms, bar, restaurants, coffee shop. Though mod-

ernized, much of the inn contains period charm, especially the Crown Bar, formerly Kendal's wool auction room.

Leamington Spa (Warwickshire; Area Code Leamington Spa 0926)

Hotel

Mallory Court ♛ ♛ ♛ ♛
Harbury Lane, Bishop's Tachbrook CV33 9QB. Tel. 30214.
2 persons in twin, $90–150.
Handsome stone mansion in the country near Warwick and the Cotswolds. 9 rooms, bar, superior French restaurant (♛ ♛ ♛), swimming pool, squash, croquet. Like a private home; stylish and spacious rooms (Blenheim's most elegant, with 2 bathtubs). Seamless service, quiet atmosphere.

Ledbury (Hereford and Worcester; Area Code Ledbury 0531)

Hotels

Feathers ♛ ♛
High St. HR8 1DS. Tel. 5266.
2 persons in twin, $48–90.
16th-century half-timbered Elizabethan inn in town center. 11 rooms, bar, restaurant, squash. Homey place, rambling floors, much charm.

Hope End Country House ♛ ♛
Hope End HR8 1JQ. Tel. 3613.
2 persons in twin, $67.50–90.
Converted coach house and stables on wooded property that once belonged to Elizabeth Barrett Browning. 7 rooms, restaurant. Handwoven spreads, crafts, wholesome home cooking provide rustic charm.

Ludlow (Shropshire; Area Code Ludlow 0584)

Hotel

Feathers Inn ♛ ♛
Bull Ring SY8 1AA. Tel. 5261.

2 persons in twin, $67.50–90.
Famous half-timbered inn in the center of a delightful
market town. 37 rooms, 2 bars, restaurant. An inn since
1521 or before, with leaded windows, oak paneling, exposed beams, antiques, some four-posters.

Malvern Wells (Hereford and Worcester; Area Code Malvern 06845)

Restaurant
Croque-en-Bouche♛ ♛ ♛
221 Wells Rd. Tel. 65612.
Average dinner: $35. (Dinner only.)
Here's one to go out of your way for. With a 5-course *prix
fixe* menu, sophisticated home cooking with a French/
English flair, and memorable desserts, it's a gem.

Manchester (Greater Manchester; Area Code 061)

Hotel
Piccadilly♛ ♛
Piccadilly Plaza M60 1QR. Tel. 236-8414.
2 persons in twin, $90–120.
High-rise modern edifice in city center. 250 rooms, 3 bars,
English restaurant, coffee shop, shops. As big, bustling
modern hotels go, here's efficiency, high standards, many
facilities.

Restaurants
Kosmos Taverna♛
248 Wilmslow Rd. Tel. 225-9106.
Average dinner: $15–20.
Good value, lively atmosphere, respectable Greek dishes.
Mr. Kuks♛
55A Mosley St. Tel. 236-0659.
Average dinner: $18–25.
Head for the Peking specialties in this popular Chinese
eatery.
Mulberry♛
400 Wilmslow Rd. Tel. 434-4624.

Average dinner: $27. (Dinner only.)
Original dishes, live music, informal setting make this a
local favorite.

Pool-in-Wharfedale (West Yorkshire; Area Code Arthington 0532)

Hotel
Pool Court ♛ ♛
Pool Bank, near Otley LS21 1EH. Tel. 842-288.
2 persons in twin, $90–150.
Georgian stone house in Yorkshire town 7 miles west of
Harrogate. 4 rooms, bar, respected restaurant (♛ ♛)
known for its original French-style cuisine, excellent wine
list, and flawless service. Spacious and well-furnished
rooms.

Ripon (North Yorkshire; Area Code Ripon 0765)

Hotel
Jervaulx Hall ♛ ♛
A6108, Near Masham HG4 4PH. Tel. (0677)60235.
2 persons in twin, $45–90.
19th-century country house on 8 acres near Jervaulx
Abbey ruins. 8 rooms, restaurant, croquet. Well-appointed
Victorian house with spacious rooms, many personal
touches.

Ullswater (Cumbria; Area Code Pooley Bridge 085-36)

Hotel
Sharrow Bay ♛ ♛ ♛
Howtown, Lake Ullswater, near Penrith CA10 2LZ. Tel.
301.
2 persons in twin, $120–150.
Comfortable Italianate country house with scenic lake
views, fishing. 29 rooms, celebrated restaurant (♛ ♛ ♛),
5-course *prix fixe* meals ($37.50) rise to climactic crescen-
do, orchestrated along elegant French/English themes.
Decor theatrical.

Wall (Northumberland; Area Code Humshaugh 043-481)

Hotel

Hadrian Inn♛
Near Hexham NE46 4EE. Tel. 232.
2 persons in twin, $37.50–57.
Compact little 1740 inn situated near Hadrian's Wall. 9 rooms, 8 private baths, bar, restaurant. Neat, tidy, publike, unpretentious; made with stones from Hadrian's Wall.

Windermere (Cumbria; Area Code Windermere 09662)

Hotel

Miller Howe♛♛♛
Rayrigg Road LA23 1EY. Tel. 2536.
2 persons in twin, $90–120.
Country-house hotel perched on a hill above Lake Windermere. 13 rooms, lounges, widely acclaimed English restaurant (♛♛♛), tennis, croquet, helipad. Showmanship is chef-owner John Tovey's forte, in room decor, orchestrated, highly original 5-course dinners, lighting, and classical music, elaborate breakfasts. Unique and memorable experience.

Restaurant

Roger's♛
4 High St. Tel. 4954.
Average dinner: $25.
Low-key French cooking done with expertise in informal setting.

York (North Yorkshire; Area Code York 0904)

Hotels

Middlethorpe Hall♛♛♛♛
Bishopthorpe Rd. YO2 1QP. Tel. 641241.
2 persons in twin, $105–150.
Handsome William-and-Mary mansion across from race-

course at edge of town. 30 rooms, 2 bars, quality restaurant (♛ ♛), croquet. Liveried footman, wood fires in wood-paneled dining rooms, handsome library, stylish Regency guest rooms, friendly service—all is formal, polished elegance. Pampering amenities.

Royal York ♛ ♛
Station Rd. YO2 2AA. Tel. 53681.
2 persons in twin, $90–150.
Massive Victorian station hotel just outside town's old walls. 130 rooms, 3 bars, restaurant, coffee shop. Recent much-needed renovations have restored grandeur to high-ceilinged spacious rooms, grand staircase, cavernous public areas.

Restaurants

Akash Tandoori ♛
10 North St. Tel. 33550.
Average dinner: $18.
Reliably spicy Indian cuisine in central location.

Betty's
6–8 St. Helens Square. Tel. 22323.
Famous Yorkshire tearoom, excellent cream teas.

Taylors Tea Rooms
46 Stonegate. Tel. 22865.
Cozy old-fashioned tea parlor.

Pubs

Cock & Bottle, Sheltergate. Supposedly haunted by George Villiers, Duke of Buckingham.

Olde Starre Inne, Stonegate. Was flourishing in 1644. Popular currently with the under-30 crowd.

Country pubs nearby:

Lord Nelson, Netherpoppleton. Farmhouse pub, great ambience.

Shoulder of Mutton, Appleton Roebuck. Convivial, lively, piano-playing pub with fun-loving local clientele.

Three Hares, Bilbrough. Farmhouse pub with fireplace coziness.

Theaters

Lyons Concert Hall, University Campus, Heslington. Tel. 59861. Concerts both classical and popular.

Theatre Royal, St. Leonard's Place. Tel. 23568. Professional productions.

SCOTLAND

Poets wax lyrical about Scotland's scenery, the beauty of the fjord-like lochs, and the ethereal islands strung like emeralds along the western coast.

Exceptional as the scenery is—and that's a guidebook in itself—Scotland has compelling man-made attractions as well. We'll try to extol *their* beauty, and let the scenery speak for itself, which it does most eloquently.

Scotland's misty beauty is prey to bad weather. Best to plan your visit for the months from May to mid-September if you want blue skies and good visibility. Late fall is almost a guarantee of rain. Note also that many of Scotland's stately homes are not open during winter months.

Begin in Borders, the southernmost Scots county you pass through, driving from Yorkshire to Edinburgh. For the acquisitive, Borders is a shopping paradise, replete with shops and discount outlets for jackets, coats, stoles, shawls, and every other woolen wearable.

INSIDERS' TIPS

Throughout Scotland are many small, family-run, country-house hotels, much like New England inns. Their food is excellent and the ambience is restful, warm and welcoming. A British Tourist Authority brochure, *BTA Commended Country Hotels*, lists many of them.

Driving through Border Forest Park, you come to Jedburgh, with the ruins of Jedburgh Abbey ♛ ♛, founded in 1147. The Abbey's small museum has medieval mementos.

Five miles north is Kelso, a recent winner of the "Britain in Bloom" citation for its exuberant town-wide floral displays. Other reasons for a visit: the romantic ruins of Kelso Abbey ♛ and Floors Castle ♛ ♛ ♛, a 1721 Adam-designed manor, with an impressive collection of English

SCOTLAND

Orkney
Islands

Kirkwall

Outer Hebrides

Thurso • John O'Groats
• Wick

•Stornoway

Ullapool
Bonar Bridge •

•Uig
Cullen
•Nairn •Elgin •Banff
Kyle of Lochalsh •Inverness
Isle of
Skye
•Barra
Carrbridge •
Fort Augustus • Aviemore • GLEN MORE Inverurie •
•Mallaig Kingussie • NAT'L
PARK Aberdeen •
Braemar • •Ballater
Fort Williams •
Tiree •Ballachulish
Tobermory • •Pitlochry
Craignure •
Obair •Montrose
Arbroath
Perth • •Dundee
Inveraray • St. Andrews
•Stirling
•Islay
Rothesay •
Paisley • •Glasgow •Edinburgh
•Hamilton
Isle of
Arran Kilmarnock • •Lanark
Campbeltown •Prestwick •Peebles
Selkirk • Melrose •Coldstream

GALLOWAY
FOREST
PARK Dumfries •
Stranraer Castle Douglas • •Gretna

SCALE OF MILES
0   25   50

and French antique furniture, as well as tapestries and
paintings by Gainsborough, Reynolds, Canaletto, and
others.

Beyond Melrose, which has its own ruined abbey ♛
(where the heart of Robert the Bruce is supposedly
buried), you'll come to Abbotsford ♛ ♛ ♛, home of Sir
Walter Scott. The 19th-century novelist designed and lived
in this fancifully turreted "castle" from 1812 until his
death in 1832. Note especially his huge collection of battle
and torture weapons and the *Madonna and Child* by Ghir-
landaio in the attached Catholic chapel.

A few miles to the south is Selkirk and one of Scotland's great stately homes, Bowhill ♛ ♛. The 1812 house

of the Scotts of Buccleuch offers a harvest of handsome antique furniture, hand-painted Chinese wallpaper, memorabilia of the Duke of Monmouth, and paintings by Reynolds, Canaletto, and Claude Lorrain.

Continue to Innerleithen and one of our favorite Scottish houses, Traquair ♛ ♛ ♛, parts of which were a royal residence in 1107. Its fascination, however, comes from its Jacobite and Mary Queen of Scots connections.

You enter Traquair House from the side because the impressive front gate, flanked by two great stone bears, is locked. Why? Because in 1745 the 5th Earl of Traquair vowed never to use the front gate until Bonnie Prince Charlie, who had just left Traquair for battle, returned as the Stuart King of England. The family is still waiting. (That's Scotland for you.)

Traquair has remarkable artifacts from that 16th–17th-century era when Catholicism was proscribed, and its ancient rooms contrast vividly with those lived in today by the present twentieth laird, Peter Stuart, and his family. Most beautiful of the rooms is the 17th-century library, which bears a decorative panel encircling the room, commemorating classical heroes (Aristotle, the Bede, Cicero, etc.), each name an alphabetical key to the books shelved below.

The lairds of Traquair were loyal both to the Stuart Prince Charles and to the Catholic religion. You will see the priest's room, hidden behind a secret staircase, and also priest's robes that could be disguised as bedspreads. There is an ornately carved cradle used by Mary Queen of Scots for her son, the future James I of England. There are many such personal objects directly related to the house and historic figures of turbulent times past.

Two miles north of Innerleithen is Peebles, a mill town, where some of the best buys in woolens can be found.

INSIDERS' TIPS

Beer buffs will head for Traquair's brewery, beneath the chapel, for some of Britain's finest ale. Don't be surprised if the laird himself hands you your bottle. Traquair ale, incidentally, sells for $10 per numbered bottle at the few New York bars where it can be found. It's about $2 at the brewery.

EDINBURGH

Edinburgh (pronounced *ED-in-burra*), 15 miles to the north, is like two distinct but connected cities. Old Town, a labyrinth of stony medieval streets, is dominated by massive Edinburgh Castle ♛ ♛ ♛ built on a rock, and extends eastward along the Royal Mile to the Palace of Holyrood ♛ ♛ ♛. New Town is airier, a series of crescents and Georgian houses.

In the castle, whose massive, brooding profile dominates the city skyline, a highlight is the bedroom in the State Apartments where Mary Queen of Scots gave birth to James VI of Scotland (England's James I). You'll see also the Crown Chamber, and the French Prisons, where Napoleon's soldiers were imprisoned by the hundreds.

Along the Royal Mile, past rows of turreted, gabled buildings, there are several stops to make: St. Giles Cathedral ♛, known for its Thistle Chapel's stalls and heraldic stained-glass windows; Lady Stair's 1622 House ♛, which features paintings and mementos of Scotland's triumvirate of writers, Sir Walter Scott, Robert Louis Stevenson, and Robert Burns; and John Knox's House ♛ ♛, home of the religious leader who founded the Scottish Presbyterian church. The house, dating back to the 15th century, is intriguing in itself, whether or not you are interested in Knox.

A real "must-see" is Holyroodhouse, through which a kilted guide will conduct you. Holyrood means "Holy Cross," but this royal palace had more than its share of less-than-holy doings. Most infamous was the murder of Mary Queen of Scots's secretary, David Rizzio, by her conspiratorial husband, Lord Darnley. You'll see the queen's private apartments, where she was dining *a deux* with Rizzio when Darnley and his men burst in and seized Rizzio. They stabbed him and carted him off to the Audience Chamber, inflicting 56 stab wounds in all.

Also in Old Town is the National Gallery of Scotland ♛ ♛ ♛ ♛, a storehouse of medieval and Renaissance masterpieces, with works by Flemish, Dutch (4 splendid Rembrandts, for example), Spanish, and Italian (several gorgeous Titians among them) painters. Upstairs in the neoclassical building are excellent Impressionist

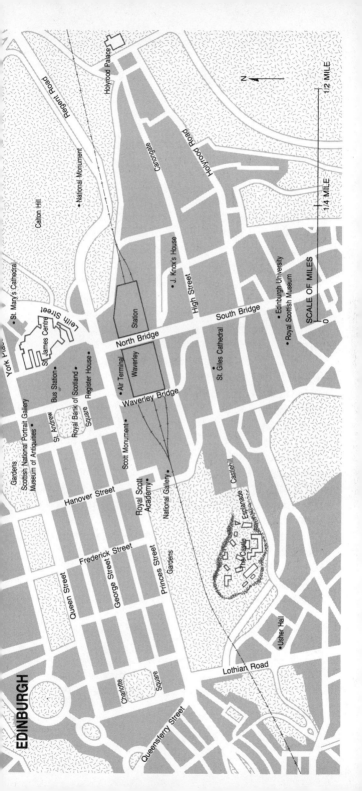

EDINBURGH

St. Mary's Cathedral
Calton Hill
National Monument
Regent Road
Holyrood Palace
Canongate
Holyrood Road
York Place
Leith Street
St. James Centre
Gardens
Scottish National Portrait Gallery
Museum of Antiquities
St. Andrew Square
Royal Bank of Scotland
Register House
Bus Station
Station
Air Terminal
Waverley
North Bridge
Waverley Bridge
J. Knox's House
High Street
South Bridge
St. Giles Cathedral
Edinburgh University
Royal Scottish Museum
Scott Monument
Hanover Street
Royal Scott Academy
National Gallery
Castlehill
The Castle
Esplanade
Queen Street
Frederick Street
George Street
Princes Street
Gardens
Charlotte Square
Queensferry Street
Lothian Road
Usher Hall

N

SCALE OF MILES

0   1/4 MILE   1/2 MILE

and Post-Impressionist works by Gauguin, Van Gogh, Degas, Monet, Cézanne, and others.

A highlight of Edinburgh's New Town is the new National Gallery of Modern Art ♛ ♛ ♛ on Belford Street. You'll know it by the 2 huge Henry Moore bronze sculptures, and one by Sir Jacob Epstein, on the spacious front lawn. Inside is a small but choice collection of every period of modern art since World War I, with works by internationally known artists such as Matisse, Picasso, Léger, Louise Nevelson, Francis Bacon, and Duane Hanson.

In addition to its art treasures, Edinburgh is famous for its annual Edinburgh Festival (August), which brings performers and music and dance lovers from all over the world. It is also a logical base for day trips.

In Linlithgow, 18 miles to the west, is the roofless Palace of Linlithgow ♛, where Mary Queen of Scots was born in 1542. Near the Forth Road Bridge, at South Queensbury, is one of Scotland's spectacular 18th-century Adams mansions, Hopetoun House ♛ ♛ ♛, seat of the Marquess of Linlithgow. Beautiful grounds, nature trails, and a Stables Museum vie for your attention, but the *creme* is the house, with its superb 18th-century furniture, paintings, and *objets.*

You needn't be a golfer to make the pilgrimage to St. Andrews, where this sport began and whose Royal and Ancient Golf Club dates back to 1754. The Scots invented the game, and they make their courses tough.

Have a look also at the ruins of St. Andrews Cathedral

and Priory, built from 1127 to 1318; another ruin, the Castle of St. Andrews, with secret passages and a dungeon; and the medieval Holy Trinity Church.

Near Scotland's east coast, north of Edinburgh, are two of the country's most famous castles, Balmoral ♛ ♛, 8 miles west of Ballater, and Glamis ♛ ♛, 12 miles north of Dundee. Balmoral was a favorite of Queen Victoria, who had it rebuilt in Scottish baronial style in 1855. As it is still used by Britain's Royal Family, only the ballroom and grounds are open to the public.

Inverness, straddling both sides of the Ness River, above Loch Ness, is the springboard to the Highlands. The city has a Gaelic museum in Abertarff House, a Clock Tower (a remnant of Cromwell's fort), and the intriguing Inverness Museum and Art Gallery ♛ ♛ ♛. The Gallery gives a wonderful overview of Highland life, with village rooms, a fine Highland silver collection, and an art gallery.

Cawdor Castle, of *Macbeth* fame, is 5 miles south of town. Six miles east of Inverness is Culloden, an important landmark in British history. It was here that Bonnie Prince Charlie's Jacobite army was crushed April 16, 1746, by English forces under the Duke of Cumberland.

GLASGOW

Glasgow is well worth your time. It is understandably Victorian and industrial, since its industrial might brought the city to the zenith of wealth in Victorian times. It also has some of the finest museums in Britain.

The Burrell Collection ♛ ♛ ♛ ♛ ♛ in Pollok Park is reason enough for a Glasgow visit. In a stunning glass and pink sandstone building are 8,000 works collected by shipping magnate Sir William Burrell over 80 years.

The collection includes Egyptian and Greek antiquities, 13th-century French Gothic doorways and arches, and 18th- and 19th-century Japanese woodcuts. There are rare

PERILS & PITFALLS

Reports persist of casual theft in Glasgow, so it is prudent to empty your car (or put everything out of sight in the trunk) and lock it when you leave it.

16th-century tapestries, Tang Dynasty horses, 16th-century suits of German armor, a superlative *Stag Hunt* by Lucas Cranach, Turkish prayer rugs, and Tudor rooms.

What makes this eclectic collection work so well are the expert, imaginative displays. For example, the many masterpieces of rare stained glass are displayed at eye level, against windows, so that natural light can flow through as originally intended.

Across Pollok Park is the Pollok House ♛♛♛, a splendidly maintained 18th-century manor house, notable for its sizable collection of first-rate Spanish art collected by Sir John Stirling-Maxwell. There are works by Velasquez, El Greco, Coello, Murillo, and Goya, plus paintings by Flemish and British artists.

In downtown Glasgow is the enormous Glasgow City Art Gallery and Museum ♛♛♛, in Kelvingrove Park. Among its many stimulating departments, one displays a revelatory exhibit of strikingly original furniture and interiors by the influential Scots designer Charles Rennie Mackintosh and his associates.

Justifiably famous is the Museum's wide-ranging art collection. It features Dutch, Flemish, British, and Italian master paintings, and many outstanding Impressionist and Post-Impressionist works by Monet, Degas, Matisse, Dufy, Rouault, Gauguin, and Van Gogh. A show-stopper is Salvador Dali's controversial *Christ of St. John of the Cross,* one of the Spanish artist's masterpieces.

For still more art, there's the Hunterian Art Gallery ♛♛♛ at the University of Glasgow. This diverse, splendid collection includes more works of Charles Rennie Mackintosh, plus paintings by Stubbs, Rubens, Corot, Pissarro, Rembrandt, and many others. It also has a remarkable print collection. But its unique feature is its collection of works by James McNeill Whistler, including the contents of his studio, bequeathed to the Hunterian by his sister-in-law.

If you aren't "museumed out," the People's Palace Museum ♛♛ on Glasgow Green has a social approach to art, displaying crafts, posters, and contemporary works that are fresh and provocative.

Less than 10 miles south of the border is Carlisle, in whose castle Mary Queen of Scots was held prisoner in 1568.

THE SCOTTISH ISLANDS

Every island buff has a favorite. Ours is tranquil Mull, in the Inner Hebrides, reached by ferry from Oban to the main town, Tobermory (a charmer). Mull is noted for its role in Robert Louis Stevenson's *Kidnapped* and is a spirit restorative—great for bird-watching, wildflowers, moors, and lochs.

PERILS & PITFALLS

Ferry timetables are tricky. To avoid missing the ferry and being stranded, check timetables and make reservations (when possible) well in advance. Then allow time for traffic jams and queues once you get to the ferry.

From Mull it is a 10-minute ferry ride to Iona, a tiny island famous as the birthplace of Christianity in Scotland and also for its "46 graves of Scottish kings" (including Macbeth and Duncan). St. Columba, it is believed, arrived from Ireland in A.D. 563 and founded the first abbey in the British Isles. The Book of Kells was written on Iona in the 8th century, and the Abbey♛♛ was an important religious center until the 13th century. It still casts a mystical spell. Or maybe it's the sea air.

The Isle of Skye tops most "favorite" lists for its remoteness and bucolic spirit. Off the beaten track is Dunvegan Castle on a remote loch, the stronghold for 700 years of the Clan McLeod chiefs.

Other islands with considerable charm are Arran, whose Brodick Castle has an eclectic collection of antiques, china, and art. Jura, fourth largest of the Inner Hebrides, is where George Orwell lived for 2 years after World War II, and where you'll see the remaining ruins of Claig Castle, home of the MacDonalds, until they were conquered by the Campbells in the 17th century.

INSIDERS' TIPS

Cars are forbidden on Iona, but you can rent bikes at the Hotel Argyll for about $1.50 per hour or $3 for 24 hours. You can easily cover the 1-by-2-mile island and still make the final ferry back to Mull.

INSIDERS' INFORMATION FOR SCOTLAND

Arisaig (Highland; Area Code Arisaig 06875)

Hotel

Arisaig House♛♛
Arisaig PH39 4NR. Tel. 622.
2 persons in twin, $67.50–90.
Stately stone 1864 manor on 20-acre wooded grounds. 16 rooms, bar, traditional restaurant, croquet. Restful, secluded, immaculate, with classic French menu a highpoint.

Auchterarder (Tayside; Area Code Auchterarder 07646)

Hotel

Gleneagles♛♛♛♛
Auchterarder PH3 1NF. Tel. 2231.
2 persons in twin, $120–150.
Enormous resort hotel in country-club seclusion. 260 rooms, bar, restaurant, gym, sauna, indoor swimming pool, solarium, shops, 4 golf courses, tennis, squash. Golfer's paradise, the *total* resort for jocks and sports activists, well run, with spacious rooms and public areas.

Bonnyrigg (Lothian; Area Code Gorebridge 0875)

Hotel

Dalhousie Castle♛♛
Near Edinburgh EH19 3JB. Tel. 20153.
2 persons in twin, $90–150.
Part of 12th-century castle facing the Esk River on 7 acres outside Edinburgh. 24 rooms, dungeon bar, restaurant, helipad. The Earl of Dalhousie's family history, stately rooms, and antiques create a medieval mood, with modern comforts, continental cuisine.

Crinan (Strathclyde; Area Code Crinan 054-683)

Hotel

Crinan♛♛
By Lochgilphead PA31 8SR. Tel. 235.

2 persons in twin, $67.50–90.
Smallish seaside hotel facing Crinan Canal and the sea.
22 rooms, 2 bars, *Loch 16* restaurant(♛ ♛), boats, coffee
shop. Water views from guest rooms are as delicious as
the fresh seafood served in the laudable *Loch 16*.

Dunblane (Central; Area Code Dunblane 0786)

Hotel
Cromlix House ♛ ♛ ♛ ♛ ♛
Dunblane FK15 9JT. Tel. 822125.
2 persons in twin, $120–150.
Austere stone house on a 5,000-acre estate. 11 rooms,
superior restaurant (♛ ♛ ♛ ♛), noted for game, fish, and
wine cellar; library, chapel, tennis, croquet, riding, shooting, fishing, helipad. Luxurious in every detail, including
silver and Wedgwood china, formal lounges, spacious
rooms with views, candlelit dining, attentive staff—a totally pampering experience.

Edinburgh (Lothian; Area Code 031)

Hotel
Caledonian ♛ ♛ ♛ ♛
Princes St. EH1 2AB. Tel. 225-2433.
2 persons in twin, $60–80.
Massive Edwardian railroad hotel (recently modernized) in
central location. A "grand hotel" in the old sense. 254
rooms, 2 bars, 2 restaurants, ballroom. Deluxe, well-
appointed rooms, many with castle views, great comfort, afternoon tea a real event, *Pompadour* restaurant
(♛ ♛ ♛), elegant and memorable (about $50 per person).

Restaurants
Aye ♛ ♛ ♛
80 Queen St. Tel. 226-5467.
Average dinner: $18–50.
One of Britain's finest Japanese restaurants, from exquisite decor to presentation of sushi, tempura, and a wide
range of delicacies.
Shamiana ♛
14 Broughham St. Tel. 228-2265.

Average dinner: $29.
Stylish restaurant featuring impeccable northern Indian dishes.

Fort William (Highland; Area Code Fort William 0397)

Hotel
Inverlochy Castle ♛ ♛ ♛ ♛
Torlundy PH33 6SN. Tel. 2177.
2 persons in twin, $150.
A Victorian castle (1863) in a dreamlike loch-and-mountain setting. 16 rooms, Great Hall, celebrated restaurant (♛ ♛ ♛), outstanding (and pricey) wine list, tennis, fishing, helipad. Luxurious (and occasionally pretentious) touches abound in this fantasy castle with Ben Nevis mountain views; a favorite celebrity hideaway. Total seclusion, fastidious maintenance.

Glasgow (Strathclyde; Area Code 041)

Hotel
Gleddoch House ♛ ♛
Langbank PA14 6YE. Tel. (Langbank 047-554) 711.
2 persons in twin, $90–120.
A 1927 former shipbuilder's home in country-club setting 13 miles from Glasgow. 20 comfortable rooms, bar, restaurant, sauna, golf, squash, riding, fishing. Clublike ambience, informal air.

Restaurants
The Buttery ♛
654 Argyle St. Tel. 221-8188.
Average dinner: $35.
Edwardian setting, 1980s Scottish/English food.
Preet Palace Tandoori ♛
Bearsden Shopping Centre, Milngavie Road, Bearsden. Tel. 942-9067.
Average dinner: $9–22.
Typical Indian specialties, to Indian music accompaniment.
Ubiquitous Chip ♛
12 Ashton Lane, off Byres Rd. Tel. 334-5007.

Average dinner: $22–25.
Converted stables form a backdrop for solid Scots dishes and superlative wine list.

Gullane (Lothian; Area Code Gullane 0620)

Hotel

Greywalls ♛ ♛ ♛
Muirfield EH31 2EG. Tel. 842-144.
2 persons in twin, $120–150.
Sir Edwin Lutyens–designed rambling house, views of the Firth of Forth. 23 rooms, library, commendable restaurant (♛), notable wine list, tennis, croquet. Comfortable, antiques-accented, well-run, family-owned hotel, a celebrity favorite, handy to Muirfield championship golf course.

Restaurant

La Potiniere ♛ ♛
Main St. Tel. 843-214.
Average dinner: $22–28.
Erratic hours; call and reserve ahead. Modern, highly personalized, expert cooking in simple setting.

Inverness (Highland; Area Code Inverness 0463)

Hotels

Culloden House ♛ ♛
Culloden IV1 2NZ. Tel. 790-461.
2 persons in twin, $120–150.
Graceful Georgian house near site of castle and Battle of Culloden in the Scottish Highlands. 20 rooms, bar, restaurant (♛), sauna, solarium, tennis, fishing. Splendid antique furnishings, stylish rooms, and spaciousness mark this idyllic, parklike setting.
Dunain Park ♛
Inverness IV3 6JN. Tel. 230-512.
2 persons in twin, $90–120.
Georgian house in 6-acre country setting, off A82 outside town. 9 rooms, quality restaurant (♛), croquet, badminton. Comfortable, informal, secluded.

Kelso (Borders; Area Code Roxburgh 05735)

Hotel

Sunlaws House♛♛
Heiton TD5 8JZ. Tel. 331.
2 persons in twin, $67.50–90.
Imposing house in a wooded park facing the Teviot River.
15 rooms, bar, restaurant, tennis, croquet, fishing, shooting, stables, helipad. Great spaciousness, comfortably furnished rooms, and a sense of privacy mark this English-Scottish border retreat.

Kentallen of Appin (Argyll; Area Code Duror 063-174)

Hotel

Ardsheal House♛♛♛
Kentallen of Appin PA38 4BX. Tel. 227.
2 persons in twin, $90–120.
1760 manor house at the end of a long one-track drive along Loch Linnhe. 13 rooms, bar, excellent restaurant (♛♛♛), tennis, garden. Bucolic setting on 1,000-acre wooded property, sophisticated cuisine (try the Stilton soup), stylish decor in a house layered with history. Friendly American proprietors.

Kilchrenan (Strathclyde; Area Code Kilchrenan 086-63)

Hotels

Ardanaiseig♛♛♛
By Taynuilt PA35 1HE. Tel. 333.
2 persons in twin, $90–120.
19th-century stone house in a remote setting, facing Loch Awe. 14 rooms, traditional restaurant (♛), tennis, croquet, fishing. Comfort is the key word in this gracious, welcoming country house, where wood fires, ample rooms, antiques, and exhilarating views abound.

Taychreggan♛♛♛
By Taynuilt PA35 1HQ. Tel. 211.
2 persons in twin, $48–90.

Old inn with a modern addition affords views of scenic Loch Awe. 17 rooms, bar, restaurant (♛), boats, fishing. Friendliness is in the air in this congenial hotel with big window views of the water; wood fires, cheerfully decorated and impeccably kept rooms. A restful spot.

Mull (Strathclyde; Area Code Tiroran 068-15)

Hotel

Tiroran House ♛ ♛ ♛
Isle of Mull PA69 6ES. Tel. 232.
2 persons in twin, $67.50–90.
Country house set on a remote hilltop amid abundant gardens and woods. 9 rooms, restaurant (♛ ♛ ♛), croquet, dinghy sailing. Personal, family-run, homelike hotel, handsomely decorated with family antiques; superior sophisticated home cooking by chef and co-owner Sue Blockey; fantastic giant crayfish are a special treat.

St. Andrews (Fife; Area Code St. Andrews 0334)

Hotel

Rufflets ♛ ♛
Strathkinness Low Road KY16 9TX. Tel. 72594.
2 persons in twin, $67.50–90.
Ivy-covered country house on 10 acres at town edge. 21 rooms, bar, restaurant, putting green, gardens. Garden-fresh, homemade Scottish food, comfy rooms, friendly folk.

Restaurant

The Peat Inn ♛ ♛ ♛ ♛
At junction of B940 and B941, 6 miles southwest of St. Andrews. Tel. (033-484) 206.
Average dinner: $30.
Gourmets flock to chef-owner David Wilson's tiny European-style inn from all over Scotland for his subtle, inventive cooking (from freshest seasonal ingredients). Exceptional wine list.

WALES

The Welsh, it is asserted by authorities of uncertain reliability, are people whose ancestors were unable to swim to Ireland to escape the invading Saxon hordes.

Today, the musical, difficult Welsh language is the major reminder of those days. Similar Celtic languages still exist in Cornwall and Brittany. Welsh literature, stemming from at least the 13th century, is alive and resonates in English translation.

Wales is smaller than Massachusetts, and you can easily peregrinate from north to south in less than a week, with leisurely visits to most major attractions. If time isn't a problem, you may want to do it by pony-trekking.

Your Wales entry point is a matter of choice. The quick way is by train from London to Cardiff (1 hour and 45 minutes). Many visitors drive into north Wales from Chester or into south Wales via the M4 motorway north of Bristol.

It's a fast 12 miles south from Chester to Wrexham in Wales, where St. Giles 1518 parish churchyard ♛ ♛ is the final resting place of Elihu Yale, benefactor of Yale University. The tower is the model for one at Yale.

Just 2 miles south you will find one of Britain's unique country-house experiences at Erddig ♛ ♛ ♛, a 17th-century manor that belonged to the Yorkes. Though the grounds, garden, and farm are immense, the focus of interest in this National Trust property is the social history of the near-feudal community that existed on the 1,900-acre estate.

The "Upstairs/Downstairs" relationships are made evident as you enter the property, not through the front door, but through the outbuildings: by the carpenter's shed, laundry and drying room, bakehouse, and stables into the downstairs hall, past the butler's pantry, the estate housekeeper's offices and kitchen, then finally into family areas.

There is a remarkable exhibit of drawings and photos of each of the staff, spanning more than 200 years. With each picture is a poem, written by succeeding heads of the family in warm, intimate terms, describing the individual and his or her duties, personality, character, and relationship to the household. Reading these, we have vivid insights into what life was like on such an estate for cooks, gamekeepers, coachmen, artisans, maids, and, by inference, the family.

While the house has its quota of exquisite furniture (the playroom and Chinese bedroom, with its Chinese wallpaper, brocaded bed canopy, lacquer screens and chests, are special delights), it is the cramped third-floor maids' rooms and glimpses of backstairs life that one tends to remember because they are so rare.

A side trip inland on A458 brings you to the town of Welshpool on the Severn River. At the town's edge is Powis (*PO-iss*) Castle ♛ ♛ ♛, a 13th–16th-century treasure trove of art, architecture, and gardens.

The building ranges from Tudor to late 20th century in a series of splendid rooms, each grander than the last, with ornate 16th-century plasterwork and wood paneling among the high points. In the Elizabethan long gallery are portraits (by Romney, Kneller, Reynolds, Gainsborough) of the Herbert family, who have lived in the castle since 1587. There are also collections of 16th-century Limoges enamel, Louis XV furniture, pewter, and miniatures.

However, the most exotic and unique items came from Lord Clive of India and the compulsive but discerning collecting of his daughter-in-law, Lady Henrietta Herbert, who married the second Lord Clive, governor of Madras from 1798. Lady Clive traveled the Indian outback in search of art and artifacts, with unflagging dedication to British standards of conduct. Her entourage included an elephant expressly to carry her daughter's harp and piano.

As a result of the Clives' collecting, you can wonder at the tiger throne, painted durbar tent, swords and guns of Tipu Sahib, the Sultan of Mysore, whose rebellion and life were ended by the British. Also on view are Indian artworks—carved ivory, metalwork, textiles and paintings—from those glory days of the Raj, when India first became part of the British Empire.

On a steep embankment below the castle are four great,

stairstep-terraced gardens ♛ ♛ ♛ ♛ of 1790, balustraded and punctuated with classical sculptures. The terraces intermingle statues, manicured borders, topiary hedges, and monumental, velvety yews with flowering dogwood, apple trees, and shrubs such as Chinese snowballs, roses, japonica, and clematis.

If you visit Wales during July, you'll find the contagious euphoria of Eisteddfod at Llangollen on the River Dee, in full force. This is a traditional celebration in Welsh song and poetry, and has been an annual event from 1568, when Elizabeth I commanded the first one to be held.

Early each July, thousands of singers and dancers compete in teams from around the world. (You'll need to reserve accommodations far ahead. The best idea is to book a farmhouse B&B through the Wales Tourist Office.)

Turning north and west, the road leads to Ruthin ♛ ♛, an animated market town with inviting craft shops and half-timbered buildings around its main street. Market day (Wednesday) is especially festive because many townspeople, including bank managers, wear medieval garb. St. Peter's Church ♛ ♛ has a splendid oak roof with 500 carved panels, given by Henry VII to acknowledge Welsh help in winning his throne. Note also the fine 15th-century screen and rood loft.

Ruthin Castle ♛ has been transformed from a medieval fortress to an Edwardian castle. It was once a Royalist stronghold. Today, as a luxury hotel, it specializes in nightly medieval banquets. On Park Road, you'll see the Ruthin Craft Centre, a complex of craft workshops fascinating to browse.

Some 22 miles northwest you reach the coast facing the Irish Sea at Llandudno, Wales's largest seaside resort. Llandudno has two beaches—one on the Irish Sea, the other on Conwy Bay—and a grand promenade along the water in front of the bulky Victorian hotels. *The* big tourist action here is taking the Great Orme Tramway ♛ ♛ to the peak for sweeping views of the north Wales coast.

Scarcely 8 miles south of Llandudno is Bodnant Garden ♛ ♛ ♛, created in 1875 by Lord Conway and famous worldwide among gardeners. The rhododendrons and camellias are standouts, but don't give short shrift to the magnolias and conifers, woodland and rock gardens.

Across the estuary from Llandudno to the west is one of

Britain's most impressive fortifications, magnificent Conwy Castle♛♛♛. You approach it broadside, via the modern highway bridge that parallels the graceful 1826 suspension bridge that is now a National Trust property.

Conwy Castle was built by Edward I in 1284 to pacify the continually restive Welsh, but Edward was besieged here himself in 1290, and a century later Richard II took refuge here. The castle commands the river and protects the town with 21 towers along the massive, mile-long walls. Called the best-preserved medieval town fortifications in Britain, they are unquestionably among the most romantic.

Castle buffs will proceed west to Bangor, then across Robert Stephenson's epochal 1850 Britannia Bridge♛♛ to Anglesey Island. Just 4½ miles east is Beaumaris Castle♛♛, the last of Edward I's fortresses. Begun in 1295, its square within an octagon is a powerful, picture-perfect outpost overlooking Conwy Bay.

CAERNARFON CASTLE

Eight miles west of the bridge on the mainland is the massive castle that millions of people have seen on TV, even if they don't remember its name. It is Caernarfon♛♛♛, the traditional site of the formal investiture of the Prince of Wales. Like so many Welsh castles, it is tremendously impressive from outside (especially when lighted at night), but only a shell of its former self inside.

Caernarfon (the preferred Welsh spelling, as Caernarvon is the English version) was begun by Edward I in 1283, and above its hulking King's Gate is a weather-worn statue of Edward II. In the inner court a black stone circle marks the spot where the last investiture ceremony took place.

In one tower are striking exhibits, with a sound and video replay of the investiture of Charles as Prince of Wales in 1969. The tradition harks back to Edward I of England, who declared his son Prince of Wales here in 1282. Since that date, the firstborn son of an English monarch takes the title of Prince of Wales at his formal investiture, making him heir to the British throne.

From Caernarfon we recommend heading south through evergreen Snowdonia National Park♛♛, with its mountain vistas, to Portmeirion ♛ ♛, a surprising resort that appears to have been transported, campanile and all, from the Italian coast. Planned that way by the architect Sir Clough Williams-Ellis, Portmeirion is a live-in put-on that is great fun, like an amusement park for adults.

The resort was the setting for the British television series "The Prisoner," where its Mediterranean buildings, palm trees, and bright colors were thoroughly disorienting. Rooms and villas are for rent and are much more reasonable than Positano or Portofino in the high season.

On Wales's south coast is Dylan Thomas's lovely, peaceful village of Laugharne, where the River Taf empties into Carmarthen Bay. You can visit the Boat House ♛ ♛ perched on Cliff Walk, in which the poet lived and wrote such works as *A Child's Christmas in Wales* and *Under Milk Wood*. There are photographs and exhibits of Thomas memorabilia. He is buried in the local churchyard.

CARDIFF

Dead east is Cardiff, Wales's major city and capital. In the city's center on Castle Street is Cardiff Castle ♛ ♛, originally Norman, but redone a century ago in high Victorian Gothic style. (Medieval banquets are offered here.) Nearby is the National Museum of Wales ♛ ♛ in Cathays Park. Its European art collection ♛ ♛ ♛ includes Rodin's *The Kiss*, a Henry Moore bronze, Lucas Cranach's small portrait of a man, the Welsh artist Augustus John's 1953 portrait of Dylan Thomas, and four larger-than-life-size tapestry cartoons attributed to Rubens (but disputed by art experts), dramatically presented in special vitrines.

You'll see notable exhibits of Welsh archaeology, artifacts, industry, and pottery.

For a review—or preview—of Wales, visit the Welsh Folk Museum ♛ ♛ ♛ in the Cardiff suburb of St. Fagan's. Set in 80 acres of park, it is an assemblage of rural buildings of various periods and styles.

The Museum's centerpiece is a whitewashed Tudor mansion, St. Fagan's Castle, whose carved wood mantels and occasional concerts (such as one by the Caerleon College Consort using ancient instruments) are delightful. Also on view are farmers' and slate quarriers' cottages, a

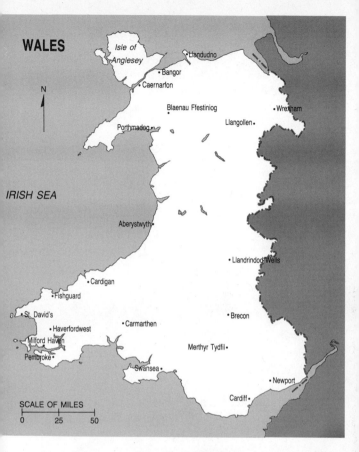

WALES

IRISH SEA

Isle of
Anglesey

• Llandudno
• Bangor
• Caernarfon

Blaenau Ffestiniog

• Wrexham

Llangollen •

Porthmadog

Aberystwyth •

• Llandrindod Wells

• Cardigan

• Fishguard

• St. David's

• Brecon

• Haverfordwest

• Carmarthen

• Milford Haven

• Pembroke

Merthyr Tydfil •

• Swansea •

• Newport

Cardiff •

SCALE OF MILES
0   25   50

rural schoolhouse, a chapel, a working smithy, and corn and woolen mills with craftsmen at work.

Looping 24 miles east of Cardiff, you will reach Chepstow on the River Wye, which forms the border with England. Highly visible above the river are the ruins of Chepstow's once-mighty castle ♛, which was begun in 1088. But the real reason for visiting Chepstow is to wander through the widely known ruins of Tintern Abbey ♛ ♛.

Made famous by Wordsworth, the Abbey is 4 miles north of Chepstow. The Cistercians began it in 1131, but what remains is mainly late-13th-century construction. Notably well preserved are the lofty walls and windows of the Gothic church and the intangible aura of romantic mystery. It's a popular tourist destination and can be overwhelmed by crowds (a rarity in Wales).

Follow the twisting Wye River north, and you'll come to Monmouth, where Henry IV was born in 1387, and its

13th-century fortified bridge. Farther up the river is Hay-on-Wye, a town of 1,500 with 16 or more bookstores. It's a noted center for old, out-of-print, and rare books and a haven for browsers and bookaholics.

INSIDERS' INFORMATION FOR WALES

Abergavenny (Gwent; Area Code Abergavenny 0873)

Hotel
The Angel
Cross St. NP7 5EW. Tel. 7121.
2 persons in twin, $67.50.
Attractive old inn in market town. 29 rooms, bar, restaurant. Unpretentious, comfortable.

Restaurant
The Walnut Tree Inn ♛ ♛
Llandewi Skirrid. Tel. 2797.
Average dinner: $30.
In cheerful, innlike trattoria, some of the best Italian food in Britain. Market-fresh ingredients, constantly changing menu, and unusual dishes (salmon and rhubarb) make this small jewel worth a detour.

Cardiff (Cardiff; Area Code 0222)

Hotels
Park ♛ ♛
Park Place CF1 3UD. Tel. 383-471.
2 persons in twin, $67.50–90.
Enormous Victorian edifice in convenient city location. 108 rooms, 2 bars, 2 restaurants. Tastefully renovated, large and well-equipped rooms, *fin de siècle* furnishings, popular with locals (especially Park Vaults Bar).
Stakis Inn on the Avenue ♛ ♛
Circle Way East, Llanedeyrn CF3 7XF. Tel. 732-520.
2 persons in twin, $67.50–90.
Modern high-rise building in garden setting just off A48. 148 rooms, bar, restaurant with French/Welsh cuisine, indoor swimming pool, sauna, gym, solarium, helipad. Total contemporary comforts for tired travelers.

Restaurants
Blas-Ar-Cymru (A Taste of Wales) ♛
48 Crwys Rd. Tel. 382-132.
Average dinner: $15–22.
A chance to sample authentic Welsh specialties skillfully prepared in tiny, gemlike setting.

Shopping
Howells Department Store, St. Mary St. Cardiff's answer to Harrods.
Pethau Cymru—Things Welsh, 3, 5, 7 Duke St. Arcade. Handicrafts.

Theaters
Concert Hall, St. David's Centre. Tel. 371-236. Classical and popular concerts.
New Theatre, Park Pl. Tel. 32446. Cardiff home of Welsh National Opera Co., also presents plays, musicals, ballets.
Sherman Theatre, Senghenydd Rd. Tel. 25855. University theater for plays, movies, exhibitions.

Chepstow (Gwent; Area Code 02912)

Hotel
Castle View ♛
16 Bridge St. NP6 5EZ. Tel. 70349.
2 persons in twin, $52.50–67.50.
10 rooms, bar, restaurant. Modest but tidy pub with rooms, convenient location.

Shopping
Stuart Crystal, Bridge St. Workshop and sales of decorated glass.

Llandudno (Gwynedd; Area Code Llandudno 0492)

Hotel
Bodysgallen Hall ♛ ♛ ♛
Deganwy LL30 1RS. Tel. 84466.
2 persons in twin, $97.50–142.50.

Commanding hilltop manor-house hotel with view of Irish Sea. 28 rooms, bar, first-class restaurant (♛ ♛), tennis, croquet, helipad. Lounges especially warm and ingratiating, beautiful gardens and well-kept grounds, all the comforts of a congenial country home.

Shopping

Mostyn Art Gallery, 12 Vaughan St. Changing exhibits of contemporary handicrafts, art, and photography.

Llangollen (Clwyd; Area Code Llangollen 0978)

Hotel

Britannia Inn ♛
Horseshoe Pass LL20 8DW. Tel. 860-144.
2 persons in twin, $45–51.
Renovated 15th-century inn at foot of famous Horseshoe Pass. 7 rooms, bar, restaurant. Comfortable rooms, scenic locale, friendly folks.

Shopping

Good town for Welsh woolens and handicrafts, many shops along main street.
Llangollen Weavers Mill and Shop. Good buys in woolens.

Monmouth (Gwent; Area Code Monmouth 0600)

Hotel

King's Head ♛
Agincourt Square NP5 3DY. Tel. 2177.
2 persons in twin, $67.50–81.
Handsome 17th-century gabled coaching inn, centrally located. 28 rooms, 2 bars, restaurant with "Taste of Wales" menu. Flower-bedecked inside and out, with sprightly guest rooms, congenial public areas, good maintenance.

Portmeirion (Portmeirion; Area Code 0766)

Hotel

Portmeirion ♛
Penrhyndeudraeth. Tel. 770-228.
2 persons in twin, $94.50–104.
Attractive guest cottages scattered through resort "village." 20 rooms, bar, 2 restaurants. Colorful "Mediterranean village" setting for "The Prisoner" TV series, facing Tremadog Bay. Hotel on grounds had a fire and is in the process of restoration.

Ruthin (Clwyd; Area Code Ruthin 082-42)

Hotel

Ruthin Castle ♛
Corwen Road LL15 2NU. Tel. 2664.
2 persons in twin, $48–90.
Authentic 13th–19th-century castle in spacious grounds at town's edge. 60 rooms, bar, restaurant (medieval banquets), fishing. Stately halls, huge rooms, oak paneling, armor and medieval adornments. Needs some refurbishing. Great potential.

Shopping

Ruthin Craft Centre, Park Rd. 14 handicraft workshops grouped around courtyard.

Tintern Abbey (Gwent; Area Code Tintern 029-18)

Hotel

Royal George ♛
Tintern NP6 6SF. Tel. 202.
2 persons in twin, $52.50–67.50.
17th-century inn next to millpond at edge of Wye Valley village. 19 rooms, bar, restaurant, garden. Simple rooms, cheerful place, handy for walks and hiking.

Welshpool (Powys; Area Code 0938)

Hotels

Dysserth House ♛
Welshpool SY21 8RQ. Tel. 2153.
2 persons in twin, $39.
4 rooms, shared baths, country house on Powys Castle estate grounds. Gracious hosts (Mr. and Mrs. Marriott), B&B "sleeper," peaceful setting.

Golfa Hall ♛
Welshpool SY21 9AF. Tel. 5444.
2 persons in twin, $72.
Restored farmhouse 3 miles from town on A458. 11 rooms, Victorian restaurant, next to 18-hole golf course. Overstuffed furniture, comfy, unpretentious. Opened 1986 as hotel.

Restaurant

Cottage Inn ♛
On B4388, Montgomery. Tel. (068-681)348.
Average dinner: $10.
Cozy pub and restaurant, simple, home-cooked foods, excellent value, 7 miles south of Powys Castle.

THE CHANNEL ISLANDS AND TWO ODD ONES

The islands, in descending order of size, are Jersey, Guernsey, Alderney, Sark, Herm, and Jethou. Ferries reach them daily (in summer) from Portsmouth and Weymouth. Frequent sea and air connections link all the islands.

Originally part of France, they are a legacy of the Norman Conquest. "We think of England as our oldest possession," a Jersey man may tell you with a wink.

What this means today is a charming split personality. Legally the islands are part of Britain, but they have an independent judicial system, many French traditions and names, and two languages. This cultural mix is fascinating, giving a French accent—in Jersey and Guernsey especially—to the food, architecture, city squares, and individualistic lifestyles. "We don't buy the local paper to find out what everyone has been doing," one Guernsey resident told us jokingly, "but to see who's been caught at it."

While each island is different, all share a climate milder and sunnier than Mother Britain's, which is why you see many escapees from mist and fog sunning themselves on the beaches of Jersey, Alderney, or Herm. Another attraction is tax-free shopping.

Large, temperate Jersey was the birthplace of the painter J. E. Millais and "Jersey Lillie" Langtry, and also home for a while to Victor Hugo, the French statesman Chateaubriand, and T. E. Lawrence. Claude Debussy wrote his memoirs on the island.

Elizabeth Castle, on St. Aubin's Bay, just off St. Helier (busy port and capital of the island), was built in Elizabeth I's time, and Sir Walter Raleigh lived here as governor. The castle's Museum of the Jersey Militia has displays from the German occupation of the island during World War II. The rock beneath Mont Orgueil Castle has been a fortified site since the Iron Age. Look as you drive through villages for the *piel du mariage* (marriage stone) in the façades of many houses—a heart with newlyweds' initials and their marriage dates entwined—a custom that is centuries old.

On Jersey, "Ask for Mary Ann." That's the slogan of a popular local malt brew that has won international awards for rich flavor.

PERILS & PITFALLS

On Jersey, don't call the ubiquitous cinnamon-brown cows Guernseys. Jerseys are smaller, but these hoofed cholesterol factories produce milk that has the highest butterfat content in the world, according to Jersey farmers.

Guernsey is a sunny land where fresh flowers, tomatoes, and other vegetables are grown for European markets. Especially scenic is the hilltop capital, St. Peter Port, winding above a pretty harbor. Street signs are in both English and French, and the tree-shaded squares have a French *je ne sais quoi.*

The prime attraction here is one of our favorite historic houses, Hauteville House ♔ ♔ ♔, Victor Hugo's home during his self-imposed exile from France from 1856 to 1870. This 23-room, 4-story Victorian house is a personal statement, full of idiosyncratic touches, such as the oak chairs that Hugo made and dubbed "Pater" and "Mater," and his hand-painted shutters and carved rococo furniture, archways, and fireplace paneling.

History buffs will look for the World War II Nazi Occupation Museum and Underground Hospital. There are also remains of German fortifications scattered throughout the island.

Good buys on both Guernsey and Jersey are navy-blue, close-knit fishermen's wool sweaters that wear for decades. Don't call a Jersey sweater a Guernsey, or vice versa; Jerseys have an anchor design, Guernseys a specific shoulder weave.

Nine miles from Guernsey is the tiniest Channel Island, Sark. This perfect getaway place is rugged and wildly beautiful, unspoiled by cars or planes. There is little to do but take long walks (most dramatic is along *La Coupée*, a rough isthmus leading to Little Sark), bike or carriage rides, and inhale the clear, fresh sea air. Sark is a feudal state, under the hereditary rule (since Elizabeth I's time) of a *seigneur.* A Court of Chief Pleas legislates local affairs, but there are no death duties, income tax, or adoption laws.

Herm is also small, with only 40 permanent residents, but several hundred types of shells along Shell Beach, and untold numbers of unusual wildflowers.

Alderney, though closest to England, and easily accessible from Guernsey by hydrofoil or plane, is also oddly remote. Yet its wide, sand-edged bays, spectacular craggy cliffs, bird sanctuary, and unusual wildlife make it a natural for vacationers and bird lovers.

THE ISLE OF WIGHT

The Isle of Wight is just a short car ferry ride from Portsmouth, Southampton, and Lymington. It's a popular summer vacation spot for Britons in search of sandy beaches, sailing, and a touch of nostalgic Victoriana. (Book your space ahead, especially summer weekends.)

Osbourne House♛♛, outside the yachting center of Cowes at Whippingham, was Queen Victoria's favorite summer residence and the place where she died in 1901. It obviously set the fashion for the Isle of Wight's many Victorian houses and cottages. In Osbourne House the State Apartments, many private, cozier rooms, and the Swiss Cottage, used as the royal children's playhouse, are all open to view.

Cowes Week in August is regatta time, Wight's high season, when the Royal Family and anyone with a boat shows up.

PERILS & PITFALLS

Balmy as Wight is in summer, it is also jammed with vacationers. It's best to go in late spring, when rhododendrons are in glorious blossom, or in September, when it is still warm but less crowded.

THE ISLE OF MAN

The Isle of Man is a favorite British resort center because of its rugged cliffs and 100 miles of sandy beaches.

Special sights: Peel Castle and Cathedral on St. Patrick's Isle (where the saint supposedly preached in 444); the Manx Open Air Folk Museum♛♛ at Cregneish, with thatched cottages depicting old-time Manx life; well-preserved medieval Castle Rushen♛♛, on the site of a Viking fortress at Castletown; and Rushen Abbey♛, Cistercian ruins dating from 1134, where concerts are held in summer in the gardens. The Celtic-derived Manx language is long gone, except in names, but look for the tailless and still-ubiquitous Manx cat.

INSIDERS' INFORMATION FOR THE CHANNEL ISLANDS

St. Peter Port (Guernsey; Area Code Guernsey 0481)

Hotels

St. Pierre Park♛♛♛
Rohais. Tel. 28282.
2 persons in twin, $67.50–90.
Rambling modern resort in out-of-town setting. 135 rooms (all with balconies), bar, restaurant, indoor swimming pool, tennis, 9-hole golf course, sauna, solarium. Idyllic for away-from-it-all vacationer, lovely grounds, lake, sports.
Old Government House♛♛
Ann's Pl. Tel. 24921.
2 persons in twin, $90–120.
Former governors' official home in handy town location. 73 rooms, bar, restaurant, swimming pool, garden, disco. Personable place, thoughtful amenities, ample space.

St. Saviour (Jersey; Area Code Jersey 0534)

Hotel

Longueville Manor♛♛♛
Near St. Helier. Tel. 25501.

2 persons in twin, $90–120.

Imposing old 13th-century manor house within a mile of the sea. 33 rooms, bar, classic French restaurant (♛ ♛), swimming pool, riding, putting green, garden. Total comfort in a pastoral setting: large rooms, elegant antiques, carved paneling, fresh flowers, attentive staff, punctilious maintenance.

St. Aubin (Jersey; Area Code Jersey 0534)

Hotel

Old Court House Inn ♛

St. Aubin's Harbour. Tel. 41156.

2 persons in twin, $67.50–120.

Old 1450 inn overlooking harbor. 8 rooms, bar, fine seafood restaurant (♛ ♛); try the fresh sardines. Great views, comfortable.

NORTHERN IRELAND

Today, most visitors to Northern Ireland arrive by air in Belfast, the largest city. We suggest a tour that begins there, dips south for a look at St. Patrick country, then loops north along the coast, with lovely green hills and seaside villages, returning to Belfast. Vistas are delightful, distances are small, roads are good and relatively uncrowded.

PERILS & PITFALLS

The tragic continuing struggle in Northern Ireland has unavoidable consequences for the visitor. Security is a pervasive concern and requires searches of luggage at airports, and of handbags and even persons before entering many public buildings. Remember, it's for your safety; be patient.

Bygone days in Northern Ireland's farms, villages, and towns can be sampled in a rambling parkland at the Ulster Folk and Transport Museum (also called Cultra Manor) ♛ ♛ ♛ in Holywood, 8 miles northeast of Belfast center. This is one of the best of folk museums—justly cited a British "Museum of the Year." Not only are the 20 diverse houses fascinating, but some of the guides at the houses are loquacious old-timers, eager to tell you about the not-so-distant past.

You'll see cottier's houses (cottages) with musical names (Meenagarragh, Duncrun, Cruckaclady), a school from County Antrim, row houses, an 1830s weaver's house, and flax-scutching and spade-making workshops. An exhibition hall at the entrance has a beautifully presented display of farm and village crafts and tools.

The Ulster Museum ♛ ♛ is located in the university quarter's Botanic Gardens. (While in the gardens, you may want to look in at the many rare plant species in the 1850 Palm House.) A modern (1972) building admirably displays exhibits of Celtic artifacts, jewelry, objects from the Spanish Armada galleon *Girona* (salvaged in 1968), some Old Master paintings, and many 19th- and 20th-century works by Irish and internationally known artists such as Bacon, Hepworth, Pasmore, Caro, Frankenthaler, Appel, and Sam Francis.

Recently refurbished and resplendent in all its 1895 flamboyant glory is the Belfast Grand Opera House ♛ ♛ on Great Victoria Street. Its brass fixtures, plush furnishings, and gilt-stucco elephants are fitting flourishes in a building that seats 1,000 and showcases internationally known entertainers and artists.

INSIDERS' TIPS

The best time to visit Belfast is November, for the annual Belfast Festival, a gala of international stars performing operas, plays, and concerts.

The Crown Liquor Saloon ♛ on Belfast's Great Victoria Street, across from the Grand Opera House, is one of the National Trust's most unusual properties. This glorious 1880s high Victorian pub is a landmark, authentic in every tiled, carved, mirrored, frosted-glass, colonnaded, and gas-lit detail.

If you wish to make a St. Patrick pilgrimage, head south to the delightful town of Downpatrick. Next to Down Cathedral ♛, with its Georgian box pews and 14th-century baptismal font, is a massive, rough stone with a Celtic cross marking the saint's burial place.

A few miles away (signposted from Downpatrick) is the village of Saul (Gaelic for "barn"), with a small church and round tower built to mark the spot where St. Patrick gave his first sermon to the Irish, and to commemorate the 1,500th anniversary of his return to Ireland.

To visit the locale where the saint tended swine for 6 years as a boy slave, you must go northeast of Belfast to Slemish Mountain. This is a focal pilgrimage point, especially on St. Patrick's day—and it offers a fine view north to the Skerry Church ruins.

One of Northern Ireland's great natural features is the Giants' Causeway ♛ ♛, on its northernmost coast, near Ballycastle. Here are 40,000 four-, five-, and six-sided basalt columns, some 40 feet tall, forming a galaxy of shapes, as suggested by their names—Amphitheatre, King and his Nobles, Giant's Granny—all the work of the Irish hero Finn McCool, according to legend, but actually the basaltic shapes are of volcanic origin. The display makes for a pleasant seaside walk.

A few miles farther west is the Old Bushmills Distillery, the oldest (legal) producer of whiskey in the world, dating from 1608, when James I granted the charter to distill. You will be welcomed here to enjoy a tour and samples of "Old Bush."

INSIDERS' INFORMATION FOR NORTHERN IRELAND

Belfast (Down; Area Code Holywood 023-17)

Hotel

Culloden ♛ ♛ ♛
Craigavad BT18 0EX. Tel. 5223.
2 persons in twin, $90–120.
Secluded 19th-century bishop's palace just outside town. 74 rooms, bar (in old chapel), restaurant, tennis, squash, pub on the grounds, beautiful gardens. Spacious rooms, great comfort; rooms in the old section have baronial character.

TRAVELER'S GLOSSARY

The Queen's English and American English aren't *quite* the same language. If you don't believe us, scan the definitions below. You will find them in common usage throughout the United Kingdom.

Accumulator	battery
Banger	sausage
Biscuit	cookie
Bonnet	the hood of a car
Boot	the trunk of a car
Caravan	house trailer
Center reservation	median strip
Chips	French fries
Clearway	arterial road, no parking
Combe	narrow valley or deep hollow
Crisps	potato chips
Digs	lodgings
Diversion	detour
Dress circle	balcony
Dual carriageway	two-lane highway
Fell	upland pasture or moor
Fen	marsh
Firth	long, narrow bay or fjord
Folly	whimsical building meant as a conversation piece
Fortnight	two weeks
Free house	independent pub free to sell various brands of ales and beers (unlike pubs tied to specific breweries)
Grot	kitsch, worthless bric-a-brac
Heath	open, uncultivated land (often with heather)
Hooter	horn
Hurst	forest clearing

Kiosk	(phone) booth
Ladder	run in a stocking
Lay-by	highway rest or passing area
Lift	elevator
Loch	lake or protected bay
Loo	toilet
Lorry	truck
Margin	shoulder or road edge
Mere	lake or pond
Moor	see *heath*, above
Off license	package liquor store
One-track road	single lane (with "turn-outs" or "lay-bys" for passing)
Petrol	gasoline
Public convenience	toilet
Punt	small flat-bottomed boat
Return ticket	round trip
Roundabout	traffic circle
Single ticket	one way
Stone	as a measure of weight, equal to 14 pounds
Subway	walkway under heavily trafficked roads
Supergrass	police informer
'Ta	thank you
Takeaway	take-out, as in fast food
Telly	television
Tube	same as American subway
Underground	see *tube*
Upper circle	second balcony
Verge	road shoulder
Windscreen	windshield

GLOSSARY OF BRITISH FOOD TERMS

The names are more bewildering than the dishes, so it may help to know before you go.

Arbroath smokies	smoked whiting
Bath Olivers	thin crackers invented by Dr. Oliver of Bath, good with cheese

Bloaters	smoked fish
Bubble-and-squeak	leftover mashed potatoes and cabbage mixed together and browned
Bucklings	baby herring
Clotted cream	thick cream skimmed from whole milk that has been specially heated and cooled
Cock-a-leekie	thick soup, principally chicken and leeks
Cornish pasties	pastry filled with diced beef, potatoes, and vegetables
Courgettes	zucchini or marrow
Crumpets	spongy (English) muffins, served at tea with jam and clotted cream (beware, the holes go all the way through!)
Devonshire cream	see *clotted cream*, above
Finnan haddie	golden smoked haddock (originally from Findon in Scotland) grilled, served with butter
Fish n' chips	deep-fried fish, served with French fries, sprinkled with vinegar or salt, traditionally served on newspapers
Flannel cakes	similar to scones, served with tea in Yorkshire
Flummery	junket-like pudding made with almonds, served with berries
Gooseberry fool	cooked gooseberry, sugar, and cream dessert
Hedgerow pudding	made with fresh fruits "right from the hedgerow"
Kedgeree	smoked haddock, cooked with rice, cream, and hard-boiled eggs, seasoned with curry
Kent cobs	a type of hazelnut in a cornsilk-like wrapper, grown in Kent
Kippers	smoked herring, grilled and served at breakfast
Lady fingers	okra
Lancashire hot pot	lamb chops and kidneys, stewed with potatoes and onions
Lemon curd	lemon juice, sugar, and egg spread for tarts
Mulligatawny soup	curried chicken soup
Navy cakes	fried fish cakes

Neep	rutabaga
Pudding	generic term for dessert, not necessarily pudding per se
Salamagundi	left-over hash of chopped veal, pork, chicken, herring, anchovies, served with lettuce and vinegar
Salsify	a root vegetable, also called "oyster plant"
Sandy soil soup	soup made with root vegetables
Scones	rough-textured, breadlike pastry, served with jam and clotted cream at tea
Scotch egg	hard-boiled egg wrapped in Spam-like pork, rolled in bread crumbs and deep fried; served hot or cold
Shepherd's pie	leftover ground lamb covered with mashed potatoes
Shepherd's purse	similar to a brownie in shape and texture, but not chocolate
Sprats	tiny smoked herring, rolled in oatmeal or flour and fried
Stargazer pie	herring pie (from Weymouth)
Swede	rutabaga
Syllabub	old English dessert of fresh milk or cream with sherry or brandy, whipped into a froth
Toad-in-the-hole	sausages topped with batter and baked
Treacle	molasses
Trifle	leftover sponge cake soaked in sherry, covered with jam, custard, and whipped cream, served cold or warm as dessert.

TYPES OF COMMON BRITISH CHEESES

Caerphilly	soft, white, light, Welsh
Catherstone	firm, creamy Bel Paese-like
Cheshire Stilton	creamy orange version of Stilton; sharp
Double Gloucester	uncolored, hard cheese; may contain onions or chives

Ilchester	a Somerset cheddar with garlic and beer
Lancashire	semisoft, loose-textured, buttery
Leicester	deep red, mild, close-textured
Maes Mawr	Welsh semisoft, creamy goat cheese
Ribblesdale	smoked goat cheese
Sage Derby	small, rindless, coated with sage flavor which permeates the cheese
Walton	Cheddar and Stilton with fine-chopped walnuts
Wensleydale	Yorkshire blue- or white-veined, hard, crumbly
Windsor Red	medium moist Cheddar marbled with elderberry wine

COMMONLY USED WINE TERMS IN BRITAIN

Claret	red Bordeaux
Hock	Rhine wine
Plonk	cheap, undistinguished jug wine, from *blanc*, as in white, wine

SCOTTISH CULINARY SPECIALTIES

Cadoc cheese	double-cream cheese, rolled in oatmeal
Crowdie	soft, low-fat cheese
Cullen skink	smoked fish soup
Haggis	Scottish wurst; sheep innards, oatmeal, and spices, encased in sheep's stomach and boiled
Hatted kit	sweet cream with nutmeg
Highland colcannon	mashed potatoes with leeks, cream, and butter
Lobster Hebridean	lobster with Drambuie
Nettle kail	boiled chicken flavored with nettles
Sweet marag	boiled pudding

SOME POPULAR NORTHERN IRISH DISHES

Barmbrack	a round, domed loaf of bread with currants and candied orange peel, usually eaten on All Souls' Day
Boxty	mashed potatoes, grated raw potatoes, melted butter, and flour, kneaded and shaped into a round loaf, then baked; with baking soda and extra milk added, it is also fried like pancakes
Champ	potatoes mashed with chives and milk, usually served with pork sausages and turnips
Fadge	potato pancakes, sometimes served with lemon juice and sugar
Fruit bannock	round bread with currants
Streaky bacon	bacon grilled, not fried
Treacle farl	sweet, molasses-like tart, cut into squares
Ulster fry	breakfast of bacon, sausage, eggs, baked tomato, potato bread, and black pudding, all fried together

INDEX